A MOMENT TO DECIDE

THE CRISIS IN MAINSTREAM PRESBYTERIANISM

Research Prepared by Lewis C. Daly
Preface by Anne Hale Johnson
Foreword by The Rev. Dr. Robert W. Bohl

INSTITUTE FOR DEMOCRACY STUDIES
New York, NY

This publication is supported by the Presbyterian Information Project,
Scarborough Presbyterian Church, Scarborough, NY 10510

Institute for Democracy Studies
177 East 87th Street
Suite 501
New York, NY 10128
info@institutefordemocracy.org
www.institutefordemocracy.org

The Institute for Democracy Studies is a nonprofit, tax-exempt organization, supported by generous contributions from foundations, corporations, and individuals.

ISBN 0-9679106-0-9

CONTENTS

Lewis C. Daly is the program associate for Religion and Democracy at the Institute for Democracy Studies. He received his M.Div. from Union Theological Seminary (NY) and Ph.D. in English Literature from the State University of New York at Buffalo. He would like to thank IDS intern Kristen Wall as well as the numerous librarians, fellow scholars, and readers, both Presbyterian and non-Presbyterian alike, who provided invaluable assistance on matters of research and interpretation during this complex undertaking.

INSTITUTE FOR DEMOCRACY STUDIES

PREFACE

On behalf of the board of directors of the Institute for Democracy Studies, I am honored to present the first in a series of reports on the serious challenges faced by a number of the mainline Protestant denominations. These denominations, in particular the Presbyterian Church (USA), or PC(USA), the United Methodist Church, and the Episcopal Church, are currently confronted with vigorous efforts to reshape their historic and vital role. It is because the Institute values these churches' role in preserving and extending democratic values and institutions that the board has authorized this series of studies. We are witnessing critically dangerous progress in this decades-long effort by well-organized and well-financed interests to weaken and even eliminate mainline commitment to social justice.

As a lay-member of the PC(USA), I am personally concerned that these interests appear motivated to dismember agencies of the church committed to social justice in the United States and in the world. As a moderate Republican, I have witnessed a similar trend in my party, as sectarian interests epitomized by the Christian Coalition seek to expand their power and influence. I am alarmed by their routine denunciation of the constitutional principle of separation of church and state. Thus I am concerned about preserving the independence of the church, from both the government and special interests of any kind. I believe that few Presbyterians want their church narrowed to a sect; we prefer reading, praying, and interpreting the Bible rather than thumping people with it. I doubt that I am alone in valuing the genuine social progress of the last century advanced by the ecumenical churches. The needs of God's world in the 21st century prompt me to work for a church for my children and grandchildren that will continue the work of social justice and peacemaking.

I believe that the publication of A Moment to Decide: The Crisis in Mainstream Presbyterianism *may be seen in the coming years as an historic turning point for the PC(USA).*

I believe that the publication of *A Moment to Decide: The Crisis in Mainstream Presbyterianism* may be seen in the coming years as an historic turning point for the PC(USA). The report contains new information viewed in the light of the history of reactionary movements in our church, as well as a rigorous analysis that I fervently hope will strengthen the resolve and inform the judgment of the broadest swath of Presbyterians. I have faith that mainstream Presbyterians will begin to awaken to the threat to their denominational integrity and tradition, and will act with a spirit and vision refreshed and invigorated by the insights offered in this report. This is indeed a major wake-up call!

The Institute for Democracy Studies was established in March 1999 to develop an interdisciplinary research and educational capacity to help generate informed public discussion on challenges to American democracy. The Institute is profoundly concerned with the challenges to the traditional values of the church as well as to the state. I am prayerfully certain that, with this critically important message, the vital conversations about the condition of our democracy and the life of our churches in the century ahead will flourish.

Anne Hale Johnson, New York, NY, April 2000

FOREWORD

The struggle for the very soul of the Presbyterian Church (USA) in the last three decades has been sharply intensified by the religious right in this denomination. This struggle has been marked by an aggressive style of partisanship that strays far from the spirit of fair-minded Presbyterianism and warmhearted evangelicalism. In the last ten years, some on the right have gone so far as to declare this struggle a "Holy War."

History is our teacher and informs us that in previous such struggles, ultra-conservatives have declared their intention to purge the church of those they have deemed unfit to be members. Their modus operandi includes a two-pronged line of attack. First, they claim that their case is based on biblical authority. Second, they seek to persuade by describing those with whom they disagree as rejecting the authority of Scripture.

This is more than a wake-up call to Presbyterians. This is a sounding of the alarm to all Americans, Christian and non-Christian alike, who value religious freedom, social justice, and the stability of constitutional democracy.

The Presbyterian Historic Principles of Church Order state clearly that "God alone is Lord of the conscience, and hath left it free from the doctrines and commandments of man which are in anything contrary to His Word, or beside it in matters of faith and worship."[1] A second set of principles declares "that truth is in order to goodness, and the great touchstone of truth, its tendency to promote holiness, according to our Savior's rule, 'by their fruits ye shall know them.'"[2]

In my 40 years as a pastor, I have worked to build a community based on the whole Gospel, in which dialogue and reconciliation are possible. Mutual understanding is necessarily based on knowledge, while ignorance is a foundation of prejudice and other false assumptions. Dialogue between people who disagree must be well informed to be meaningful and effective. Belatedly, we are learning that we need much more information to have a truly informed dialogue about the future of our church.

A Moment to Decide clearly documents the fruits by which exclusionary elements in the church have come to be known. The study also details the determined efforts of the religious right to undermine the freedom of conscience—the democratic hallmark of the Presbyterian Church (USA). This study does not seek to present motives of the various groups, which indeed differ. Rather it is a well-documented account of their origin, activities, and leadership. The five major organizations described in this book have no cohesive organic relationship, but they do share what they would call a common opponent. One rightist leader speaks about this opponent in military terms: "You talk about an aversion to blood on the floor . . . to fighting . . . . I submit to you that the bloody battle is exactly what we need to be engaged in . . . we need to fight until the battle is won."[3]

Every Presbyterian who cherishes the principles on which this denomination was established, the freedom of conscience, and our heritage of democratic traditions, would be wise to read the following chapters to see the determined and often ruthless campaign that is being waged to capture the power to take over this denomination. The religious right groups have a common strategy, which has been made public, and which must not be ignored or casually dismissed. These groups are planning to take over the leadership in church governance and have a longterm focus on the fiduciary assets of the church. They are also reviving the mechanisms of church discipline to enforce their views regarding church programs and leadership. Part of this includes efforts to increase their influence and power over seminary education, which some currently claim is harboring "alien ideologies."

I personally watched such machinations in the takeover of the Southern Baptist denomination and its large seminary in Fort Worth, Texas. While those at the center of the church were declaring it would not happen, it did. These far right groups have access to millions of dollars and key political lay people who are being used as consultants to dismantle the denomination as we know it.

The Presbyterian denomination has been a bulwark of freedom and hope because it proclaimed the liberating news of the Gospel, the good news of Jesus Christ, who welcomes all who believe in him to follow him and to try to be like him. The news was good because it was based on God's love, grace, and compassion. Its fruits were spiritual maturity, freedom from intolerance, support for civil and human rights, peacemaking and healing ministries, and brave advocacy for justice.

This carefully documented report has provided invaluable context to my personal knowledge and experience in the Presbyterian Church (USA), of which I am a pastor and former elected moderator of the General Assembly. It has also expanded my knowledge of the history of my church and some of the influential figures within it. It has reminded and underscored for me the divisiveness of "offering plate boycotts" and campaigns against national staff. Taken together, I fear for the future of my church and its heritage. I regret that so many of my conservative brothers and sisters in Christ take the view that social justice in public life is inconsistent with advancing the Gospel. I deplore the reactionary views that women must be placed "in submission" to men. I object to the persecution of gays and lesbians by the far right of my church. Finally, I am deeply concerned about the efforts of a growing coalition of rightist groups to transform the church that I love into an agency of the radical right—as was done to the Southern Baptist Convention.

Early in *A Moment to Decide,* the study notes that the rise of the radical right inside and outside the church "has benefited from the relative absence of strong and effective counter movements." This is more than a wake-up call to Presbyterians. This is a sounding of the alarm to all Americans, Christian and non-Christian alike, who value religious freedom, social justice, and the stability of constitutional democracy.

This report is the work of the Institute for Democracy Studies, an independent nonprofit organization that was founded in 1999 to study anti-democratic religious and political organizations and trends in the U.S. and internationally. The Institute initiated a series of studies of rightist trends in the mainstream denominations, beginning with the Presbyterian Church, because it seems to be the most endangered in the wake of the takeover of the Southern Baptist Convention.

I believe you will find that this report puts the picture up front for all of us to see, and represents the organizations and individuals mentioned in a fair and nuanced manner. How the story unfolds in the struggle for the soul of the Presbyterian Church (USA) will be determined by what the great center of the church decides to do.

It is time for each of us to decide not only how much we value fellow Presbyterians and other human beings as equals in the eyes of God and the laws of the United States. It is time to plumb the depths of our values and our commitments to the institutions of our society that make these values manifest. It is a moment to decide, and therefore it is time to act.

The Rev. Dr. Robert W. Bohl, Prairie Village, Kansas, April 2000

---

1 *Book of Order of the Presbyterian Church* (USA), G-1.0301.
2 *Ibid.* G-1.0304.
3 Parker T. Williamson, chief executive officer, the Presbyterian Lay Committee.

"Mainline Protestantism has historically championed the ideals of liberal democracy, and in doing so it has comfortably regarded society as a social extension of the church. That accommodation is no longer possible—if it ever was. The pluralism of modern culture is not only not compatible with the great ends of the church, but increasingly inimical to them."

> — James R. Edwards, writing in the May/June 1998
> issue of Theology Matters, the publication of
> Presbyterians for Faith, Family and Ministry[1]

"You talk about an aversion to blood on the floor . . . to fighting . . . . I submit to you that the bloody battle is exactly what we need to be engaged in. We need to stand for the truth of Jesus Christ, the veracity of his Word, and we need to fight until that battle is won."

> — Parker T. Williamson, chief operating officer of the
> Presbyterian Lay Committee, speaking from the
> floor of the Presbyterian Coalition's Gathering IV,
> September 20, 1999[2]

INTRODUCTION

The Presbyterian Church (USA), or PC(USA), has reached an historic moment in its denominational life. This mainstream church of 2.6 million members is the largest Presbyterian denomination in the U.S. and is embroiled in controversy. A range of conservative, evangelical, and sometimes reactionary groups, operating under the rubric of religious "renewal," have recently forged a powerful campaign to challenge the 20th century tradition of Christian social witness and the values of democratic pluralism.

Early in this century, a conservative revolt against Darwinism and modernism in science and in culture, and against progressive social witness in the church, led to a movement that gave fundamentalism its name. Today, fundamentalism continues to inform and strain the life of the church. The renewed conservative insurgency has roots in the earlier theological and social struggles, although its contemporary character and players are necessarily different.

Since the mid-1960s, conservative renewal movements (see Glossary) have arisen in all of the mainline churches, notably, the PC(USA), the United Methodist Church, and the Episcopal Church. Of these, the Presbyterian renewal movement has the longest history and stands as the most successful such grouping in mainline Protestantism.

Presbyterian renewal is about much more than religious conservatives reacting to liberal trends in theology and biblical interpretation and the sexual revolution. It is deeply political and unambiguously part of the growth of right-wing political power in the United States. This dimension of the Presbyterian renewal movement—and similar movements across mainline Protestantism—is little discussed in contemporary scholarship and denominational history.

This oversight is especially remarkable given that one of the most profound and sustained right-wing objectives since World War II has been to neutralize or eliminate mainline Protestant churches as socially conscious institutional forces in public life. In the late 1970s, in the midst of debates around U.S. military intervention abroad, nuclear disarmament, and domestic racial and gender policies, conservative groups both inside and outside the church gained significant political power and momentum. Over the past few decades, their efforts have helped catalyze a significant rightward shift in American public religion and have contributed to the decline of the mediating role of mainline Christianity in the social and cultural conflicts that mark American public life. The denominational renewal movements, not least of all in the PC(USA), have been a pivotal factor in this broader dynamic of rightist ascendancy and mainline decline.

This report focuses primarily on the history, political context, and leadership of key elements of the conservative renewal movement in the PC(USA). The first chapter discusses in depth the origins, leaders, and political involvements of the original and most strident organization in the movement, the Presbyterian Lay Committee. However, it is the efforts of two relatively new organizations to contest the entire 20th century direction of the church and to control the next century that provided the impetus for this study. These two groups, the Presbyterian Coalition and the Presbyterian Forum, are discussed throughout this report and in detail in the later chapters.

While most people are inevitably focused on the issues of the day inside and outside the church, the historical struggles behind these issues are particularly relevant to the current situation in the PC(USA). Indeed, the ideology and ambitions of a relatively small group of ultraconservative businessmen, who initially underwrote the movement, live on. In their time, these men bitterly opposed modernism, the labor movement, and the New Deal, among other things. In our time, this legacy has made its way into certain defining elements of what is now broadly called Presbyterian renewal.

From the 1930s through much of the 20th century, the leaders of what scholars call the Old Right unfairly tarred everything they opposed with the brush of what they labeled the "communist menace." The old epithets may not work as well anymore, but new menaces have been identified and are being used to help propel the conservative drive for power. The Presbyterian Coalition, for example, claims to have discovered "alien" ideologies in church-affiliated seminaries and seeks to root them out. The leading charismatic group (see Glossary) in mainline Presbyterianism has identified the church's official women's ministry as a "demonic stronghold." The absolute conviction that some people hold regarding such matters should not be underestimated. Nor should the determination and, in some cases, the seeming ruthlessness with which such ideologically driven actors seek to accomplish their goals.

PRESBYTERIAN RENEWAL: PARADIGM OF INTERNAL DESTABILIZATION

Over the past three decades, the renewal movement in the PC(USA) has substantially eroded the denomination's legacy and capacity for advancing change in the interest of social justice. In 1998, the stakes escalated when the Presbyterian Coalition unveiled an ambitious agenda complete with a bold statement of doctrine and strategy—almost an alternative confessional statement (see Glossary). This comprehensive evangelical vision and open takeover plan marks a dramatic advance in the renewal movement's strategic vision and capacity. What's more, the purgative goals of the Coalition are indicative of the conservatives' general vision for the church. For example, in 1999, the Coalition's agenda began to emerge in four high-profile ecclesiastical trials held in the Synod of the Northeast, which will be discussed in some detail in Chapter 6.

The organizational roots of the contemporary Presbyterian conservative renewal movement date to the mid-1960s, when the mainline churches became deeply involved in such areas of concern as civil rights, world peace, economic justice, and the war in Vietnam. Until recently, however, renewal groups have been primarily reactive to these issues and to the socially enlightened vision, policies, and programming that have defined the major initiatives of the PC(USA) and mainline Protestantism generally for much of this century.

The history, character, and composition of the major players of the renewal movement are integral to any understanding of the recent history of the church and the current state of social witness in mainstream Christianity.

In recent years, matters of gender and sexuality, notably feminist theology and gay and lesbian rights, have served as "wedge" issues for conservative efforts to gain political leverage inside the denomination. At the same time rightists in the church, usually invoking a claim of doctrinal orthodoxy as well as fiscal and political control or accountability, have established a climate in which individual staff, funding streams, and official programs are constantly questioned, challenged, undermined, and attacked.

The history, character, and composition of the major players of the renewal movement are integral to any understanding of the recent history of the church and the current state of social witness in mainstream Christianity. This report is an initial examination of some of the major organizations and leaders of the conservative renewal movement in the context of the history and contemporary struggles of the PC(USA).

PSEUDO-POPULISM OF RENEWAL

Presbyterian renewal groups (especially the Presbyterian Lay Committee) have tended to characterize renewal as a popular rebellion from the pews against a tyrannical and elite denominational leadership and its supposedly "secular humanist" (see Glossary) agenda. Paradoxically, renewal theology and ecclesiology typically reflect and support the prevailing social order and its rightward drift since the 1980s. Thus, renewal is better understood as a strategic challenge to faith-based social witness within the church and in public life. This challenge varies greatly in expression and form, ranging, for example, from the inquisitorial hyperbole of *The Presbyterian Layman* (generally referred to as *The Layman*) to the earnestly conservative focus on church growth and youth evangelism of Presbyterians for Renewal.

The rise of Presbyterian renewal is coterminous with and integral to the growth of the political and religious right. This movement, both inside and outside the church, has benefited from the relative absence of strong and effective countermovements. Part of the reason for this is the dynamic of single-issue politics, which often consumes the attention of many groups and individuals to the exclusion of all else. The attendant sense of urgency sometimes leads to an atmosphere in which monitoring and engaging the wider rightist mobilization may be considered a distraction from, and even a betrayal of the cause. In the context of the situation in the PC(USA), it is essential to engage not only the single issues, but the comprehensive agenda that the conservative renewal movement has for the church, and to understand the formidable array of organizations and resources that have been mobilized thus far. Moreover, it would be limiting to view this struggle in terms of a single denomination rather than the wider conflict in mainline Protestantism, and the still wider context of right-wing mobilization against democratic pluralism and social justice in the United States.

It would be limiting to view this struggle in terms of a single denomination rather than the wider conflict in mainline Protestantism, and the still wider context of right-wing mobilization against democratic pluralism and social justice in the United States.

Very briefly, the major renewal organizations profiled in this report are:

- **The Presbyterian Lay Committee (PLC):** Founded in 1965, the Lenoir, North Carolina-based PLC is the historic starting point of Presbyterian renewal and probably the most significant organization of its kind in mainline Protestantism. Its main role has been to attack and neutralize the church's social witness with an unremitting stream of inquisitorial campaigns against national church agencies.

- **Presbyterians for Renewal (PFR):** Headquartered in Louisville, Kentucky, PFR is a network of churches linked to conservative politics in the church. It is largely a post-1983 reunion reorganization of the historic Covenant Fellowship of Presbyterians from the southern Presbyterian Church (PCUS).

- **Presbyterians Pro-Life (PPL):** A major advocacy and anti-abortion resource organization based in Burke, Virginia, PPL works to reverse the PC(USA)'s historic support for reproductive rights. PPL closely collaborates with national right-wing anti-abortion rights networks.

- **The Presbyterian Coalition:** Headquartered in Birmingham, Alabama, the Coalition is an historic consolidation of renewal forces organizing for comprehensive conservative evangelical control of the PC(USA).

- **The Presbyterian Forum:** Generally referred to as the Forum, the group is the chief political agent for the conservative forces vying for control of the church. It operates from Pasadena, California.

In addition to these key groups, there are other significant entities in the renewal movement, which are touched on briefly in this report:

- **Presbyterian Action for Faith and Freedom**, generally known as Presbyterian Action, is an advocacy group that has primarily opposed the PC(USA)'s work on international social justice concerns. In 1990, Presbyterian Action became an affiliate of the Washington, D.C.-based Institute on Religion and Democracy (IRD), which emerged in the early 1980s as the major national right-wing organization targeting the mainline churches (see Glossary). Presbyterian Action says that it challenges "national church pronouncements when they are unbiblical, unwise, or unbalanced."[3] Incorporated in 1985, Presbyterian Action was formerly called Presbyterians for Democracy and Religious Freedom (PDRF). It was founded by Nashville insurance executive John L. Boone in consultation with the IRD.

- **Presbyterians for Faith, Family and Ministry (PFFM)**, based in Blacksburg, Virginia, emerged as a leading forum for developing intellectual currents in Christian orthodoxy and the Christian worldview, largely in reaction to the controversy over the ReImagining conference on Christian feminism in 1993 (see Glossary). Among other things, PFFM publishes a journal called *Theology Matters,* which seeks to defend its view of Christian orthodoxy against such concepts as religious pluralism and Darwin's theory of evolution.

- **The Presbyterian Renewal Network (PRN)**, an unincorporated association of renewal leaders and organizations, has been in place for many years. Many of the more extreme leaders of the renewal movement participate in the ongoing strategic work of this network, including Parker Williamson of the Presbyterian Lay Committee and Terry Schlossberg of Presbyterians Pro-Life. Under the influence of the closely related Presbyterian Forum, the PRN has begun to play an increasingly important strategic role in the conservative movement's bid for power in the church.

- **Presbyterian Frontier Fellowship** in Portland, Oregon, the **Presbyterian Center for Mission Studies** in Pasadena, California, and the **Presbyterian Outreach Foundation** in Franklin, Tennessee, are all members of the Presbyterian Renewal Network. Each has significantly influenced the character of global missions in the PC(USA). One man whose influence has been particularly important is Ralph Winter, who was for many years the president of Presbyterian Frontier Fellowship. Founder of the evangelical U.S. Center for World Mission, Winter is a pioneering figure in the "unreached peoples" mission movement, which employs sophisticated anthropological analysis in order to weaken indigenous cultural resistance to Christian evangelization. Winter has also served as a board member and chief financial officer of the Presbyterian Center for Mission Studies.

- **Presbyterian-Reformed Ministries International (PRMI)** is the historic charismatic organization in mainline Presbyterianism. Formerly known as Presbyterian & Reformed Renewal Ministries International, PRMI is based in Black Mountain, North Carolina. In the summer of 1999, PRMI called for a campaign of "spiritual warfare" against PC(USA) agencies and special interest groups supportive of feminist theology and gay and lesbian ordination.

- **Voices of Orthodox Women (VOW)** is a newer antifeminist network within the Presbyterian renewal movement. Based in Loveland, Colorado, it is led by Sylvia Dooling, wife of Presbyterian Forum founder Robert Dooling.

1999: THE LAY OF THE LAND

The various renewal groups have historically collaborated to orchestrate conservative actions at the General Assembly—most notably in defeating gay ordination in the late 1970s and again in the 1990s. However, the renewal groups have in recent years sought to clearly identify and institutionalize their shared agenda. Since its founding in 1993, the Presbyterian Coalition has served as the main organizational vehicle for this effort. The common agenda and accompanying strategy were crystallized in the publication of the Coalition's 1998

Declaration and Strategy Paper. This effort gained a powerful new political dimension with the emergence of the Presbyterian Forum as an outgrowth of the Coalition in 1997. The campaign to transform the church into a right-wing evangelical institution has not yet peaked.

One of the Forum's key leaders is Clarke Reed, who has a history of involvement in Presbyterian renewal groups. Less well known in church circles is Reed's career as a leader of the Republican Party in the South since the late 1960s. The "Republican South" in turn has provided the base for the ascendancy of the political far right. Reed's role as a behind-the-scenes strategist in denominational politics may be taken as a measure not only of the stakes in the struggle for control of the PC(USA), but of the increased capacity of the renewal movement to prevail.

Reed's role may be taken as a measure of the stakes in the struggle for control of the PC(USA).

MODERATE IMAGES, EXTREME GOALS

Since its founding in 1965, the Presbyterian Lay Committee (PLC) has served as the historic vanguard of Presbyterian renewal. The broader political history and significance of the PLC is a key, in turn, to gauging the ever-shifting currents and coalition building in the renewal movement.

The prominence of the PLC has led, however, to certain misperceptions about the politics of Presbyterian renewal. The PLC's characteristic hard-right stance has tended to provide a kind of political cover for other groups—particularly Presbyterians for Renewal and the Presbyterian Coalition—whose roles in the renewal movement are often underestimated due to the moderate appearance they cultivate in relation to the PLC and other more extreme groups.

What gets lost in this type of analysis is the strategic role of moderate politics in rightist movements. Indeed, sometimes moderate and even progressive frameworks of rhetoric and debate have provided mainstream cover for extreme political goals. This phenomenon has tended to be the rule rather than the exception in every contested area of public policy including affirmative action, education, economic justice, and separation of church and state. A good example of this is the "civil rights" model of anti-abortion politics in recent years, which masks an agenda of religious oppression of women through public policy by using a legal posture of defending the rights of the fetus.

Sometimes moderate and even progressive frameworks of rhetoric and debate have provided mainstream cover for extreme political goals.

Differences among Presbyterian renewal groups primarily revolve around process and method in advancing a shared set of political goals. The overall purpose of this political effort is to diminish mainline social witness tradition and achieve conservative evangelical control of the church. Presbyterians for Renewal (PFR) is noteworthy in this respect because its local networks of conservative pastors serve as the infrastructure for right-wing campaigns by more overtly politicized groups, such as the Presbyterian Lay Committee. In the PC(USA), where the membership franchise is the primary means of setting policy, such local infrastructure is an important foundation for political change.

PROMOTING INFORMED DISCUSSION

The conservative renewal movement is both politically and theologically varied and complex. It is most usefully explained in terms of the contours and trajectory of its history and how it has arrived at this juncture. Knowledge of this history, the major and minor players inside the church, and the relevant actors outside the church, is vital to the discussions and debates that will shape the direction of the church in the new century.

The shadow of the rightist drive to dominate the Southern Baptist Convention looms large over the PC(USA).

The shadow of the rightist drive to dominate the Southern Baptist Convention looms large over the PC(USA). The conservative Baptists have ultimately prevailed after a struggle of more than 15 years. Historian Gary North, a leader of the theocratic Christian Reconstructionist movement—the far-right wing of Reformed thought today (see Glossary)—cheered the takeover as an historic victory, calling it "the most remarkable ecclesiastical reversal of the past three centuries."[4]

North is a student of Presbyterian history who looks back with the eye of a reactionary and wonders what went wrong. His belief is that the key to liberal ascendancy in the 1920s and 1930s was the conservatives' loyalist refusal, and inability, to use judicial power to sanction and eliminate liberal control of the church. Instead, the liberals defeated orthodoxy, in part by way of judicial power—culminating in the trial of fundamentalist leader J. Gresham Machen in 1935. To reverse the outcome, North clearly implies, purgative judicial power is the key, but this time exerted *against* "modernism."[5] Whether a reversal of Southern Baptist proportions will occur in the PC(USA) remains to be seen.

The renewal movement's current emphasis on judicial power is epitomized by the Presbyterian Coalition's task force on church discipline.

In certain respects, the Presbyterian renewal movement is already acting as if North had written the script. The renewal movement's current emphasis on judicial power is epitomized by the Presbyterian Coalition's task force on church discipline—of which Julius Poppinga, a longtime leader of the Christian Right legal movement, was appointed chair in 1999. The revival of church discipline was a central focus at the Coalition's September 1999 conference in Dallas and was implemented in the four ecclesiastical trials that took place in the Synod of the Northeast in the fall of 1999—the political effects of which will be felt for years to come.

The renewal movement's drive for power in the PC(USA) has reached an advanced stage. How far it will continue to advance will depend on the degree to which supporters of the social progress of 20th century Presbyterianism can mobilize. The efficacy of any such movement will be enhanced, if not determined, by a clearer picture of these historic opponents of social progress inside and outside the church.

CHAPTER 1

THE PRESBYTERIAN LAY COMMITTEE

I. Significance

The Presbyterian Lay Committee (PLC) is among the best-funded and most politically oriented right-wing organizations in mainline Protestantism. It is a powerful watchdog agency for right-wing forces trying to eliminate the social witness tradition of the PC(USA). As part of the broader movement of right-wing renewal, which includes groups ranging across theological, pastoral, and political lines, the PLC's role has been to target, attack, and neutralize key leadership sectors and initiatives within the national structure of the church.

PC(USA)-supported initiatives that the PLC has historically opposed include economic justice for African Americans,[6] the anti-war movement,[7] the labor movement,[8] the anti-apartheid movement,[9] nuclear disarmament,[10] feminist theology,[11] and international solidarity with the oppressed.[12] This nexus of associated social witness movements, with shifting emphases over time, was the focus of right-wing resurgence within the Presbyterian Church for three decades. Gay and lesbian sexuality, which is a central focus of the PLC today, has been a target of attack since the early 1970s as well. The United Presbyterian Church, or UPC(USA), a national denomination that is still sometimes called the "northern church," initiated consideration of gay and lesbian rights in its 1970 report on human sexuality. By the 1990s and the fall of communism, the PLC (like the broader Christian Right) focused increasingly on wedge issues, especially gay ordination and religious feminism.

The PLC essentially operates as a standing inquisition aimed at crippling the church's moderate, but profoundly important institutional support for this body of democratic initiatives. The resulting erosion of support among PC(USA) leaders for social witness initiatives is in part a testament to the PLC's impact. The PLC's efforts are but one aspect of what has become a kind of "open season" on the structure of the church, which has suffered an attrition in leadership as social witness agencies have been reduced to pursuing survival tactics instead of carrying forward their stated mission. This history of political inquisition against church leadership is the foundation of the renewal movement's bid for institutional power, even as the

The PLC's history of political inquisition against church leadership is the foundation of the renewal movement's bid for power.

Presbyterian Coalition's 1998 *Declaration and Strategy Paper* has set the parameters for the drive for denominational control over the next few years.

Part of the historic significance of the Presbyterian Lay Committee also lies in the context of its development as a denominational entity amidst the ascendancy of the religious and political New Right (see Glossary) since the late 1960s.

II. Background

The Presbyterian Lay Committee was founded in 1965 by a group of corporate executives led by J. Howard Pew, scion of the Sun Oil natural resource empire. Pew served as a director and primary benefactor of the PLC until his death in 1971. The original group also included George Champion, chairman of Chase Manhattan Bank, Roger Hull, president of Mutual Life Insurance of New York, and Hugh MacMillan, senior vice president of Coca-Cola Exports. The latter three were all members of Noroton Presbyterian Church in Darien, Connecticut.[13]

As recounted by Paul Cupp, the first vice president of the PLC and chairman of American Stores Company, Pew helped organize Presbyterian laymen to discuss what he called "troubling developments in the church." There was "evidence of a fundamental shift in the mission of the church," according to Cupp. "In place of a mission to preach the Gospel and make disciples in the name of Jesus Christ, the new church leaders introduced a mission to change the structures of society by political and economic means."[14] In particular, the circulation of drafts for a projected new confession, what would become the Confession of 1967 (see Glossary), galvanized the founding of the PLC.[15] The Confession of 1967, which contained a moderate affirmation of institutional commitment to the social justice movements of the time, has become the symbol for conservatives of liberalism gone awry and has informed their vision of church conflict ever since.

Cupp recalls an important meeting that took place in George Champion's Chase Manhattan offices in New York City.[16] Notable attendees at this meeting, according to Cupp, included Arthur Langlie, former governor of Washington, as well as two Pittsburgh-based executives: M.M. Anderson, a chemical warfare expert and former director and executive vice president of Aluminum Company of America, part of the Mellon empire;[17] and Carlton Ketchum, a pioneer in the field of professional fundraising and founder of Ketchum, Inc., until recently one of the nation's largest fundraising firms.[18] Ketchum is credited with introducing modern fundraising methods into politics. He was national finance director of the Republican

Party from 1937 to 1941 and from 1949 to 1957.[19]

On January 29, 1965, a meeting called by Arthur Langlie and Roger Hull was held at George Champion's Chase Manhattan offices.[20] Langlie, who chaired the McCall Corporation in New York in the early 1960s, was instrumental in starting the PLC, but died in 1966. The January meeting was called, according to the minutes, to review what would become the PLC's founding document, "A Call to Presbyterian Laymen," which was published in *Presbyterian Life* in the fall of 1965.[21] They also decided to form a permanent organization to carry out this agenda. A board of directors was created, led by an executive committee consisting of Roger Hull, Paul Cupp, Arthur Langlie, Hugh MacMillan, Clarence McGuire (president of Hoover Brothers, Inc.), John Humphrey (one-time vice president of International Telephone & Telegraph and later president of Philip Carey Manufacturing Co. in Lockland, Ohio, until his retirement in 1967), and J. Howard Pew.[22] The PLC submitted its certificate of incorporation in New York State on May 14, 1965.[23] The incorporating board members included Hull, MacMillan, Cupp, and John Humphrey.

As Cupp describes the sequence, prior to the founding of the PLC, Champion, Hull, and MacMillan had met with Presbyterian Stated Clerk Eugene Carson Blake, who was also a longtime leader of the National Council of Churches, to air their concerns. Blake politely suggested that if they were unhappy with the new direction of the church, then they could leave it. This is when they called Pew, who would remain the predominant force behind and patron of the PLC until his death in 1971. Early board member William C. Mullendore, former chairman of the Southern California Edison Company and a close friend of Pew, asserted that Pew was "the real spark plug and the man who is 90% responsible for the organization of the Lay Committee."[24]

THE PLC AND COLD WAR ULTRACONSERVATISM

Important insights into the Presbyterian Lay Committee's agenda for the church can be gleaned from its political affiliations and affinities, which in many ways have remained unchanged since the committee's founding. At the PLC's first national convention in 1973, president Paul Cupp emphasized the influence of Pew. "Mr. Pew," Cupp explained, "expressed the belief that Protestantism—historical and Biblical Christianity—is the great guardian of the freedom given us by God and that if the church fails, if it strays from its primary mission, and we lose our religious freedom, we stand to lose—progressively—all our freedoms and would come under some form of state socialism, some form of dictatorship."[25]

This notion animated the historic linkage between right-wing libertarian politics and evangelical anti-mainline activism of which Pew was the dominant force in the postwar period. Pew essentially held that any government intervention apart from national security and law enforcement was by definition a form of collectivism, a view he shared with fellow ultraconservative manufacturing leaders in response to the New Deal in the 1930s. These industrialists became alarmed when public interventions in the economy threatened to extend beyond industrial recovery into support for labor rights and such programs as Social Security and unemployment insurance.[26]

Bankrolled by Pew and his colleagues, laissez-faire economics became an ideological pillar of the dominant trend in right-wing mobilization in the decades that followed—the "fusionist" combination of social traditionalism and in some cases evangelical Christianity, with libertarian politics focused on rolling back the policies of the New Deal.[27]

Pew's politics are rooted in a Depression-era context that journalist George Seldes and others have characterized as "native fascism."

Throughout the postwar period, Pew and his allies routinely equated such contemporary advances as labor laws, Social Security, and civil rights legislation with Soviet dictatorship.[28] But the distinct perspective that Pew brought to such matters was his view that the church was crucial for maintaining "freedom," which for him meant freedom in property above all else.

Pew's politics are rooted in a Depression-era context that journalist George Seldes and others have characterized as "native fascism." Native fascist groups were far more alarmed by what they termed the "communist menace" than by the spread of fascism in Europe and domestically. Of course, there were many openly fascist groups in the United States at the time, such as the German American Bund and William Dudley Pelley's Silver Shirts. Far more important, however, were the business sectors that played off of fascist currents, which sometimes directly supported business-led attacks on the New Deal.

Not least among these native fascist business sectors was the right wing of the National Association of Manufacturers (NAM), of which Pew was a leader, and its political counterpart, the American Liberty League.[29] While the American Liberty League operated as a chief backer of Alf Landon's failed presidential bid against Roosevelt in 1936, its leaders simultaneously subsidized a network of native fascist organizations, such as John H. Kirby's Southern Committee to Uphold the Constitution, which sought to create a racialist states' rights backlash movement against Roosevelt and the labor movement. The League also financed the anti-Semitic Sentinels of the Republic, a lobbying and intelligence network dedicated to repealing New Deal legislation right down to child labor laws.[30] J. Howard

Pew served on the executive committee of the American Liberty League and was a chief funder of the organization and several of its affiliates.[31]

Pew also served as chairman of an important NAM front organization, the National Industrial Information Committee (NIIC), founded in 1934 by General Motors executive Alfred Sloan. The NIIC was an anti-New Deal propaganda mill, which targeted public opinion through educators and the press.[32]

THE NATIONAL LAY COMMITTEE: THE NEW EMPIRE STRIKES BACK

The 1940s were marked by what historian Elizabeth Fones-Wolf has called a "postwar employer counteroffensive." This included the creation of organizations both inside and outside the mainline Protestant churches in an effort to contain and control the cultural authority of mainline Protestantism.

Part of this was an effort by the National Association of Manufacturers (NAM) to challenge what it called "doctrines inimical to the American system of freedom." To do this, it formed the Committee on Cooperation with Churches, which was led by long-time Pew ally and DuPont executive Jasper Crane.[33] By the end of 1943, 2,600 business and clerical leaders had participated in meetings convened by the NAM. The Jackson, Mississippi, Chamber of Commerce claimed that cooperation between business and clergy would weaken "subversive forces that would destroy [our] Way of Life and at the same time blow out Christianity and American Business."[34]

During this period, J. Howard Pew was at the hub of several conservative business-backed evangelical anti-mainline entities. One such enterprise, called Spiritual Mobilization,[35] had a reported 17,000 clergy representatives and a circulation of 100,000 for its publication *Faith and Freedom*. The group has been characterized as "[the] most influential of the clergy-oriented bastions of unrestrained individualism." Spiritual Mobilization leader James Fifield, pastor of the 4,500-member First Congregational Church of Los Angeles, was known for using his pulpit to promote racial prejudice as well.[36] Leonard Read, who founded the right-wing libertarian Foundation for Economic Education in 1946, got his start with Spiritual Mobilization.[37] Both organizations received substantial support from Pew.[38]

Pew was also the driving force behind the Christian Freedom Foundation (CFF), formed in 1950 and bankrolled by the J. Howard Pew Freedom Trust until the early 1970s. This influential organization distributed its publication, *Christian Economics,* to 175,000 clergy members at its peak, established a speakers' bureau, and sent free inserts for church bulletins to interested clergy.[39] CFF also played an important role in the development of the new Christian Right in the 1970s, and maintained links to the Presbyterian Lay Committee (see page 30).

CONTAINING THE ECUMENICAL MOVEMENT

The formative stages of Pew's fight against the ecumenical movement and the growing social gospel movement took shape in his attacks on the Federal Council of Churches (FCC), the forerunner of today's National Council of Churches. Founded in 1908, the FCC "offered the social gospel its highest platform," according to historian Donald Meyer.[40] The social gospel, among whose founders in the early decades of the century was Baptist leader Walter Rauschenbusch, focused on creating a more egalitarian social order. As such, it was situated in a prophetic tradition of devotion to the plight of working people and the poor.[41] The FCC's Social Creeds of 1912, 1919, and 1932 were touchstones in mainline Protestantism's growing embrace of social justice as a theological and institutional norm. This coincided with the fundamentalist-modernist controversies that embroiled the mainline churches, especially the Presbyterian church. The linkage of conservative theology with regressive politics, which crystallized in the mainline churches in the 1920s and 1930s, is also a hallmark of today's mainline renewal movements. Most important, however, is the corporate-sponsored reconfiguration and expansion of this fundamentalist agenda, coupled with its growing interface with right-wing libertarian politics, in the postwar period.

In a 1932 speech, President Roosevelt declared that he was "as radical as the Federal Council." But as historian Donald Meyer notes, Roosevelt "by no means swept into his ranks the church leaders who had written into the Social Creeds of 1912 and 1919 something like a checklist of principles that the New Deal was soon to make law."[42] Despite misgivings about its sufficiency, the FCC strongly supported the New Deal.

In the 1940s, the FCC sponsored several major conferences that tried to generate business and clergy dialogue on social issues. These discussions resulted in certain political gains in the eyes of the business community. In February 1950, however, the FCC sponsored a National Study Conference, which pitted United Auto Workers leader Walter Reuther against NAM secretary Noel Sargent. Reuther won the day with a speech reminiscent of the Hebrew Prophets, according to Methodist bishop and future NCC leader G. Bromley Oxnam. The resulting FCC report was viewed by Pew and his allies as being disproportionately pro-labor.[43]

The following fall, the National Lay Committee (with Pew as its chair) was formed in tandem with the National Council of Churches. Unable to split up or sufficiently undermine the FCC, Pew and his allies apparently shifted strategy and sought to make the NCC (which incorporated the FCC and 11 other Protestant ecumenical bodies) substantially dependent on his and his colleagues' largesse.[44] Fones-Wolf explained: "Pew had been a prominent critic of the Federal Council of Churches, charging that it promoted socialism and collectivism. Indeed, just two years earlier, Pew had agreed to finance a book exposing 'the subversive activities of the Federal Council.' But, by 1950, he had decided that rather than fight the Council from outside, more could be 'accomplished from within.'"[45]

The right-wing challenge to the NCC during its first few years was more threatening than anything until the 1990s. Pew and a core group of executives (notably Jasper Crane) with shared political roots in the anti-New Deal backlash of the mid-1930s, dominated the National Lay Committee. Pew broadened the group to include government officials, educators, and a handful of conservative labor leaders. Pew figured that in this way the NCC would be subject to their control and they would be able to extend their advisory role into one of de facto political censor.

Pew did not, however, rely entirely on inside leverage. He maintained longterm and continuing political and financial commitments to groups whose purpose it was to attack mainline liberalism and its ecumenical institutions, some of which are discussed in this report.

After a five-year struggle, the National Lay Committee (NLC) was defeated in its bid for power.[46] The defeat of the Pew faction marked a significant moment in the alignment of mainline Protestantism with social progress in the postwar years. Even in defeat, however, the NLC served as a forerunner of the Presbyterian Lay Committee and the denominational renewal movement as a whole. Four members of the NLC would go on to become founding or early board members of the PLC ten years later: Pew, Crane, Champion, and Lemuel T. Jones (president of Russell Stover Candies).[47]

After a five-year struggle, the National Lay Committee was defeated in its bid for power. The NLC served as a forerunner of the Presbyterian Lay Committee.

Pew's business colleagues on the National Lay Committee also included:

- Charles Hook, president of American Rolling Mill Company, former president of the National Association of Manufacturers, and chief backer of the Committee to Uphold Constitutional Government, a far-right antilabor organization.[48]
- Admiral Ben Moreell (USN-ret.), president and chairman of Jones and Laughlin Steel, a trustee of the right-wing libertarian

Foundation for Economic Education, and founding chairman of Americans for Constitutional Action—an electoral support vehicle for right-wing congressional candidates, financed in part by a group of far-right oil executives.[49]

- Henning Prentis, a former president of the National Association of Manufacturers who gained notoriety for supporting Spanish dictator Gen. Francisco Franco in the 1930s. He also served as lay consultant to the general board of the NCC.
- B.E. Hutchinson, a senior executive of the Chrysler Corporation, also served as a lay consultant to the NCC. Hutchinson and J. Howard Pew financed the purchase of the estate that housed the Foundation for Economic Education in Irvington, New York.[50] Following the dissolution of the NLC, he joined the John Birch Society (see Glossary).

Two of Pew's closest colleagues on the National Lay Committee were Olive Beech and Jasper Crane. Beech was president of Beech Aircraft, pioneer in the field of small commuter aircraft. She was also a financial backer of the private National Economic Council, a notorious anti-Semitic right-wing news and publishing operation based in Manhattan, whose leader, Merwin K. Hart, was an American lobbyist for the Spanish dictatorship of Gen. Francisco Franco.[51] Hart was also a Nazi apologist who opposed the Nuremberg Trials.[52]

Crane was elected vice president of the NCC and served on 18 different committees. A trustee of both Princeton University and Princeton Theological Seminary, he was a pivotal figure in the development of the DuPont munitions and chemical empire, serving as director of European operations from 1919 to 1926 and then as a member of the board of directors until 1946. In the 1930s, Crane helped to negotiate market-sharing and cooperative research agreements between DuPont and Nazi conglomerate I.G. Farben, as well as Lord McGowan's Imperial Chemical Industries in England.[53] McGowan was a member of The Link, which historian Charles Higham has described as "the British organization of highly placed Nazi sympathizers, which included in its membership some of the most prominent aristocrats in England." One of Crane's connections to these circles was Lammot du Pont, who Crane declared was "the finest man I ever knew." Lammot du Pont often dined at the Chrysler Building's Cloud Room with Charles Bedaux, who was a German industrial spy as well as Nazi leader Heinrich Himmler's liaison to the Duke of Windsor.[54]

Such dealings aside, Crane was personally a right-wing libertarian—a trustee of the Foundation for Economic Education, an incorporating member of the conservative Mt. Pelerin Society, and director of Van Nostrand Publishers, which published books by libertarian economist Ludwig von Mises in the 1950s. He maintained an extensive correspondence with Rose Wilder Lane, book review editor of Merwin K. Hart's National Economic Council.[55]

Pew and his colleagues viewed with deepening alarm the developments in both domestic and foreign policy during Harry Truman's second term as president. The growth of the labor and civil rights movements coupled with the rise of communism in China and the stalemate of the Korean War helped set the stage for a domestic ultraconservative resurgence under the banner of anticommunism.

Conservatives had viewed the founding of the National Council of Churches as a step toward the development of a mainline "superchurch" that would coordinate mainline Protestant support for progressive social policy.[56] Thus Pew viewed the NCC's need for start-up funding as an opportunity to use his considerable financial leverage to influence and control the NCC's deliberations and policies in its formative years.[57] During this period, the National Lay Committee sought to become a standing body with overarching powers of review.

Neither Pew's money nor his influence was sufficient to compel the NCC to conform to his views.

Bishop Oxnam led the opposition to this plan and alternatively sought to integrate National Lay Committee members into existing committees and agencies in an apparent effort to minimize the committee's role. Nevertheless, the group was able to leverage its financial weight against NCC policy initiatives through 1952. For example, it successfully blocked NCC pronouncements against the Bricker Amendment, which would have severely limited presidential authority to make treaties. This reflected the resistance among conservatives to agencies of international cooperation such as the United Nations.[58]

The National Lay Committee also forced the National Council of Churches Department of Church and Economic Life to rewrite its statement on Christian principles of economic life. Led by Bishop Oxnam, NCC leaders sought to unhinge themselves from National Lay Committee control. They were able, for example, to bypass the NCC General Board—where NLC review powers could be applied through the presence of delegates—to make a series of policy pronouncements on such matters as McCarthyism, federal aid to education, and public housing. Pew led a movement within the NLC threatening mass resignation if the NCC continued to engage in political activities of which he did not approve. However, neither Pew's money nor his influence was sufficient to compel the NCC to conform to his views. Pew stepped aside and let the NLC go out of existence in 1955. He later said that forming the NLC was "the most unfortunate decision of my life."[59]

Pew then narrowed his sights to his own denomination and formed the Presbyterian Lay Committee (PLC). The founding of the PLC signaled the emergence of a distinct denominational platform for this effort to gain control of the church from within rather than attacking it from without. Pew's legacy of right-wing patronage cuts across this transition and is illustrative of the broader political movement that the PLC brought into the church in the mid-1960s.

III. Agenda, Activities, and Political Ties

WORKING WITHIN THE CHURCH — The driving principle of the Presbyterian Lay Committee is to remain within the mainline church at all costs.[60] This emphasis, which is reflected in the broader Presbyterian renewal movement, also has roots in the anti-schismatic stance of the Covenant Fellowship of Presbyterians in the former Presbyterian Church in the U.S. (sometimes called the "southern church," see Glossary). This stance is sometimes mistakenly taken as a sign of political moderation when compared with conservative schisms such as that of the Presbyterian Church in America in 1973 (see Glossary).

Merely refusing to go into schism is not, however, a reliable indicator of mainstream values. In the case of PLC founder J. Howard Pew, for example, the avoidance of schism reflected his interest in gaining or influencing institutional power (even as he helped to advance the agenda of extreme groups outside the church, such as the John Birch Society).[61]

THE PLC REACHES INTO THE PEWS — The PLC's first publication, a biweekly newsletter called *The Restorer,* was aimed at denominational leaders.[62] When this proved ineffective, the PLC decided to reach into the pews, adopt a more populist tone, and with a boost of $50,000 from the J. Howard Pew Freedom Trust, launch *The Presbyterian Layman* in 1968.[63] Respondents to an earlier national ad campaign against the Confession of 1967 comprised *The Layman's* original mailing list, which was expanded through the use of church directories supplied by the original recipients.[64]

The publication's circulation climbed steadily, reportedly reaching over 340,000 by 1973 and the 600,000 mark in 1987, making it the most widely distributed Presbyterian publication in the world. In 1970, the PLC inaugurated a short-lived weekly national radio show heard in more than 70 cities at its peak.

The PLC developed a network of local chapters, the most active of which in the early days were in Pittsburgh, Philadelphia, Detroit, Washington, D.C., and Chicago. These urban chapters featured nationally known Presbyterians at their events, including J. Howard Pew, former U.S. Senate chaplain Richard Halverson, and Grove City College president Charles Mackenzie. By 1971, the PLC had formed at least 50 local chapters. The greatest concentration of PLC chapters was in the mid-Atlantic States, particularly New Jersey and Pennsylvania, as well as the Midwest, especially in Ohio, Indiana, and Michigan. There were also four chapters in California.[65] These chapters helped to establish regional leverage for the PLC's agenda of destabilizing the national leadership and programming of the church.

In the early years, the PLC's opposition to efforts in the UPC(USA) to support racial justice crystallized around two major figures: James Forman and Angela Davis. In 1969, Forman was given a General Assembly platform to unveil the National Black Economic Development Conference's *Black Manifesto*, perhaps the most controversial political program supporting racial justice ever to cross the threshold of public debate in the United States.[66] This document represented an authentic cry for economic justice in black communities, which remained deeply impoverished despite the political gains of the civil rights movement. The church took the stand of being open to this cry despite, not because of, the *Manifesto's* radical vision of challenging institutional racism in U.S. society, ultimately offering support on a much smaller scale than Forman proposed.

Provocative coverage of the *Black Manifesto* in *The Layman* set off a wave of outrage. This laity revolt reached catastrophic proportions when, two years later, the Council on Church and Race issued a $10,000 grant to the Angela Davis legal defense fund in 1971.[67] In addition to this, over the next few years, UPC(USA) support for the World Council of Churches (WCC) became controversial. This was at a time when the WCC's Fund to Combat Racism was giving humanitarian aid to African anti-colonial movements.[68] Two articles printed in early issues of *The Layman* set the tone for the PLC's sustained attack on the National Council of Churches and the World Council of Churches. The WCC was accused of promoting "Social Gospel, Revolution, Violence, Humanism, [and] Share the Wealth," while the NCC was accused of endorsing "Revolution."[69]

The church was also providing direct support for grassroots education and organizing in Colombia and in Native American communities through its Committee for the Self-Development of People in the early 1970s.[70] Moreover, the first denominational sexuality report was released in 1970, having been initiated by the church's Council on Church and Society in 1966. This report marked the church's commitment to liberalization on sexual issues, including homosexuality, as they relate to the church. It was received, but not endorsed, by the General Assembly in 1970 and was tempered with an attached motion reaffirming the church's commitment to biblical teachings on sexual activities deemed sinful.[71] Presbyterians Pro-Life credited this report with helping pave the way for the church's current pro-choice position on abortion.[72]

Fueled by the PLC, the controversies of this period, particularly those surrounding James Forman and Angela Davis, resulted in what Presbyterian writer John R. Fry has called the "great offering-plate boycott" in the early 1970s. This response by conservative laity to liberal trends in the denomination was the final surge in an eight-year downward trend in general or unrestricted mission giving, which declined 34 percent between 1965 and 1973. During the same period, however, *total* contributions steadily increased, demonstrating the political nature of the decline in general mission giving. "Finally surfaced," Fry asserts, "[this boycott] was a naked political effort calculated to punish the General Assembly agencies and force them to change policies." Fry goes on to claim that this decline in general mission giving fueled an historic "trivialization" of the Presbyterian church—its general diminishment as an institutional force in national public life.[73]

Seeking to seal this trend, in 1978 the PLC board passed a resolution calling for the dissolution of the Advisory Council on Church and Society (formerly the Council on Church and Society), the key agency for shaping denominational commitment to social justice.[74]

The growing political power of the conservative renewal movement became apparent in 1978, when, responding to a campaign fueled primarily by *The Layman*, the UPC General Assembly approved a "definitive guidance" (see Glossary) prohibiting gay ordination, in response to two presbytery overtures requesting such guidance.[75] Stated Clerk William Thompson later stipulated that presbyteries were bound by this General Assembly policy as an interpretation of the church's constitution, effectively ending the possibility of ordination for non-celibate gays and lesbians.

The definitive guidance of 1978 provided the foundation in church policy for a constitutional ban on gay ordination, which passed the PC(USA) General Assembly in 1996 and is generally referred to as Amendment B (see Glossary). Amendment B served the purpose of removing the issue of gay ordination from interpretive control of the General Assembly.

The PLC's development generally mirrored that of the New Right in the 1980s. Its close association with the Washington, D.C.-based Institute on Religion and Democracy (IRD) epitomizes this trend (see Glossary). PLC board members, including then-vice president J. Robert Campbell and Langdon S. Flowers (see page 32), were prominent on the founding steering committee of Presbyterians for Democracy and Religious Freedom (PDRF) in 1985. PDRF officially affiliated with IRD in 1990. Several early PDRF leaders, including founder John L. Boone, Q. Whitfield Ayres, Luke G. Williams, and William I. Monaghan, would go on to join the board of the PLC. Norman McClelland, at one time a member of the PDRF advisory board,[76] has been a longtime director, as well as chairman, of the far-right Rockford Institute.[77] Rockford, in turn, has several significant links to the PLC (see page 29).

Like the IRD, the PLC has attacked church support for economic justice and human rights in Central America, as well as the sanctuary movement (see Glossary), a national effort to shield Central American refugees from deportation by the U.S. government. The anti-apartheid movement was also targeted by both organizations. The IRD, notable for its close alignment with Reagan-era foreign policy, initially gained national attention for its campaign against the National Council of Churches in 1983.[78] In many ways, the IRD and its related denominational projects have functioned much like J. Howard Pew's Christian Freedom Foundation (see page 30) in its relentless attacks on mainstream social justice institutions.

In 1983, the "northern" United Presbyterian Church (USA), or UPC(USA), and the "southern" Presbyterian Church in the United States, or PC(US), united to form the PC(USA), which added conservative strength to the Presbyterian church nationally.

In 1985, a letter protesting Presbyterian social policy, signed by 20 Presbyterian members of Congress, was circulated throughout the church by Presbyterians for Democracy and Religious Freedom. *The Layman* reprinted this letter, along with an article denouncing the sanctuary movement (see Glossary) written by an organization that maintained close ties to Latin American military dictatorships.[79]

The IRD influence in the PC(USA) deepened in 1985 when IRD's director of research, Kerry Ptacek, joined the staff of the PLC as director of planning and projects.[80] He focused on developing a Presbytery Liaison Network, which sponsored regional training institutes for the development of congregational leadership in church politics.[81] As of 1988, about 1,100 congregations were linked in this network.[82]

The PLC's allegiance to the militarist politics of the New Right crystallized around its opposition to an internal church position paper called *Presbyterians and Peacemaking: Are We Now Called to Resistance?* The document, produced in 1986 by the Advisory Council on Church and Society, supported nonviolent civil disobedience against militarism in U.S. foreign policy.[83] Following a barrage of overtures (requests for action by the General Assembly) against the report sent to the 1987 General Assembly, the report was revised and the 1988 General Assembly accepted a new version of the policy paper, renamed *Christian Obedience in a Nuclear Age* (CONA). Prior to the 1988 General Assembly, PDRF issued a report attacking CONA. At the time of this report, four of the eight members of the PDRF executive committee were also staff or board members of the Presbyterian Lay Committee. Then-PLC president J. Robert Campbell was a member of the board of PDRF.[84]

PLC leader Parker Williamson expressed the organization's apparent animus towards the anti-apartheid movement in a 1985 article in *The Layman,* in which he supported the South African government, even as support was waning in conservative circles.[85] Six months later, *The Layman* ran an interview with Jonas Savimbi, leader of the right-wing terrorist movement UNITA in Angola, which was covertly backed by the government of South Africa.[86]

SEX AND THE PLC

In the wake of the fall of communism in 1989, the PLC shifted its focus to sexuality-based issues, especially feminism and gay and lesbian rights. The first wave of conservative dissent in this arena came in response to the 1991 report *Keeping Body and Soul Together: Sexuality, Spirituality, and Social Justice,* written by a Special Committee on Human Sexuality. This report, which, among other things, called for acceptance of sex outside of marriage, caused tremendous upheaval in the church, including a 2,000-member schism in renewal leader Clayton Bell's Highland Park Presbyterian Church in Dallas.[87]

In the wake of the fall of communism, the PLC shifted its focus to sexuality-based issues.

The PLC waged a sustained campaign against the report, beginning with the January/February 1991 issue of *The Layman,* which helped to generate 86 presbytery overtures (see Glossary) and 2,140 session resolutions (public statements of individual churches, but not binding on General Assembly deliberations) against the report. PLC president J. Robert Campbell hand delivered 10,000 letters of protest to the 1991 General Assembly committee charged with considering the report.[88]

The controversy generated considerable national attention and spurred a conservative mobilization on sexuality issues in the major denominations. During this time, the PLC joined forces with two activists from the far-right Presbyterian Church in America (see Glossary) to attack the PC(USA) sexuality report. Rev. George Grant and Mark Horne authored two books stemming from the controversy, the first of which, *Unnatural Affections: The Impuritan Ethic of Homosexuality and the Modern Church*, was published in 1991 and was mailed to PC(USA) pastors around the country. Among other things, this book claims that the "scourge of AIDS amply demonstrates [that] when a culture departs from Christ's standard of justice, frightful consequences are meted out to the wicked and innocent alike."[89] The book jacket is emblazoned with endorsements from two PC(USA) renewal leaders: Herbert Schlossberg (current president of Presbyterian Action), and then-PLC president J. Robert Campbell. Campbell wrote that the book "will answer many of the questions we have all been asking about these issues over the years."[90]

Grant and Horne come out of the Christian Reconstructionist movement, which seeks to impose a theocracy in the U.S. Reflecting this orientation, the authors claim that "[as] Christians, our longterm goals for the civil government must include the positive enforcement of justice as defined by Scripture...To begin with, this means campaigning for the restoration of moral constraint laws—ranging from alimony exaction precepts [sic] to anti-sodomy statutes."[91]

Both books uphold the biblical sanction of capital punishment for homosexuality.

Grant and Horne published an expanded version of *Unnatural Affections* in 1993 under a new title: *Legislating Immorality—the Homosexual Movement Comes out of the Closet.* Both books uphold the biblical sanction of capital punishment for homosexuality.[92] In the acknowledgements in *Legislating Immorality*, the authors complain of the difficulties of combating a "homosexual movement" whose growing strength they felt was reflected in the PC(USA) task force report, *Keeping Body and Soul Together.* According to Grant and Horne, their task "involved research into unspeakable obscenities...traumatic personal encounters with both the victims and the perpetrators of unimaginable perversions...[and] the fiercest spiritual warfare that either of us has ever experienced."[93] Grant and Horne thank the PLC for its support in the acknowledgements of both books.[94]

THE REIMAGINING CRISIS: "CLEANING HOUSE"

From the winter of 1993 through the spring of 1994, the PLC gained national news coverage for its attack on the PC(USA)-supported ecumenical ReImagining conference in Minneapolis, Minnesota. This event, supported with funding and staff primarily by the PC(USA) and the United Methodist Church, provided a groundbreaking platform for woman-centered theological exploration. One of the central purposes of ReImagining is to "challenge the system of patriarchy and other sinful structures that deny equality."[95]

In all, 2,200 women participated in this event, including 409 Presbyterians. It was co-sponsored by the Ecumenical Decade Churches in Solidarity with Women Committee of the Greater Minneapolis/St. Paul Area and the Minnesota Council of Churches. The PC(USA) contributed $66,000 and provided support for staff persons to attend the conference.[96]

Following the lead of the PLC, conservative churches mobilized to punish the denomination for supporting ReImagining.

Following the lead of the PLC, conservative churches mobilized to punish the denomination for supporting ReImagining, which was described as heretical. The protest contributed to a multimillion-dollar budget shortfall in the PC(USA) and the forced resignation of a key executive, Mary Ann Lundy, director of the church's Women's Ministry Unit and associate director of churchwide planning at the time.

The campaign against ReImagining, and the attack on the PC(USA) for its partial sponsorship, was coordinated with Presbyterians for Renewal and the Institute on Religion and Democracy (IRD), and gained national attention and media coverage. A key figure was *Layman* freelancer Rev. Susan Cyre, who attended the conference and coordinated with IRD in covering it.[97] After ReImagining, IRD hired Cyre as a part-time consultant.[98] Cyre is now executive director of Presbyterians for Faith, Family and Ministry (PFFM) and editor of its journal, *Theology Matters.*[99]

Parker Williamson, executive editor of *The Layman,* believes that the backlash to ReImagining may lead to a break between the liberal minority that allegedly controls the church and the broad middle of theologically conservative, but institutionally loyal church members. He believes this could result in "enough movement to tilt the denominational balance" to the right. "By the summer of 1994," he claimed, "the de facto leftist/institutional loyalist hegemony had been dealt a crippling blow, one whose consequence in plummeting financial support for the national church leadership has been so dramatic as to appear irreversible."[100]

Interestingly, Williamson's analysis echoes Gary North's views on earlier Presbyterian conflicts. According to North, the failure of the "institutional loyalists" led to the liberal-modernist takeover of mainline Presbyterianism—definitively marked by the expulsion of fundamentalist leader J. Gresham Machen in 1936.[101] If Williamson is correct, the ReImagining backlash augurs an historic reversal of the liberal-moderate alliance, which North believes captured the church in the 1930s.

In 1995, *The Layman* continued its attack on feminism in a series of articles by Judy Theriault. Religious feminism, in Theriault's view, prioritizes civil rights over duty to God. Theriault is associate director of the Presbyterian Center for Mission Studies in Pasadena, California, a member organization in the right-wing Presbyterian Renewal Network. Playing on the double entendre of "cleaning house," she explains that women should "clean the Lord's house" by returning to a time "a century ago when women were perceived as the guardians of faith," not by holding office, but "as they taught children and exerted influence on their fathers, brothers, husbands, and sons." Having been "guardians of the faith," she continues, "Presbyterian women are now often seen as the opponents of it."102

The PLC waged an aggressive campaign against the National Network of Presbyterian College Women (NNPCW) in 1998 and 1999. NNPCW, a PC(USA) campus ministry with activities on 85 campuses, was formed in 1993 during the tenure of Mary Ann Lundy. The attack on NNPCW featured an attempt to claim that the young women's organization was a continuation of the ReImagining movement, and therefore implicated in the spread of heretical theologies including worship of the goddess Sophia.

The Presbyterian right has cast feminist currents as heretical with the epithet "Sophia-worship." As a result, ReImagining-related feminist groups and individuals within the PC(USA) have been unfairly accused of attempting to replace the Bible with pagan traditions. In fact, ReImagining embraces a wide-ranging "wisdom tradition" in biblical understanding and scholarship. Sophia is the Greek word for wisdom, which is also personified as the goddess. Sophia as wisdom is specifically included in several books of the Bible, notably Proverbs. The wisdom tradition, of which Sophia is but one part, stands well within mainstream biblical scholarship and Christian tradition.103 The primary focus of ReImagining is to seek the ongoing relevance of biblical and Christian tradition to issues of women's role in society. To facilitate this, the group cultivates continuing, rather than static, understandings of divine revelation.

Seizing on a routine request for continued funding, critics attacked the NNPCW at the 1998 General Assembly, leading to a vote to defund the network. In a remarkable turn of events, General Assembly moderator Douglas Oldenburg permitted a demonstration of hundreds of spectators and commissioners late in the evening. A motion to reconsider the vote from Assembly vice moderator James Mead led to a restoration of funding—although a special review committee was established to bring recommendations concerning the NNPCW to the 1999 General Assembly in Fort Worth, Texas.104

Following the 1998 General Assembly, the PLC's campaign

The Layman featured a series of articles by Judy Theriault, explaining that women should "clean the Lord's house" by returning to a time "a century ago when women were perceived as the guardians of faith."

focused on the NNPCW's curriculum, *Young Women Speak*, as well as its web site. The NNPCW was accused of supporting views on sexuality that did not conform to the constitutional standards of the church, which emphasize heterosexual relations within marriage. Specifically, the network was accused of advocating acceptance of premarital sex, homosexual sex, and gay ordination.[105]

Perhaps the nadir of this effort was an unusual "investigation" by Parker Williamson. Starting at the official PC(USA) web site, Williamson followed the standard link to the web site of the church-funded college women. From there, Williamson followed the hyper-links on their site. In a press release, *The Layman* declared that it "found troubling material including suggested links to web sites that were linked to pornography" on the NNPCW site.[106]

In a method reminiscent of McCarthyism, *The Layman* detailed a succession of links. According to an account in the fundamentalist *World* magazine, "[t]wo links on the NNPCW's pages, 'Sexuality and Spirituality' and 'Christian Views on Homosexuality,' pointed to off-site pages of other groups, which in turn contained links to porno sites and dating services for lesbians and gay men. *Layman* staffers easily clicked their way from the PC(USA) site into porno sites via the NNPCW's links. They concluded the NNPCW was leading some college women into pornography."[107] In early July 1998, the college women's web site was taken down. Williamson later declared that the NNPCW was a "gateway to hardcore homosexual pornography."[108]

In a hearing sponsored by the General Assembly Council Special Review Committee in January 1999, Parker Williamson, Sylvia Dooling (of Voices of Orthodox Women), and Terry Schlossberg (of Presbyterians Pro-Life) engaged in further attacks on the NNPCW. Williamson suggested that Campus Crusade for Christ, Bill Bright's right-wing evangelical parachurch (see Glossary) organization, would be a better recipient of PC(USA) support than the NNPCW.[109] While the NNPCW remains a funded project of the church, it operates in a diminished mode.

The broader politics of the attack on social concerns in recent years have been evident in the context of the "Building Community Among Strangers" document, which deals with questions of religious diversity and the rapidly changing racial and cultural demographics of U.S. society. Characterized in *The Layman* as a "controversial study paper that calls for building community by denying the lordship of Jesus Christ," the project was deferred for further revision at the 1998 General Assembly. The resulting rewrite, influenced by evangelicals, made more explicit a conservative Christian framework for the social vision of the original.[110] The main thrust of this revision was to counter the focus on inclusivity in the original. The revised "Building Community Among Strangers" was accepted at the 1999 General Assembly.

IV. Political Ties

In addition to the political affiliations mentioned above, PLC directors, advisors, and staff have been directly involved in many right-wing organizations over the years. These involvements not only inform an understanding of the history of the PLC, but suggest its contemporary direction as well.

- **The Rockford Institute:** Formed in the late 1970s, the Rockford Institute is the center of a resurgent "Old Right," loosely grouped under the banner of "paleo-conservatism" in the current discourse. Paleo-conservatism combines traditional business and property rights libertarianism with extreme cultural traditionalism and a streak of nativism and racism.[111] According to conservative author William Rusher, Rockford "has served the paleo-conservatives as an important institutional base." Paleo-conservatives, he says, "tend to identify themselves with the views of Pat Buchanan."[112] *Layman* editor Parker Williamson and longtime PLC ally Charles MacKenzie have both served as members of the Rockford advisory board.[113] Rockford characterizes the role of its advisory board, called the Main Street Committee, as one of assisting "the Institute in research, writing, planning, and communication. Members are listed in a *Directory of Experts*, which is distributed to the press and friends of the Institute."[114] When it was founded in 1990, the Main Street Committee described itself as a network of educators and policy analysts with different backgrounds but shared commitments to Rockford's goals.[115]

  Paleo-conservatism combines traditional business and property rights libertarianism with extreme cultural traditionalism and a streak of nativism and racism.

- **The Plymouth Rock Foundation:** A far-right Christian Reconstructionist network, which for many years was led by the late Rus Walton, an organizer of Barry Goldwater's 1964 presidential campaign. PLC board member Phyllis Moehrle (the first woman vice president of the National Association of Manufacturers) has served on the advisory board.[116] Rev. Lane Adams, the former pastor at Key Biscayne Presbyterian Church, is the Plymouth Rock Foundation's national minister-at-large. Among Adams' successors at Key Biscayne was Presbyterians for Renewal founder John Huffman.[117]

- **Council for National Policy (CNP):** This umbrella group of top right-wing corporate, civic, and religious leaders is devoted to comprehensive policy and strategy development. It emerged in the early 1980s essentially out of John Birch Society circles, led by Nelson Bunker Hunt, oil magnate and former member of Clayton Bell's Highland Park Church in Dallas. Since then, it has become a key behind-the-scenes strategy organization and a virtual *Who's Who* of rightist politics.[118] PLC director W. Robert Stover is a longtime member of the CNP.[119]

- **Christian Freedom Foundation (CFF):** Started by Howard Kershner with a $50,000 grant from J. Howard Pew in 1950,[120] CFF was an important promoter of right-wing libertarian politics aimed at church leaders of the postwar period. CFF's chief economic advisor in the 1950s was Percy Greaves, a disciple of libertarian economist Ludwig von Mises and frequent contributor to the CFF newsletter, *Christian Economics*, which reached a circulation among clergy of more than 175,000 at its peak. Greaves had formerly worked as a researcher for Rep. Fred A. Hartley, best known for the Taft-Hartley amendment, which significantly undermined the political power of labor unions. He was a founding member of the far-right Constitution Party, which arose as an electoral vehicle for General Douglas MacArthur, in the wake of the Republican nomination of Eisenhower in 1952 (MacArthur declined to be their candidate). Greaves also served on the initial advisory board of Liberty Lobby in 1958, a far-right organization that has been described by the Anti-Defamation League as "the nation's leading anti-Semitic propagandist,"[121] and by author Russ Bellant as "quasi-Nazi."[122] Longtime CFF president Kershner was notably racialist in his otherwise laissez-faire worldview, stating once to a reporter who questioned him on racial integration, "Well, the Negroes must first catch up with us anthropologically."[123] Various Pew family related trusts contributed millions of dollars to CFF from the late 1950s through the early 1970s.[124] In 1975, a group of rightist businessmen including Richard DeVos (Amway), John Talcott (Ocean Spray) and Arthur De Moss (National Liberty Insurance Co.) took control of CFF and transformed it into an agency focused on getting Christian conservatives elected to Congress in 1976. As Art De Moss put it, "The vision is to rebuild the foundations of the republic as it was when first founded—a 'Christian Republic.'"[125] This effort was the brainchild of Rep. John B. Conlan (R-AZ). Its central text was a political manifesto titled *One Nation Under God*, by Christian Reconstructionist Rus Walton, and published by Third Century Publishers. Rightist activist Howard Phillips called the book "a valuable survey of God-ordained authority in the family, church, and civil government."[126] CFF also launched what was probably the first conservative evangelical voter education and mobilization project and laid the ground-

"Well, the Negroes must first catch up with us anthropologically."
—longtime CFF president Kershner to a reporter who questioned him on racial integration

Various Pew family-related trusts contributed millions of dollars to CFF from the late 1950s through the early 1970s

CFF launched what was probably the first conservative evangelical voter education and mobilization project.

work for the Religious Roundtable, a key organization of the Christian Right in the 1980s.[127] As of 1975, PLC founding board member W. Robert Stover was also a board member of CFF, along with Kershner, DeVos, Talcott, and DeMoss, among other businessmen.[128] *The Presbyterian Layman* ran an editorial by John B. Conlan in 1975 entitled "Christians Needed in Politics," in which he promoted *One Nation Under God* and Third Century Publishers' "Good Government Kit."[129]

- **Grove City College (GCC):** The PLC has held its annual convention at Grove City College in Grove City, Pennsylvania, since 1973. PLC founder J. Howard Pew was the college's primary benefactor and chairman of the board of trustees for many years. Pew shaped the college into a cornerstone institution of conservative Christian higher education. GCC gained national prominence in the early 1980s by launching one of the most significant assaults on civil rights protection since the passage of the Civil Rights Act of 1964.[130]

The PLC has held its annual convention at Grove City College in Grove City, Pennsylvania, since 1973.

Christian Reconstructionist author Gary North has hailed Pew's "entrepreneurial and ecumenical" vision in persuading Hans Sennholz, a Lutheran, to join the GCC faculty and "serve as a beacon in the department of economics,"[131] which he went on to head from 1956 to 1991. Sennholz was a German *Luftwaffe* pilot in WWII, fighting in France, the Soviet Union, and North Africa.[132] He has developed a substantial following within the libertarian wing of the Christian right. North cites Sennholz as among the most important theorists of Christian or biblical economics, a theocratic variant of classical business and property-rights libertarianism.[133] After retiring, Sennholz became president of the Foundation for Economic Education, another Pew-funded agency and perhaps the most significant right-wing libertarian institution of the post-World War II period.

As president of Grove City College, Charles McKenzie hosted and convened PLC conventions throughout his tenure from 1971 to 1990. In the early stages of the PLC's development, he served as the featured speaker at chapter and prospective chapter events. MacKenzie is currently a professor of philosophy at Reformed Theological Seminary (RTS) in Orlando, Florida. RTS President Luder Whitlock, who preached at the PLC annual convention in 1995,[134] has been involved in such Christian Right projects as the International Council on Biblical Inerrancy (precursor to the theocratic Coalition on Revival; see Glossary) and the Council on Biblical Manhood and Womanhood, which advocates "male headship" of the family and the church.[135]

MacKenzie is also a prominent endorser of the Separation of

School and State Alliance, which advocates the complete privatization of education and characterizes the Christian Right's school voucher agenda as a liberal plot against American families. The Alliance awarded MacKenzie its de Tocqueville award in education in 1998.[136] Fellow Alliance endorsers include Gary North and right-wing libertarian Llewellyn Rockwell, as well as Howard Phillips and columnist Joseph Sobran,[137] who are, respectively, the presidential and vice presidential candidates of the far-right Constitution Party in the 2000 election. PLC director Warren Reding, a Pittsburgh attorney, is also listed as a member of the Alliance.[138]

V. Key PLC Leaders

W. Robert Stover, a founding board member, served as PLC chairman from 1985 to 1989. Born in Philadelphia in 1921, he attended Waynesburg College, the University of Illinois, and the Wharton School of Business. In 1948, in Walnut Creek, California, he founded Western Temporary Services, which went on to become one of the largest temporary employment services in the world. Stover served as CEO as well as chairman of the board of directors.[139] He served as a director of the Christian Freedom Foundation in the 1970s. Stover has also been a longtime member of the Council for National Policy.[140]

Stover has been a central figure in the West Coast conservative evangelical movement since the late 1940s. He found Christ under Rev. Robert Munger at First Presbyterian Church of Berkeley, California. Munger, a former dean of the School of Theology at Fuller Theological Seminary, has mentored many evangelical leaders, including Rev. Lloyd Ogilvie, the current U.S. Senate chaplain and who was for many years pastor of the conservative evangelical Hollywood First Presbyterian Church.[141]

Stover has served as national fundraising chairman for Young Life, a major right-wing youth ministry; chairman of the Oakland Billy Graham Crusade;[142] and chairman of Fuller Theological Seminary, an influential nondenominational seminary and a key training ground for much of the leadership of the right-wing renewal movement within the PC(USA).[143] Stover has also been deeply involved in international evangelical mission work, serving as chairman of the Los Angeles-based African Enterprise, and as a member of the General Council of Latin America Mission.[144]

Langdon S. Flowers, a longtime member of the PLC board of directors, is credited with bringing Parker Williamson to the attention of the organization in the mid-1980s.[145] Flowers was born in

Thomasville, Georgia, in 1922 and led Flowers Industries, Inc., from 1965 to 1985. He was president and CEO from 1965 to 1976, vice chairman and CEO from 1976 to 1980, and chairman from 1980 to 1985. Flowers Industries is a multibillion-dollar baked-goods conglomerate that includes the Keebler, Cheez-it, Famous Amos, Nature's Own, and Mrs. Smith's labels. Flowers has served on the executive committee of the National Association of Manufacturers.[146]

Langdon Flowers is a financial contributor to many politicians, both as an individual and through the Flowers Industries Political Action Committee. In addition to substantial "soft-money" contributions, the Flowers PAC has donated more than $1.5 million to individual candidates (almost all Republicans) over the last 20 years. In 1994, for example, the Flowers PAC donated $5,000 each to the campaigns of 33 Republicans, including such leaders as Rep. Bob Barr (R-GA), Sen. Rick Santorum (R-PA), Sen. James Inhofe (R-OK), and Sen. Spencer Abraham (R-MI). These four candidates also received 100 percent ratings from the Christian Coalition.[147] The Flowers PAC gave Oliver North two contributions, totaling $10,000, for his Senate race in 1994. In 1996, highlights included three contributions, totaling $8,000, to the Senate campaign of Woody Jenkins (R-LA). The Flowers PAC also made $5,000 contributions to Sen. Jesse Helms (R-NC), Sen. Strom Thurmond (R-SC), Sen. Bob Smith (R-NH) and Rep. Steve Stockman (R-TX).[148] Sen. Smith made news in the fall of 1999 for leaving the GOP to entertain the possibility of running as the presidential candidate of the far-right U.S. Taxpayers Party (see Glossary).[149] Upon his election in 1994, Rep. Stockman took a "Christian oath of office" from Baptist minister Rev. Rick Scarborough, founder of a "Reconstructionist-oriented political organization called Vision America."[150] Langdon Flowers personally contributed to the 1996 presidential campaign of Sen. Phil Gramm (R-TX) as well.[151]

Flowers Industries has long had close family and corporate ties to the Atlanta-based Southeastern Legal Foundation, a right-wing public interest law firm. Among the founders of Southeastern Legal in 1976 were former Rep. Ben Blackburn (R-GA)[152] and William H. Flowers, Langdon's older brother and the first chairman of Flowers Industries.[153] William Flowers served on the board of Southeastern Legal for 14 years. Southeastern Legal Foundation made news in 1999 for its campaign to abolish Atlanta's affirmative action program.[154]

Ben Blackburn's eight-year congressional career was notable for its perfect record on civil rights: he opposed every major piece of civil-rights legislation.[155] President of Southeastern Legal from 1976 to 1985, Blackburn was once quoted as saying, concerning public housing, "if it was up to me, we would go back to public hangings, and we would not have any more trouble collecting rent."[156] Adorning the walls of Southeastern Legal's office is a photograph of Lester Maddox, former segregationist governor of Georgia.[157]

In 1983, William Flowers was elected chairman of Southeastern's board of trustees and served in that position until 1987.[158] A threatened boycott of Flowers Industries by the Georgia Black Chamber of Commerce caused Amos R. McMullian, the current chairman and CEO of Flowers Industries, to resign from the board of Southeastern Legal in 1999. He had served on the board since 1990. Although McMullian claimed that Flowers Industries' financial support for Southeastern Legal would end,[159] he has also asserted that he continues to support the work of the organization, which he says "embraces the philosophy the nation was founded on."[160] Langdon Flowers' family and business ties to Southeastern Legal appear to have been severed with the McMullian resignation, however.

Chapman Cox, a PLC board member since 1997, is also on the boards of both the Presbyterian Church USA Foundation and its for-profit arm, the New Covenant Trust Co. He is currently senior vice president of Lockheed Martin IMS. Born in Dayton, Ohio, in 1940, Cox was educated at the University of Southern California and at Harvard University, where he received a J.D. in 1965. He began his law career as an associate at Adams, Duque & Hazeltine in Los Angeles (1968–1972) and then moved to Sherman & Howard in Denver, where he was a partner from 1972 to 1981 and again from 1987 to 1990. He served as general counsel to the Colorado Republican Party from 1977 to 1981.

From 1981 to 1987 he held a series of positions in the Pentagon: deputy assistant secretary, Department of the Navy (1981–1983); assistant secretary, Department of the Navy (1983–1984); general counsel, Department of Defense (1984–1985); and assistant secretary, Department of Defense (1985–1987), where he was in charge of special operations and low-intensity conflict.[161] He has been a member of the American Bar Association standing committee on law and national security since 1988.[162]

After leaving government, he became president and CEO of United Service Organizations (1990–1996) and moved to Lockheed Martin in 1996. He is currently on the board of the Fund for American Studies—a rightist recruiting and leadership development forum started in the late 1960s by conservative leaders Charles Edison,[163] William F. Buckley, and Marvin Liebman. The Fund is currently divided into four separate program institutes and run in cooperation with Georgetown University.[164]

Robert L. Howard, the chairman of the Presbyterian Lay Committee, joined the executive committee of the Presbyterian Coalition in 1999 and has chaired its communications and development task force.[165] He was previously a member of the Coalition's steering committee (1996–1997).

Howard is chairman of Foulston and Siefkin, one of the largest law firms in Kansas.[166] The firm's clients include such corporate giants as Boeing, Cargill, Dow Corning, and Koch Industries. Howard was chief legal adviser to Koch Industries, the second largest privately held corporation in the United Sates, during its 1983 buy-out of family shareholders Bill and Fred Koch. A spectacular family battle ensued, culminating in a billion-dollar lawsuit brought against Koch Industries by Bill and Fred Koch, among others, who claimed that their stock was undervalued in 1983. In 1998, Howard successfully defended Koch Industries in this suit.[167] Koch Industries executives Charles and David Koch, defendants in the suit, are both directors of major foundations supportive of right-wing organizations—notably the libertarian Cato Institute and the Heritage Foundation.[168] The Cato Institute has received $21 million from Koch Industries over the years.[169] David Koch was the vice-presidential candidate of the Libertarian Party in 1980. The Koch brothers' father, Fred Koch, was a member of the national council of the John Birch Society.[170]

Howard is a former naval intelligence officer, has an LL.B. from the University of Kansas and has served as a trustee of Sterling College. Fellow Sterling College trustee J. Robert Campbell, then-president of the PLC (1986–1993), invited Howard onto the PLC board.[171] Formerly a Monsanto chemist and more recently academic dean of the College of the Ozarks, Campbell has also been a member of Rev. Benjamin Sheldon's Bethany Collegiate Church in Havertown, Pennsylvania.[172]

Howard is currently a ruling elder at Eastminster Presbyterian Church in Wichita, Kansas. Howard's wife Joanne, also an elder, is a director of Presbyterians for Renewal.[173] Robert and Joanne Howard each contributed money to Pat Buchanan's campaign for the GOP nomination for president in 1992.[174]

Eastminster was long pastored by Dr. Frank N. Kik, a former vice chairman of Presbyterians United for Biblical Concerns (see Glossary), and an editorial advisor to *The Presbyterian Layman*.[175] Kik is now professor of practical theology at Reformed Theological Seminary in Charlotte, North Carolina. He has chaired the advisory board of World Impact, Inc., a national urban "discipling and church planting" ministry whose advisors include such right-wing evangelical leaders as Bill Bright of Campus Crusade for Christ, Bill

McCartney of Promise Keepers, and Los Angeles black Republican evangelist Rev. E.V. Hill.[176] Kik published a seminal attack against the National Council of Churches and the World Council of Churches in *The Presbyterian Layman* in 1987 (September/October). Former Grove City College President Charles MacKenzie served as senior pastor at Eastminster Presbyterian Church in 1993.[177]

Q. Whitfield Ayres, a member of the PLC board since 1995, served as president of Presbyterians for Democracy and Religious Freedom from 1994 to 1996[178] (see Glossary). He is the principal of the Atlanta-based Ayres and Associates, a prominent Republican research and polling firm that focuses on the South. Ayres worked on Lamar Alexander's 1996 presidential campaign, as well as the campaigns of U.S. senators Paul Coverdell (R-GA), Strom Thurmond (R-SC), Jeff Sessions (R-AL), and GOP governors of South Carolina David Beasley and Carroll Campbell[179]—for whom he also worked as senior executive assistant for budget and social policy.

Ayres specializes in candidacies that unite traditional Republicans and religious conservatives and has called for an anti-affirmative action agenda in Republican electoral strategy in the wake of the passage of the Civil Rights Act of 1991.[180]

Ayres is a member of Alpharetta Presbyterian Church in Alpharetta, Georgia. A graduate of Davidson College, Ayres received a Ph.D. in political science from the University of North Carolina at Chapel Hill.

Parker Williamson joined the editorial advisory board of *The Presbyterian Layman* in 1984 and was appointed editor in 1987.[181] He is currently executive editor of *The Layman* and chief operating officer of the Presbyterian Lay Committee. He has also played a major role in the Presbyterian Coalition and continues to serve on the nominating committee of its board of directors.

Parker Williamson is the son of the late Rene de Visme Williamson and was raised in Baton Rouge, Louisiana. The elder Williamson, a right-wing specialist in political theology (he was an early critic of liberation theology), chaired the political science department at Louisiana State University from 1955 to 1963.[182] For more than a decade (1978–1989), he was a director of the Covenant Fellowship of Presbyterians, the southern church precursor to Presbyterians for Renewal.

Parker Williamson attended Rhodes College in Memphis, Tennessee, and received his theological training at Union Theological Seminary in Richmond, Virginia, where he was a student of orthodox Calvinist theologian John Leith. Interestingly, Williamson says

Q. Whitfield Ayres is the principal of the Atlanta-based Ayres and Associates, a prominent Republican research and polling firm that focuses on the South.

he was one of three Union students to join Martin Luther King Jr. on his historic march to Selma.[183]

Ordained in 1965, Williamson was previously pastor of First Presbyterian Church in Lenoir, North Carolina, beginning in 1972. Williamson served the wider Presbyterian Church (US) as a member of the Committee on Church and Society of the Synod of North Carolina, and as a member of the General Assembly Mission Board from 1974 to 1977, where he was chair of its Division of National Missions. Active briefly as a "hunger action enabler" for the PC(US) mission board, Williamson says he turned toward conservative renewal after Rhodesian guerrillas, which he claims were funded by the World Council of Churches, shot down a plane and allegedly murdered several Christian missionaries who survived the crash.[184]

Echoing South African government propaganda of the time, Williamson later claimed that white control in South Africa was "not a case of colonialism" and that apartheid was created not to sustain white supremacy, but to "maintain historic boundaries among disparate ethnic communities."[185] He further argued that negative views of white control in South Africa are a product of "Marxist" revisionism. He claimed that "Whatever is of economic value [in South Africa] is the result of white activity . . . Primitive Africans lived above those resources for many generations, lacking the motivation, technology, organization, and managerial skills necessary to make use of the potential wealth [there]. . . ."[186] Apparently, Williamson did not oppose apartheid as a system, but only what he called its "more offensive aspects." He even went so far as to claim that "apartheid is not unique to South Africa. . . it is typical of social policy throughout the continent. . . ."[187]

Williamson has often used the pages of *The Layman* to keep a spotlight on Southern Africa, continuing the PLC's longterm efforts to undermine the African National Congress of South Africa (ANC) and related liberation movements.[188] In his important study of the right, *Funding the War of Ideas,* Presbyterian journalist Leon Howell points to an obituary Parker Williamson wrote upon the death of Johan Heyns of South Africa. This is a good example of "the attack mode he [Williamson] uses and how distorted his judgment can be," according to Howell. Williamson stated that "In 1991. . . endorsed by the South African Council of Churches, ANC terrorists wreaked havoc in the townships, spilling blood into the streets. Millions of South African blacks were unemployed, many of their jobs having been sacrificed on the altar called sanctions . . . Mandela's ministers, and the scores of former ANC lieutenants they have brought into the infrastructure, are paying themselves exorbitant salaries . . . Incompetence reigns . . . ."[189]

Williamson's "attack mode" in this instance is just one example of a PLC legacy going back to the early 1970s, when the World Council of Churches' Fund to Combat Racism gained international attention for its humanitarian support of African anti-colonial movements.

At the 50th anniversary meeting of the World Council of Churches in Harare, Zimbabwe, in 1998, Williamson rebuked the WCC for supporting Robert Mugabe's Patriotic Front. "Rhodesian blacks were in no position to run this sophisticated and highly efficient infrastructure," Williamson declared. "Theirs had been a tribal life, governed by a worldview that could not easily comprehend ideological assumptions on which the Rhodesian economy was formed."[190]

The occasion for Williamson's broadside stemmed from his leadership role as a member of the steering committee of the Association for Church Renewal (ACR), an IRD-sponsored coalition of right-wing "renewal" executives founded in 1996 to oppose the social justice traditions and objectives of the mainline churches. ACR published a challenge to the World Council of Churches called *Proclaim Liberty: A Jubilee Appeal* in 1998. In an accompanying position paper, ACR leader Faye Short declared that "much of contemporary Western feminist ideology is antithetical to biblical values" and "seeks systematically to dismantle the very biblical witness that has ennobled and liberated women."[191]

Williamson has served on the advisory board of the Rockford Institute since at least 1992.

Williamson has served on the advisory board of the Rockford Institute since at least 1992,[192] and provided Rockford founder John Howard with substantial space in the pages of *The Layman*.[193] Thomas Fleming, Rockford's current president and longtime editor of its magazine, *Chronicles*, was a founder of *The Southern Partisan* and is currently on the board of the League of the South.[194] The League is a central network in the far-right neo-Confederate movement (see Glossary). Apparently resonating with these currents, in 1999 Williamson delivered a speech entitled "Who Are Our People?" in New York City, in which he emphasized his Deep South roots and suggested a Southern sensibility, where "genes and chromosomes count" as the best way of gauging the question "[what] does it mean to be a Presbyterian?"[195]

In 1997, Rockford president Allan Carlson stepped down to head a new Rockford initiative, the Howard Center for Family, Religion & Society,[196] to which Williamson serves as an adviser.[197] The Howard Center is the founder and co-convener of the World Congress of Families, the most significant international formation opposed to United Nations family planning policy.[198]

Williamson's 1996 book, *Standing Firm: Reclaiming Christian Faith in Times of Controversy,*[199] attempts to read current controversies in the church in light of the Council of Nicea (325 A.D.), which pitted the "forces of Christian faith" against "cultural accommodation." *Standing Firm* was endorsed "heartily" by Christian Right leader Bill Bright, whose relationship with the PLC dates back to at least 1987, when he was the PLC's featured "Conference Preacher."[200] The PLC sent the book free of charge to PC(USA) pastors across the country.

VI. Funding

The Presbyterian Lay Committee's effectiveness is closely linked to the breadth of its funding. Between 1989 and 1997, total revenue was approximately $13.4 million. In 1997, the PLC recorded an income of approximately $1.5 million.[201]

The PLC has received more than $4 million in grants from the J. Howard Pew Freedom Trust since 1968. In 1996 and 1998, the Pew grants increased from a two-year increment of $375,000 to a two-year increment of $560,000.[202]

The bulk of PLC income apparently derives from small contributions. Former PLC vice president William Hoppe, a retired Bethlehem Steel executive, reported that the PLC received "no large donations except for one $10,000 gift last year" (1994).[203] However, in 1995, the PLC received at least four contributions of $10,000 or more, including one grant of $185,000.[204] 1996 saw grants of $35,000 and $25,000, among other large donations. In 1997, one donor contributed $39,785.[205]

In 1994, the PLC claimed that 21,500 donors provided 80 percent of its income.[206] While this statistic suggests an image of significant grassroots financial support, it downplays the substantial support PLC receives from large donations. The PLC's 1997 Form 990 (Schedule A, Part IV, item 26b), for instance, reveals that, of a total revenue stream of $5,888,444 between 1993 and 1996, $1,077,041 came from contributors granting more than $117,769 over that period.[207] According to a study by Leon Howell, in 1993 a $165,000 grant came from financier and former PLC board member, John Templeton.[208] In 1992, PLC received a bequest of "over $1.3 million" from Helen McFayden Straitiff, at the time an unknown supporter.[209]

The PLC had net assets worth close to $3.5 million as of 1997, part of which is an endowment started with a grant of $250,000 from Mary and Foster McGaw in 1977.[210] On average, close to 90 percent of the PLC budget is devoted to printing and distributing *The Presbyterian Layman,* coupled with educational services for local chapters, as well as religious education publications. In recent years, the PLC has paid more than $100,000 per year in editorial advisory fees, except in 1997 when the fees dipped to $66,900.

CHAPTER 2

PRESBYTERIANS PRO-LIFE

I. Significance

Presbyterians Pro-Life (PPL), initiated in 1976, is a key mainline agency of the national anti-abortion rights movement. PPL was a founding member of the National Pro-Life Religious Council (NPLRC), formed in 1987 as a religious affiliate of the National Right to Life Committee. As such, PPL is an integral part of a broader campaign to establish anti-abortion policies in all of the denominations of mainline Protestantism.[211] Within the PC(USA), PPL's role in the conservative renewal movement is indicative of the broader issues at stake, as anti-abortion, antifeminist, and anti-gay agendas intertwine in the catch-all agenda of a return to scriptural orthodoxy and confessionalism, and move the church in the direction of conservative evangelical control.

Anti-abortion, antifeminist, and anti-gay agendas intertwine in the catch-all agenda of a return to scriptural orthodoxy and confessionalism, and move the church in the direction of conservative evangelical control.

In contrast to the battle over gay ordination, in which renewal forces are fighting to protect and deepen an already conservative PC(USA) stance, the anti-abortion campaign seeks to erode the existing pro-choice church policy. Although the policy seems to enjoy broad support, PPL and its allies have progressed, not only in constantly raising the issue of "balance" in the churches' published materials, but also in shifting the debate on reproductive choice onto conservative theological grounds in an effort to curtail human and civil rights perspectives.

II. Background

In 1970, the United Presbyterian Church's first human sexuality report signaled a reversal in Presbyterianism's historic position that life begins at fertilization and that the fetus should be protected by criminal law. A new, essentially civil stance in support of abortion rights was developed and reaffirmed in subsequent policy papers until 1988, when the PC(USA) General Assembly voted to revisit the church's historic pro-choice position.[212]

EARLY DEVELOPMENT

Three PCUS ministers first conceived of an anti-abortion rights group operating inside the church at a 1976 conference in Montreat, North Carolina.[213] Rev. J. Andrew White of Bristol, Tennessee, Rev. Bruce Davis of Thompson, Georgia, and Rev. Thomas Warren of Memphis, Tennessee, called their group Southern Presbyterians Pro-Life (SPPL). The result is a long history of caucusing and national networking that has produced several important victories and prepared the groundwork for the reconsideration vote at the 1998 General Assembly.

In its first few years, SPPL worked to establish itself while encouraging churches to take up the abortion issue. White served as the SPPL coordinator in these early years, sending out mailings, organizing the first general meeting in March of 1979, and editing a small monthly newsletter, *Southern Presbyterians Pro-Life*. By 1978, SPPL had a checking account, a growing membership, and a full-time editor, Thomas Warren.[214]

SPPL held its first general meeting on March 21, 1979, at Columbia Theological Seminary in Decatur, Georgia, established a formal board, and changed its name to Presbyterians Pro-Life (PPL). Eleanor Blizard of Columbia, South Carolina, was the first chair of the PPL board; J. Andrew White was vice chair; Thomas Warren, secretary; and Bruce Davis, treasurer.[215]

THE CHRISTIAN ACTION COUNCIL AND MAINLINE ANTI-ABORTION MOBILIZATION

The second PPL annual meeting was held in Montreat, North Carolina, in April 1980. Presbyterian minister Curtis Young, executive director of the Christian Action Council (CAC) of Washington, D.C., was invited to speak.[216] Dr. Harold O.J. Brown, founder of the CAC and an influential evangelical theologian, keynoted PPL's March 1981 national meeting in Atlanta. Brown's address, titled "The Pro-Life Political Agenda," focused on legislative initiatives in the wake of the 1980 election of Ronald Reagan.[217]

The Christian Action Council was formed in 1975[218] at the home of Rev. Billy Graham in Montreat, North Carolina, the same city where the idea for PPL's precursor, Southern Presbyterians Pro-Life, was conceived only a year later. Along with Harold O. J. Brown, the founders of the CAC included influential evangelical Presbyterian theologian Rev. Dr. Francis Schaeffer and his wife Edith Schaeffer.[219]

Francis Schaeffer (1912–1984) spent nearly two decades (1937–1956) as a pastor under Rev. Carl McIntire in the Bible Presbyterian Church, a schismatic far-right by-product of the historic split in modern Presbyterianism following the dismissal of fundamentalist leader J. Gresham Machen and the formation of what would become the Orthodox Presbyterian Church in 1936 (see Glossary). After leaving McIntire's church, which gained notoriety primarily for its vehement attacks on the NCC and the WCC, Schaeffer belonged to a succession of smaller evangelical denominations until 1982, when he joined the Presbyterian Church in America (see Glossary).[220]

In an age of widespread dispensationalism (see Glossary) in evangelical circles, marked by the popularity of apocalyptic "end-times" authors such as Hal Lindsey, Schaeffer was a key source of inspiration for the development of the new Christian Right beginning in the 1970s. The rise of the new Christian Right, epitomized by Rev. Jerry Falwell's Moral Majority and by Pat Robertson's educational, political, legal, and broadcasting empire, was marked by an anti-dispensationalist agenda which gave priority to political and social change as a necessary part of God's plan for world dominion. Schaeffer's influential work, *A Christian Manifesto*, was a seminal text in this development, urging evangelical Christians to save the United States from "secular humanists."[221] The book played a catalytic role in the development of militant anti-abortion rights organizations, such as Operation Rescue.[222]

Edith Schaeffer is currently on the advisory board of Care Net, CAC's 500-unit network of "crisis pregnancy centers."[223] This arm of the anti-abortion movement operates not on a medical model of reproductive services but rather on a religious model of evangelism, based on anti-abortion propaganda.[224] Care Net's president is Guy Condon, a member of the Council for National Policy who has also served as president of Americans United for Life, the Chicago-based anti-abortion legal think tank.[225] Christian Right leader and 2000 presidential candidate Gary Bauer has written fundraising letters for Care Net. Televangelist D. James Kennedy, senior minister of Coral Ridge Presbyterian Church and a leader in the Presbyterian Church in America (see Glossary), is a member of the Care Net advisory board.[226] PPL board member Peggy MacLeod counsels churches on how to set up "abortion restoration" ministries linked to the Care Net network.[227]

Since its inception, PPL has looked to the Christian Action Council for information, ideas, and national connections. The earliest newsletters of Southern Presbyterians Pro-Life recommend publications of Harold Brown and Edith Schaeffer, as guides to the abortion issue.[228] During PPL's early years, newsletters informed Presbyterian subscribers of CAC events and projects, including conventions,[229] religious vigils and marches,[230] Human Life Amendment progress,[231] the formation of "crisis pregnancy centers,"[232] and general educational and contact information, including screenings of Francis Schaeffer's film series, *What Ever*

Schaeffer's influential work, A Christian Manifesto, *urged evangelical Christians to save the United States from "secular humanists." The book played a catalytic role in the development of militant anti-abortion rights organizations, such as Operation Rescue.*

Happened to the Human Race?[233] In March 1984, immediately following PPL's incorporation and during a "strategic" time of "renewed theological and Biblical reflection" on the abortion issue, the legislative coordinator and Capitol Hill liaison for CAC, Douglas Badger, addressed the PPL Steering Committee at an open meeting.[234]

FORSAKE RESISTANCE! JOYFULLY SUBMIT!

Dr. Harold O.J. Brown, founder and former chairman of the Christian Action Council, was for many years professor of theology and ethics at Trinity Evangelical Divinity School, one of the most important nondenominational academic centers for right-wing evangelical politics.[235] PPL coordinator J. Andrew White and *PPL News* editor Thomas Warren were both recent graduates of Trinity Evangelical Divinity School when they started PPL.[236]

Brown, who currently teaches at Reformed Theological Seminary in Charlotte, North Carolina, was for many years director of the Center on Religion and Society at the Rockford Institute, where he edited its influential monthly newsletter, *The Religion & Society Report*.[237] He is a longtime member of the steering committee of the theocratic Coalition on Revival and currently on the board of reference for the Council on Biblical Manhood and Womanhood,[238] an organization that espouses "male headship" in family life and the church, asserting in its mission statement that "wives should forsake resistance to their husbands' authority and grow in willing, joyful submission to their husbands' leadership."[239]

BEYOND REUNION

When the northern and southern Presbyterian churches merged in 1983, PPL hosted a meeting in Atlanta, Georgia, with the goal of establishing itself as a strong force within the unified PC(USA). PPL established an advisory council and planned to establish a network of contacts in presbyteries around the nation. At this pivotal meeting the current president of PPL, the Rev. Donald Elliot, was welcomed into PPL. Rev. Benjamin Sheldon was made chairman of the steering committee.[240]

Sheldon served as president from 1984 to 1995, except for a one-year hiatus in 1985.[241] In 1986 Terry Schlossberg of Minneapolis, Minnesota, became PPL's first executive director—a position that she still holds today. During these years the national organization was institutionalized, with a board of directors and an advisory board of reference providing oversight as organizational efforts were extended to local outreach. By the spring of 1986 the PPL board had 23 members, including 12 Presbyterian ministers, mainly from the South and Midwest.[242]

In 1983, PPL became a Special Organization under the rules of the Book of Order of the Constitution of the Presbyterian Church (USA).[243] A year later, PPL registered as a nonprofit corporation with the state of Georgia.[244] Around this time, plans to develop a local chapter network were announced.[245] PPL currently has between 70 and 90 chapters in the U.S.[246] *PPL News*, a quarterly newsletter published since 1983, claims about 30,000 subscribers. PPL's revenues totaled $260,000 in 1996.[247]

III. Agenda, Initiatives, and Activities

Presbyterians Pro-Life seeks to "affirm Scripture as the authority for the Church's proclamation and teaching."[248] PPL's positions on reproductive rights, sexuality, and family issues are rooted in a broader concern that the church is abandoning Christian orthodoxy.[249]

AGENDA

PPL's stated purpose is to "protect the right to life of every human being from the moment of conception to the moment of natural death," which leads them to take a position against euthanasia as well as abortion. PPL opposes abortion even in such circumstances as rape, incest, and fetal deformity.[250] PPL's position on sexuality is based on what it calls "a return to the Biblical teaching concerning the sacred value of the family [which] is essential to recovering respect for the sacred value of individual human lives."[251] The main objective of PPL, given this theological backdrop and the broader sexual parameters of the "renewal" worldview that PPL supports, is to reverse the historic pro-choice course in church policy that began in 1970.

PPL opposes abortion even in such circumstances as rape, incest, and fetal deformity.

PPL's advocacy stems from a somewhat conspiratorial view of institutional malfeasance in regard to issues involving sexuality and reproductive rights. This approach has especially characterized PPL's ongoing campaign against the Presbyterian Health, Education, and Welfare Association (PHEWA), a social justice-oriented coalition that receives denominational funding and has been in conflict with PPL over issues of membership. PPL has waged a campaign to become a member of PHEWA despite its unwillingness to affirm PHEWA's Statement of Inclusion and to submit to financial oversight by the PHEWA board.[252] PPL currently supports efforts to cut denominational funding for PHEWA on the grounds that it includes groups that are supportive of the ordination of gays and lesbians.[253]

PPL executive director Terry Schlossberg advocates reviving the machinery and ethos of church discipline to eliminate those deemed to have violated "biblical faithfulness."

PPL executive director Terry Schlossberg advocates reviving the machinery and ethos of church discipline to eliminate those deemed to have violated "biblical faithfulness."[254] This position is generally consistent with the most conservative wing of Presbyterian renewal, namely the Presbyterian Lay Committee, Voices of Orthodox Women, and the Presbyterian Forum. Church discipline is a priority of the Presbyterian Coalition (see Chapter 4). It should be noted in this regard that the current president of Presbyterians Pro-Life, Don Elliot, is also secretary-treasurer of the Presbyterian Coalition.

PPL Initiatives: To Oppose and To Opt Out

Among PPL's efforts to promote its agenda as policy in the denomination was a successful lobbying campaign to create a "relief of conscience" option in the PC(USA) medical plan for pastors. This option, now Board of Pensions policy in effect since January 1998, allows churches to divert a percentage of the congregational dues earmarked for medical plan coverage—the percentage corresponding to coverage for abortions—into a fund for medical claims of adopted newborn dependents.[255]

PPL persuaded the 1988 General Assembly to revisit PC(USA) policy on abortion. This political shift, prompted in part by the dramatic appearance of Mother Teresa in a PPL pre-Assembly event, was coupled with the election of C. Kenneth Hall as General Assembly moderator. Hall was "[the] only candidate who clearly voiced his disapproval of abortion," according to PPL.[256] Hall appointed the task force commissioned by the General Assembly to revisit the PC(USA) abortion policy. The outcome was a weaker policy adopted in 1992, which gave significant weight to moral concern about abortion and curtailed the medical and civil rights perspectives that had previously been emphasized. Despite significant gains, PPL rejected the 1992 majority report, supporting instead a more conservative minority report drawn up by three dissident members of the committee, two of whom were members of PPL.

The hallmark of the earlier trend was the 1983 policy statement *Covenant and Creation: Theological Reflections on Contraception and Abortion.*[257] In that document, influenced strongly by the women's movement, abortion was defined as potentially an act of "stewardship responsibility."[258]

One year after the PC(USA) began to retreat from its pro-choice policy (1988), the Evangelical Lutheran Church and the United Church of Christ began a similar retreat. In fact, since the late 1980s all mainline denominations have begun to revisit their pro-choice positions.[259] In 1997, the PC(USA) became the first mainline denomination to officially condemn so-called partial birth abortion.[260]

Most importantly, in 1992 the pro-life position within the PC(USA) was officially recognized as a legitimate policy viewpoint and therefore as a standard by which programming can be measured.[261] This may have implications for the PC(USA)'s involvement with national abortion rights networks such as the Religious Coalition for Reproductive Choice (RCRC). PPL aims to stop denominational funding for the RCRC, which is the political counterpart and theological rival to the National Right to Life Committee's religious affiliate, the National Pro-Life Religious Council.[262]

PPL aims to stop denominational funding for the Religious Coalition for Reproductive Choice.

Part of PPL's objection to RCRC stems from disagreements over sexuality education.[263] RCRC advocates teaching teens about contraceptives as part of a broad educational program, while PPL insists that abstinence is the only biblically acceptable practice for youth.[264] In 1999, the PC(USA) General Assembly called for a revised sexuality curriculum, one that advocates abstinence outside of marriage. Among the other problems PPL found in the curriculum as it stood was its representation of the church's position on homosexuality as something still open to debate. For PPL, the case on gay ordination is closed.[265]

PPL works locally and nationally to change church policy and take its message to churches and individuals. At the General Assemblies, PPL hosts informational booths, publishes the *Daily Delivery*, a daily newsletter on the proceedings, and sponsors anti-abortion lecturers. Since the PPL-hosted lecture by Mother Teresa in 1988, other General Assembly speakers have included Richard John Neuhaus (1989), neoconservative director of the Institute on Religion and Public Life, which challenges the "abortion regime" in the name of a "culture of life";[266] Cardinal John O'Connor (1991); Dr. Bernard Nathanson (1992), producer of extreme anti-abortion videos such as "Silent Scream"; Rev. Howard Edington (1997), pastor of First Presbyterian Church in Orlando; and Rev. William Willimon (1999), Dean of the Chapel at Duke University, editor-at-large for *The Christian Century* and editorial advisor to *Leadership*, an offshoot of *Christianity Today* aimed at church leaders.

ACTIVITIES

PPL's presence at General Assemblies is marked by pre-assembly events, daily morning prayer sessions, and protest-style leafleting of commissioners.

PPL's presence at General Assemblies is marked by pre-assembly events, daily morning prayer sessions, and protest-style leafleting of commissioners. PPL is very active in shaping policy by presenting reports to task force committees,[267] writing and publishing critiques of PC(USA) policy and programs,[268] and educating its members in the political processes of denominational change—using overtures, resolutions, minority reports, and other polity mechanisms.[269]

PPL functions as a resource and referral center for local churches and individuals. Speakers on life and family issues are offered through PPL's speakers bureau. PPL also maintains a hotline that refers women to crisis pregnancy centers, encourages adoption as an alternative to abortion, distributes materials to pastors concerning post-abortion counseling,[270] and offers pastors sample sermons. Additionally, PPL publishes and distributes educational materials, including audiotapes, videos, pamphlets, books, and a resource packet for creating a biblically based abstinence curriculum for youth in local churches titled "Pure Hearts! Pure Minds! New Human Sexuality Program."

PPL also holds leadership training workshops and assists in the formation of new chapters. Once established, local chapters organize study groups and workshops and distribute PPL's publications and informational materials.

NATIONAL CONNECTIONS

PPL is closely connected to national anti-abortion organizations. Former PPL president Rev. Benjamin Sheldon is now executive director of the National Pro-Life Religious Council, a group of religiously based anti-abortion rights groups. Co-founder and treasurer of NPLRC is Ernest Ohlhoff, who doubles as director of outreach for the National Right to Life Committee (NRLC), the largest and most influential anti-abortion organization in the United States.[271] In 1999, Sheldon addressed the annual convention of the NRLC,[272] whose next strategic goal is the "[f]ight to restore [the] pro-life position in major Protestant churches."[273]

PPL has twice joined other religiously affiliated anti-abortion groups in submitting *amicus curiae* briefs to the Supreme Court. In 1989, Walter M. Weber, then associate general counsel for the Catholic League for Religious and Civil Rights[274] and later attorney for six members of Operation Rescue,[275] filed an *amicus curiae* brief in *Webster v. Reproductive Health Services* for PPL and other religious organizations.[276] PPL also submitted an *amicus* brief in the 1992 *Planned Parenthood v. Casey* decision that upheld a restrictive abortion law in Pennsylvania.[277]

IV. Key Leaders

OFFICERS

Terry Schlossberg has been executive director of Presbyterians Pro-Life since 1986. She describes herself as a former feminist and formerly pro-choice. In the early 1980s, her viewpoint radically changed.[278] She previously worked as a special education audiologist in the public schools.[279] During her tenure at the helm of PPL, she has also emerged as a national and international activist leader.

In 1995, Schlossberg represented the Ecumenical Coalition on Women and Society (ECWS) at the U.N. International Conference on Women in Beijing, China.[280] ECWS is a project of the Washington, D.C.-based Institute on Religion and Democracy (IRD), which has a long history of campaigning against social justice initiatives of the mainline denominations. ECWS was formed in July 1994 in reaction to the ReImagining conference.[281] The IRD states that the purpose of ECWS is to monitor the "development of radical feminism within our church institutions" and to teach "Christian women how to recognize it and respond to it."[282]

The Ecumenical Coalition on Women and Society is a project of the Washington, D.C.-based Institute on Religion and Democracy, which has a long history of campaigning against social justice initiatives of the mainline denominations.

Prior to the Beijing conference, Schlossberg represented ECWS at a summit hosted by Concerned Women for America, the largest Christian Right women's organization. At this summit, 30 conservative groups allied themselves in opposing what they called the "gender perspective" of the Platform for Action that was to be presented in Beijing. Among the ideas they found objectionable was what they called the "demand for recognition of sexual and reproductive rights," including the acceptance of homosexuality and the right to "abortion on demand," and a position which they contended "blame[d] the problems of women on male power and control."[283]

In 1996, she participated with all seven U.S. Catholic cardinals and more than 50 bishops in a national ecumenical prayer service focused on partial birth abortion.[284]

In 1998, Schlossberg spoke at the annual convention of Oregon Right to Life, a state affiliate of the National Right to Life Committee.[285] The keynote speaker at this event was Gregg Cunningham, director of the Center on Bioethical Reform. His organization currently tours campuses around the U.S. with a highly controversial exhibit, the Genocide Awareness Project, which presents large, graphic pictures of aborted fetuses alongside images of victims of the Holocaust, as well as lynchings in the South.[286]

Terry Schlossberg's husband Herbert is an important intellectual historian in right-wing religious and national security circles. He is currently president of the IRD project, Presbyterian Action.[287] Formerly a senior analyst for the Central Intelligence Agency,[288] Herbert Schlossberg's ties to the Christian Right include his role as international liaison of Christians for Justice International, the political arm of Caribbean Christian Ministries.[289] Caribbean Christian Ministries, headed by Rev. Geoff Donnan, has been described by sociologist Sara Diamond as a support structure for destabilization of the Sandinista regime in Nicaragua in the 1980s.[290]

Terry Schlossberg's husband Herbert is currently president of the IRD project, Presbyterian Action.

Herbert Schlossberg has also served as the historical consultant to Alive & Free,[291] a Santa Rosa, California-based political network headed by Rev. Dennis Peacocke that organizes Reconstructionist and charismatic churches around the country. Peacocke is a disciple of right-wing charismatic shepherding movement founder Rev. Bob Mumford[292] (see Glossary). Like Peacocke, Schlossberg signed the Coalition on Revival's founding manifesto in 1986, which calls for biblical dominance in all spheres of life.[293]

Schlossberg has been employed as a project director with the Fieldstead Institute in Irvine, California.[294] Fieldstead co-published Schlossberg's 1991 book *A Fragrance of Oppression: The Church and Its Persecutors.*[295] Fieldstead president Howard Ahmanson is perhaps the leading financier of Christian Right politics in California.[296] He has also bankrolled the Chalcedon Foundation, the seminal think tank of the theocratic Christian Reconstructionist movement. Ahmanson served as a board member of Chalcedon for many years as well.[297]

Rev. Benjamin Sheldon heads the Donegal Presbytery (Pennsylvania) chapter of PPL. He joined the PPL board in 1982 and became chairman of the steering committee in 1983. He served as president of PPL in 1984 and again from 1986 through 1995. Sheldon was the first PPL representative to the annual convention of the National Right to Life Committee in 1982[298] and has since spoken on abortion to a range of organizations and events, including the milestone Presbyterian Congress on Renewal in 1985.[299]

In 1987, Sheldon helped found and became vice president of the National Pro-Life Religious Council.

In 1987, Sheldon helped found and became vice president of the National Pro-Life Religious Council (NPLRC).[300] In 1995, he became executive director of NPLRC, a position he still holds, but stepped down from the PPL presidency while remaining on its board of directors.[301] As executive director of NPLRC, Sheldon spoke on a panel at the 1999 Convention of the National Right to Life Committee. Sheldon joined other clergy on a "Pastor's Track" program that addressed the perceived lack of pastoral leadership in the anti-abortion rights movement. His co-panelists included Fr. Frank Pavone of the Catholic anti-abortion rights group Priests for Life,[302] Dr. James Lamb of Lutherans for Life, and Rev. Will Dodson of Baptists for Life.[303]

Benjamin's brother, Rev. Lou Sheldon, chairs the Anaheim, California-based Traditional Values Coalition, a powerful Christian Right lobbying network that claims 32,000 member churches.[304] Benjamin's son Daniel, who represented PPL at the 1999 General Assembly, worked for many years under J. Robert Campbell, long-time president of the Presbyterian Lay Committee. As noted above, Benjamin Sheldon was at one time Campbell's pastor.[305] Another son, John S. Sheldon, is the chief complainant in a church judicial case brought against the Presbytery of West Jersey in 1999, which has been appealed to the Permanent Judicial Commission of the PC(USA) General Assembly, the highest court in the church. The complaint seeks to reverse the Presbytery's decision to accept an openly gay man into candidacy for ordination to the ministry. John S. Sheldon was formerly vice president of Presbyterians Pro-Life.

Rev. Dr. Don Elliott is currently the president of Presbyterians Pro-Life. Before he became president, he served on the board of directors. He has been involved with PPL since the first open meeting in 1983.[306] In 1986 he served as chairman of the nomination committee of the PPL board and was in charge of PPL's presence at that year's General Assembly.[307] Originally from Fayetteville, Georgia, Elliot attended Belhaven College (B.A.), Reformed Theological Seminary (M.Div.), and Fuller Theological Seminary (D. Min.). Since 1985, he has served as pastor to First Presbyterian Church in Corinth, Mississippi.[308]

Burl S. Watson of Tulsa, Oklahoma, has served as the treasurer of PPL and in 1999 was listed as its chief financial officer. From 1957 to 1983, he worked for Cities Service Co., a major Midwestern oil company, and was director of corporate finance from 1979 to 1983. In 1967, Cities Service Co. (the chairman of which was Watson's father, Burl S. Watson Sr.) was a defendant in a cartel conspiracy case brought against seven major oil companies for mounting a global boycott of Iranian oil in the wake of Iran's nationalization of British Petroleum in 1951.[309] Watson is also a trustee of the College of the Ozarks (where former PLC president J. Robert Campbell served as academic dean) and he has served on the board of directors of Presbyterian Action since 1998.[310]

BOARD OF REFERENCE

Rev. Jerry Kirk has been affiliated with Presbyterians Pro-Life for more than a decade, serving as a member of its advisory board[311] and board of reference.[312] Until 1989, he served as a pastor of College Hill Presbyterian Church in Cincinnati, Ohio, and in 1982 he formed Citizens for Community Values (CCV), the group that protested the exhibition of Robert Mapplethorpe photographs in Cincinnati in 1990.[313] Kirk also founded the National Coalition Against Pornography (now the National Coalition for the Protection of Children and Families)[314] and served as its chairman and CEO.[315]

Kirk was also a founder of the Religious Alliance Against Pornography in 1986, which he co-chaired with the late Cardinal Joseph Bernardin for many years. A key adviser on pornography to the Reagan and Bush administrations,[316] he has been a member of the Council for National Policy, and is the author of *The Homosexual Crisis in the Mainline Church*.[317] He holds an honorary Doctor of Divinity degree from Sterling College and an honorary Doctor of Letters degree from Grove City College.

E. Peb Jackson has served on the board of reference of Presbyterians Pro-Life since at least 1991.[318] During this time he has also served as senior vice president of Focus on the Family,[319] James Dobson's Christian Right media empire, and as a member of the board of directors of Promise Keepers.[320] Jackson has been a member of the Council for National Policy and served on its board of governors in 1985. Currently he is senior vice president for public affairs at the Colorado Springs-based Young Life, a conservative evangelical recruiting network aimed at high school students.[321] PLC leader W. Robert Stover is on the board of Young Life.[322]

E. Peb Jackson has also served as senior vice president of Focus on the Family, and as a member of the board of directors of Promise Keepers.

Dr. John Jefferson Davis, a professor at Gordon-Conwell Theological Seminary, has been on the board of reference of Presbyterians Pro-Life since at least 1987.[323] He has served as vice president and chair of the board of directors of the Massachusetts Citizens for Life and has served on the board of the Value of Life Committee.[324] Both of these anti-abortion rights organizations were founded by Mildred Jefferson, former chair of the National Right to Life Committee.[325] In 1997, Davis and Jefferson both served as vice presidents for Massachusetts Citizens for Life, the state affiliate of the National Right to Life Committee.[326]

Dr. Richard Lovelace has been a member of the board of reference of Presbyterians Pro-Life since at least 1987.[327] An expert on Protestant revivalism, Lovelace is professor emeritus at Gordon-Conwell Theological Seminary, and is currently on the board of directors of Presbyterians for Renewal.[328] He also served on the advisory board of IRD in 1986.[329] In 1987, he was a member of the National Prayer Committee, whose National Day of Prayer is arguably the religious right's most successful longterm mainstreaming initiative in public intercessory theology.[330] He helped to draft the "Definitive Guidance" against gay ordination passed by the 1978 General Assembly of the UPC(USA).

OTHER SUPPORTERS **Rev. Elizabeth Achtemeier** has been a member of the board of directors of Presbyterians Pro-Life since 1993 and joined PPL's board of reference in 1999.[331] In 1992, she was the primary author of the conservative minority report to the General Assembly during the church's reconsideration of its abortion position.[332] She taught for 38 years at Lancaster Theological Seminary and later at Union Theological Seminary in Richmond, Virginia. She recently retired as adjunct professor of

Bible and homiletics at Union.[333] Her husband, Paul J. Achtemeier, Th.D., is professor emeritus of biblical interpretation at Union.[334]

Achtemeier is known in the U.S. and Canada as a preacher, lecturer, and writer. In 1995, she co-authored *Not My Own: Abortion & the Marks of the Church* with Terry Schlossberg.[335] In 1998 she was awarded a Groneman Memorial Lectureship at the A&M United Methodist Church and university, a lectureship established to bring Christian communicators to that community.[336] At a 1998 conference in Fairfax, Virginia, sponsored by the National Pro-Life Religious Council, Achtemeier spoke alongside such influential figures as Richard John Neuhaus of the Institute on Religion and Public Life and Richard Land of the Southern Baptist Convention.[337]

Rev. Timothy Bayly was a frequent contributor to *PPL News'* coverage on sexuality and abortion from the mid-1980s until 1991, at which point he left the PC(USA) to join the more conservative Presbyterian Church in America (PCA).[338] He was also a member of the 1988 PPL team that succeeded in passing an overture calling on the General Assembly to reconsider the church position on abortion.[339] Bayly is a graduate of Gordon-Conwell Theological Seminary.[340] He is currently executive director of the Council on Biblical Manhood and Womanhood, an organization that insists on "male headship" in the family and the church.[341]

V. Funding

Presbyterians Pro-Life is funded primarily by individuals. Between 1987 and 1996, contributions to PPL ranged from $118,000 (1987) to $251,699 (1996). Major gains came in 1989 ($170,863),[342] in 1994 ($227,000), and in 1996 ($251,699).[343] The largest individual contribution in recent years was $80,000 (1996–1997).[344]

A review of PPL's federal tax records from 1991 to 1996 shows that it allocates approximately 20–25 percent of its funding to its annual General Assembly campaigns, and another 25 percent to *PPL News*. Approximately 40 percent is allocated for outreach (e.g., chapter development, educational speaking, and contributions to other ministry publications). Approximately 10–15 percent is allocated for "other" interaction with denominational entities.

CHAPTER 3

PRESBYTERIANS FOR RENEWAL

I. Significance

Formed in 1989, Presbyterians for Renewal (PFR) has developed into a broad-based force for conservative change within the PC(USA). The ten-year anniversary issue of PFR's staple publication, *reNews,* claims dynamic organizational growth and emphasizes a continuing process of linking pastoral and congregational revitalization to political developments within the PC(USA).

PFR is the closest thing to a "parachurch" organization operating within mainline Presbyterianism. As an independent, service-based evangelical agency, PFR functions as a "shadow church," operating in tension and even competition with the official structure of the church. Thus, PFR offers services and resources that allow people to circumvent official structures in pursuit of religious objectives deemed more important than those of the national church.

OUT OF THE SHADOWS

PFR functions as a "shadow church," operating in tension and even competition with the official structure of the church.

Parachurch pastoral programming notwithstanding, conservative political impact is and has always been a central pillar of PFR.[345] Thus, it is precisely the more mainstream appeal of PFR that makes it more, not less, dangerous as a political force in the PC(USA). Conservative Presbyterians put off by the inquisitorial methods of the Presbyterian Lay Committee can find a far more broadly conceived and pastorally structured vehicle for denominational change in PFR, carried out under the evangelical rubric of church growth through a return to orthodoxy. This does not necessarily mark a political dividing line within the renewal movement, but rather the emergence of a comprehensive pastoral depth-structure to undergird the continuing encroachment of conservative power on the institutional structures of the PC(USA).

PFR's leaders emphasize stylistic rather than political differences with other conservative groups. For example, PFR board member Harry Hassall, referring to ostensibly more extreme groups such as Presbyterians Pro-Life, Presbyterians for Democracy and Religious Freedom, and the Presbyterian Lay Committee, once explained, "We support many of their objectives, but we ever seek to moderate and modify their methodology, as today they appear to be alienating much of the church against their views."[346] Former PFR executive director Betty Moore claims that the organization has a "constructive" approach to politics and links institutional change to a broader movement of pastoral growth and congregational service.[347] In 1999, PFR's policy recommendations for the General Assembly were consistent with the rest of conservative renewal: against gay ordination, against the National Network of Presbyterian College Women, against same-sex "holy unions," in favor of gay conversion therapies, in favor of cutting ties with the Religious Coalition for Reproductive Rights, and in favor of the conservative revision of "Building Community among Strangers," the PC(USA)'s project on diversity and multiculturalism.[348] PFR's conservative politics is characterized by an attitude of "speaking the truth in love," as they put it in an official statement against holy unions adopted in April 1999.[349]

PFR's pastoral focus goes hand in hand, however, with political organizing aimed at the policies and institutional structure of the church. This is epitomized by the pivotal role of PFR in the establishment of the Presbyterian Coalition. Among other things, PFR staffer Jackie Holland was the legal incorporator of the Presbyterian Coalition in 1993, and PFR executive director Joseph Rightmyer served simultaneously as executive director of the Presbyterian Coalition in 1997.

While the political methodology of PFR members may not be as extreme as that of their colleagues in the PLC, this moderate stream of conservative renewal plays a central role in the broader dynamics of the movement, and specifically the mainstreaming objectives of the politics of the Christian Right.

Despite indicating a certain measure of progress in terms of what is no longer permissible at the surface of politics, the political danger of the right may actually be far greater, precisely because it is increasingly masked by mainstreaming rhetorical strategies and methods. White male Christian domination can no longer be openly displayed in national public life, as it was up to the late 1960s, the crucial period for the rise of conservative Presbyterian renewal. Indeed it has become fashionable and expedient for conservative leaders to invoke the legacy of the great moral crusade of modern America in the service of their interests. Former Christian Coalition leader Ralph Reed, for example, has suggested that the fight against women's reproductive choice is a struggle in the tradition of Martin Luther King Jr.[350]

Viewed in this light, PFR does not function as a mediating force between right and left as it has often been portrayed. Rather, PFR is a mainstreaming arm of the right, nearly identical in its politics if more palatable in its style. As such, PFR has tended to support only those institutional objectives for which there is significant popular support and an easily manipulable framework of debate, such as the authority of Scripture argument against gay ordination.

II. Background

Presbyterians for Renewal is rooted in two influential evangelical movements going back to the late 1960s: the Covenant Fellowship of Presbyterians, active in the southern PC(US), and Presbyterians United for Biblical Concerns, active in the northern UPC(USA). After the historic reunion of the northern and southern branches of mainline Presbyterianism in 1983, conservative renewal groups also merged. PFR is arguably the most important such merger of northern and southern conservative streams in the united church.

PFR's HISTORICAL CURRENTS

Two key events mark the early development of PFR. The first was a "Call to Renewal," held in Dallas in the spring of 1988. This meeting was convened by Rev. Dr. B. Clayton Bell, pastor of Highland Park Presbyterian Church in Dallas, Rev. Dr. J. Murray Marshall of First Presbyterian Church in Seattle, Washington, and Rev. Dr. John A. Huffman Jr., of St. Andrews Presbyterian Church in Newport Beach, California. The second important event was a follow-up "Gathering of Presbyterians," held in St. Louis, Missouri, in the spring of 1989. Rev. Dr. Paul Watermulder of Burlingame Presbyterian Church in California and Rev. Kathleen Goodrich of Wyomissing, Pennsylvania, led the St. Louis Gathering.

A 60-member board was elected at the St. Louis Gathering, with 12 members representing each of five regions. The original regional representatives included Rev. Linda Jaberg of Altoona, Pennsylvania (East); Dr. Myers Hicks of Florence, South Carolina (Southeast), who was concurrently a director of the PLC; Rev. Dr. Robert Hunter of Indianapolis, Indiana (Midwest); Gary R. Terrell of Lubbock, Texas (Southwest); and Janice Sperry of Sierra Madre, California (West). The first officers were J. Murray Marshall, president, Rev. Dr. Virgil Cruz, vice president; Mrs. Linda Baker, secretary; and Mr. James Hargrove, treasurer. Also prominent in St. Louis were PC(USA) moderator Kenneth Hall and famed Presbyterian missionary to Asia, Samuel Moffett.[351]

In the south, the Covenant Fellowship of Presbyterians (CFP) was considered the moderate renewal group compared to more extreme groups such as Presbyterian Churchmen United, Concerned Presbyterians, and *The Southern Presbyterian Journal.*[352]

SOUTHERN STREAM: THE JUMPER SHIFT

Concerned Presbyterians, led by Florida real estate developer Kenneth Keyes, would play a pivotal role in the schism that produced the right-wing Presbyterian Church in America (PCA) in 1973.[353] The turning point for the various conservative factions was the 1971 PCUS Assembly, where the CFP joined with the above-mentioned groups in a "Grand Coalition" assembled by Keyes in an effort to defeat a restructuring plan intended to help facilitate reunion with the North. CFP founder Andrew Jumper, a former Synod of Texas progressive turned conservative by way of charismatic conversion, was the lead strategist in this effort to thwart reunion.[354]

CFP's rejection of schism is not so much an index of relative moderation, but primarily a matter of institutional design in the vein of recapturing the church from liberalism.

In the mid-1960s, Jumper played an important role in building a general progressive movement in the denomination. This movement culminated at the 1969 PC(US) General Assembly and set the stage for reunion with the North.[355] Jumper's charismatic conversion to conservative renewal in the summer of 1969 in many ways epitomizes the religious dynamic underlying political conflict in the church both then and now.

When the right lost by only one percent in 1971, Jumper called it "the death knell of the Southern Presbyterian Church."[356] CFP then distanced itself from the Grand Coalition and sought to create a reputation as a "centrist" group that refused to join in the schism. Like the PLC's foundational mandate of working within the mainline church, the CFP's rejection of schism is not so much an index of relative moderation, but primarily a matter of institutional design in the vein of recapturing the church from liberalism.

The Covenant Fellowship of Presbyterians sought increased lay empowerment and local church autonomy while fighting gay ordination and other liberal concerns that occupied much of the dialogue leading up to reunion in 1983. Indeed CFP played a defining role in preventing further schism within the PCUS by exercising a conservative influence over the Plan for Union (1981).[357] Conservatives who rejected schism came to rely on CFP's *Open Letter* to inform their understanding of developments in the church.[358]

NORTHERN STREAM: THE ANTI-GAY ALLIANCE

The northern stream of Presbyterians for Renewal flows from Presbyterians United for Biblical Concerns (PUBC), which was formed in 1965 in response to drafts of what became the UPC's Confession of 1967 (see Glossary). PUBC evolved into a multi-issue renewal organization in the 1970s, launched a quarterly publication, *Presbyterian Communiqué*, and gained a membership of nearly 1,600, representing some 250 churches. Unlike the CFP, which essentially functioned as a shadow church, PUBC was an executive agency with an essentially diplomatic mission to the "northern church" denominational leadership.[359]

Just as the CFP appeared moderate compared with the faction of the southern church that became the schismatic PCA, PUBC appeared moderate compared to the Presbyterian Lay Committee in the North.

PUBC was notable for its historic conferences on denominational issues and its strategic alliance with the PLC beginning in the late 1970s, when the gay ordination issue first came to a head. Indeed, PUBC played a key role in the nearly ten-year battle over gay ordination inaugurated in 1970 by the report of the first Task Force on Human Sexuality. As noted above, this watershed document advocated greater religious acceptance of homosexuality and reversed the UPC position opposing abortion.[360]

In 1976, PUBC formally allied with the Presbyterian Lay Committee, two advisors of which, George Fuller and August Kling, joined the PUBC board.[361] Two years later, PUBC, the PLC, and the Presbyterian Charismatic Communion (now called Presbyterian-Reformed Ministries International) formed an *ad hoc* Evangelical Coalition against gay ordination at the 1978 General Assembly.[362]

At PUBC's Chicago mission consultation in 1975, Ralph Winter, who began as a UPC missionary in Guatemala, presented his United Presbyterian Order for World Evangelization. Winter went on to found the U.S. Center for World Mission, which has played an important role in conservative evangelical mission analysis and implementation, and has led the current wave of evangelical mission coordination known as the "unreached peoples" movement.[363]

Winter has been a key link between the overseas mission development movement and the Christian Right, partly through his membership on the steering committee of the theocratic Coalition on Revival (see Glossary).[364] Despite such involvements, Winter remains a key figure within the PC(USA). As noted above, he was for many years president of Presbyterian Frontier Fellowship, which is a member of the Presbyterian Renewal Network. He addressed the Evangelical Presbyterians Pastors' Fellowship, also a member of the Presbyterian Renewal Network, in 1991.[365] In 1999, PFR awarded Ralph and Roberta Winter its Bell-Mackay award for mission service.[366]

The Covenant Fellowship helped to forge North-South evangelical alliances before reunion in 1983 and was principally responsible for the series of discussions and events that constitute the prehistory of PFR within the PC(USA). CFP also created a presbytery-level National Evangelical Network to develop

RENEWAL AFTER REUNION

greater participation in conservative renewal activities and initiatives within the newly united church.[367] In fact, the CFP proposed a three-way merger with PUBC and the Presbyterian Lay Committee in 1980. While the CFP was closer to the PLC, according to Hassall, the PLC, itself already at odds with PUBC, refused to merge out of fear of losing its focus as a watchdog agency with tremendous grass-roots support in that capacity.[368]

Perhaps the pivotal event for conservative evangelical unity in the aftermath of reunion was the 1985 Congress on Renewal, which drew 5,000 people, had a $1.25 million dollar budget, and was directed by Dr. Ernest J. Lewis. This event sparked regional evangelical conferences in Philadelphia, South Bend, and California.[369] In 1988, CFP founder B. Clayton Bell, along with John A. Huffman (CFP) and J. Murray Marshall (PUBC), pulled together a group dedicated to creating a united evangelical front within the PC(USA). This was the Dallas "Call to Renewal" meeting which led to the CFP-PUBC merger and the origins of Presbyterians for Renewal.

III. Agenda, Structure, and Activities

AGENDA: STRATEGIC MODERATION   With an expected $5 million budget and the largest membership constituency among Presbyterian renewal groups, including 750-member congregations and "a network of 4,000 congregations in sympathy with our theological convictions and ministries,"[370] PFR models itself as an evangelical service organization oriented toward reviving the church through renewed individual faith and commitment to working for general renewal through the structures of the church.

While PFR includes social issues in its charter, notably resistance to racism and sexism, they exhibit little evidence of action.[371] Moreover, PFR is paradoxically aligned with the historic opponents of the social justice policies of the PC(USA) and the agencies and leaders assigned to advance them. PFR has, like much of evangelicalism, approached race as a matter of personal transformation, with little or no historical context or sense of political and economic conditions. This is perhaps epitomized by a 1994 presentation on "racial reconciliation" to the PFR board by representatives of the John Perkins Foundation.[372] The notion of racial reconciliation was developed by conservative African American Rev. John Perkins (for whom the foundation is named) and has swept the evangelical community in recent years. While often authentic in promoting the experience of Christian brotherhood across racial boundaries, agencies of the Christian Right such as the Christian Coalition and Promise Keepers have effectively utilized this personal transformation approach to sidestep or undermine efforts to use the law and public policy to redress the legitimate concerns of racial minorities. It is worth noting here that the late John Perkins' principal funder was financier Howard Ahmanson, one of the major bankrollers of the Christian Right in California and particularly the theocratic Christian Reconstructionist movement.[373] Perkins was a longtime member of the steering committee of the Coalition on Revival and signed its founding document, *A Manifesto for the Christian Church,* in 1986.[374]

In contrast to the political style and agenda of such established right-wing groups as the PLC and Presbyterians Pro-Life, PFR's operating mode is one of strategic moderation aimed at broadening support for its basic goals through a gradual process of institutional realignment.

PFR's constituency-centered approach emphasizes efforts perceived to be winnable, primarily concerning sexuality issues. PFR's position on the National Network of Presbyterian College Women is instructive. While not attacking the NNPCW in the frontal style of the Presbyterian Lay Committee, PFR emphasized the deficiency of the NNPCW in terms of the needs of the young Christian women themselves, thereby framing the political agenda of reining in NNPCW in terms of pastoral concern.[375]

STRUCTURE AND ACTIVITIES

In building a broad pastoral base for conservative institutional realignment of the PC(USA), PFR has adopted the CFP "shadow church" model of conservative renewal, operating through nine parachurch ministry divisions, with oversight by six committees which are accountable to a regionally distributed 59-member national board of directors.

As of the fall of 1999, the executive committee of the national board consisted of:

President: Rev. Tamara Letts, pastor in Yellowstone, Montana
President-Elect: Jim Cahalan, retired accountant from Edmond, Oklahoma
Vice President: Jim Hartman, management consultant from Cincinnati, Ohio
Treasurer: Dr. Ann Hunt, chemist from Indianapolis, Indiana
Secretary: Nancy Scott

There are three main categories of PFR ministries:

PERSONAL RENEWAL

• Annual **Christian Life Conferences**, held in Montreat, North

Carolina—A CFP tradition since 1971, these conferences bring together evangelical scholars, preachers, and laity in an intellectual workshop setting and serve as the main forum for networking renewal throughout the broader church.

- **Youth Ministry**—The CFP's extensive youth ministry program was essentially folded into PFR in 1989. Former CFP staffer Chuck Neder runs the PFR Youth Ministry, based in Chattanooga. Serving more than 10,000 youth each year, mainly in the south, PFR Youth Ministry runs regional evangelical conferences for high school students (Fun in the Son) and junior high students (The Great Escape), retreats for training youth to become leaders in their churches, wilderness adventure camps (The Rock), and short-term mission trips to places like Jamaica and Mexico (Son Servants).

CONGREGATIONAL RENEWAL

- A **Congregational Renewal Ministry**, directed by Joe Woods, provides revitalization services for individual churches. This entity is largely a legacy of Robert Fenn, who left the CFP in 1985 to start his Lay Renewal Ministries affiliated with the Evangelical Presbyterian Church, and Dr. Myers Hicks of Florence, South Carolina, who committed his life to Jesus at one of the first Renewal Weekends sponsored by the CFP in the late 1960s.[376] Hicks became director of Congregational Renewal for the CFP in 1986 and has also served as a board member of the Presbyterian Lay Committee.
- **Wee Kirk Conferences** provide support for small churches. Harry Hassall currently directs this CFP legacy.
- **Family and Christian Marriage Seminars**
- **Church Officer Development**

DENOMINATIONAL RENEWAL

- PFR's **Issues Ministry** is another legacy of the CFP, designed to inform the church about biblical and confessional positions through written materials as well as at the General Assembly. Since 1991, this ministry has fielded resource teams at PC(USA) General Assemblies to assist commissioners in pursuit of evangelical goals. The first PFR issues task force chair, Roger Kvam, was the last president of the CFP and formerly the CFP's vice president for the task force on issues.[377]
- The **Network of Presbyterian Women in Leadership** (NPWL) was launched at the 1994 General Assembly.[378] NPWL has been a PFR ministry since 1995, providing resources and support for evangelical women involved in the institutional life of the church. NPWL, which has been holding regional conferences since 1998 and publishes the *Lydian Network* newsletter,

approaches gender and sexuality issues in a way similar to Christians for Biblical Equality (CBE). CBE is a national women's clergy network which, despite its advocacy for women's equality, opposes homosexuality as a sin.[379] CBE leaders have defended Promise Keepers from its feminist critics as well. Gretchen Gaebelein Hull, a former CBE board member, is currently on the board of PFR. NPWL assumed oversight of PFR's Lydia Fund women's scholarship in 1997.[380]

- PFR's **Seminary Ministry** is designed to build and coordinate evangelical presence in denominational as well as nondenominational seminary student bodies, faculties, and boards of trustees. This ministry publishes *Catalyst*, a quarterly journal of evangelical and Reformed scholarship with a circulation approaching 3,000. PFR's first major seminarian conference, hosted by the Mars Hill student group at Austin Theological Seminary, took place in August 1999. A report posted on the Presbyterian Forum web site described this event as marking "the beginning of renewed evangelical interest in the theological education of PC(USA) seminarians."[381] As of December 1999, PFR has engaged with evangelical student groups at ten seminaries, including the major Presbyterian-affiliated seminaries as well as conservative nondenominational institutions such as Fuller Theological Seminary and Trinity Evangelical Divinity School. In addition, a Theological Enrichment Fund, with a goal of raising $2.5 million in scholarship support for evangelical students and seminarians, has been set up.[382]
- **Evangelism Celebrations**—These periodic events are co-sponsored with the denomination.

RESOURCES

- An extensive **Publications Ministry** oversees five PFR publications: *reNews*, a quarterly journal; *reConnect*, a quarterly newsletter; *reSource*, covering denominational issues; *reForm*, a semiannual theological journal for church officers; as well as *Catalyst* (see above).
- **PFR Referral Service** brings together evangelical churches and pastors.

The CFP legacy is strongly reflected in PFR's program structure and leadership. Harry Hassall, a founder of CFP, has served as an advisor on issues and strategy to PFR and is currently a Southeast regional board member.[383] Betty K. Moore, the first executive director of PFR, is a former CFP leader from South Carolina.[384]

One could arguably describe Presbyterians for Renewal as the CFP writ large across the body of united Presbyterianism. Put another way, there appears to be a re-emergence of a "southern stream"

One could arguably describe Presbyterians for Renewal as the CFP writ large across the body of united Presbyterianism.

within the PC(USA)—perhaps a rebirth of the conservative wing of the PCUS in the united church.

LOGAN'S SLOGAN PFR mounted a comprehensive political program at the PC(USA) 1999 General Assembly in Fort Worth—supplying many of the advisors, resource people, intercessors, and others deployed on behalf of the conservative agenda. This effort included a commissioner orientation luncheon; a high-profile breakfast assembly which drew several hundred people; daily lunch-hour briefing sessions for commissioners involved in General Assembly proceedings; and joint sponsorship of evening briefings with such groups as the Presbyterian Forum and the Presbyterian Coalition.[385]

PFR mounted a comprehensive political program at the PC(USA) 1999 General Assembly in Fort Worth.

Two of the General Assembly morning worship services were led by PFR-affiliated preachers: Rev. James H. Logan Jr., pastor of South Tryon Presbyterian Church in Charlotte, North Carolina, and a former PFR board member; and Rev. Craig Barnes, pastor of National Presbyterian Church in Washington, D.C. Barnes, a *reNews* columnist and a member of PFR's editorial board, was the keynote speaker at this year's PFR General Assembly breakfast. Logan took the opportunity presented by his position as a General Assembly preacher to make a political statement against gay ordination. Logan's slogan, "Don't lower the bar," punctuated the subsequent debate on the plenary floor. Presbyterian Coalition moderator Jack Haberer later wrote, "'Don't lower the bar,' they shouted again and again. 'Don't lower the bar,' they quoted again and again. Echoing the refrain sounded by Jim Logan . . . the commissioners determined not to lower the church's standards of morality, theology, accountability, and unity-amid-diversity."[386]

Logan's slogan, "Don't lower the bar," punctuated the subsequent debate on the plenary floor.

IV. Key PFR Leaders

Thirty years ago, **Rev. Dr. B. Clayton Bell's** Highland Park Presbyterian Church in Dallas, Texas, then led by William Elliot Jr., was the focal point for the beginning of the Covenant Fellowship of Presbyterians, of which Bell was a founder, a major fundraiser, and a longtime leader.[387] Bell began his pastorate at Highland Park in 1973, was a founder of the CFP and early board member of PFR, and was elected moderator of the Presbyterian Coalition for 1999.

He is the son of L. Nelson Bell, a renowned medical missionary to China and father-in-law of Billy Graham. The elder Bell joined with J. Howard Pew in starting *Christianity Today* magazine in 1954[388] and was previously the founder of the *Southern Presbyterian Journal* in 1942. Openly segregationist, the *Southern Presbyterian Journal* became the chief publication of the evangelical far right within the southern church, most notably linking to Kenneth Keyes' Concerned Presbyterians in the period leading up to the PCA split in 1973. By 1966, the *Journal* had abandoned open segregationism in keeping with the evangelical movement of the period.[389] B. Clayton Bell is currently executive chairman of the board of *Christianity Today*, perhaps the major organ of conservative evangelicalism in the United States today.

Educated at Wheaton College, Columbia Theological Seminary, and Gordon-Conwell Theological Seminary, Clayton Bell served as student assistant evangelist for the Billy Graham New York Crusade in 1957. He has pastored churches in Alabama and Georgia, and emphasizes his struggle against institutional segregation within his early pastorates. He recently retired as senior minister of the 7,800-member Highland Park Presbyterian Church, the second largest in the PC(USA). He has also served as a presbytery moderator, as a member of numerous General Assembly committees, and as a board member of the Texas Presbyterian Foundation as well as Austin Theological Seminary.[390]

Highland Park hosted the 1985 Congress on Renewal, an evangelical initiative ostensibly celebrating the Presbyterian reunion of 1983, but clearly intended to consolidate the forces of conservatism, particularly given the influx of a distinct "southern stream" of right-wing evangelical politics from the former PCUS.[391] Bell's church boasted the membership and financial support of both Ross Perot and oil magnate Nelson Bunker Hunt.[392] In 1991, his church lost more than 2,000 members in a schismatic split over continuing liberal influence within the leadership structures of the PC(USA).[393] A precipitating factor in this schism (reputedly spearheaded by Hunt) was the church's controversial sexuality study, *Keeping Body and Soul Together*. More importantly, 1991 was the cut-off point for former southern churches to leave the united church with their property, as provided for by the reunion agreement of 1983. The Highland Park schism was a result of the failure of the dissenting group to obtain enough votes to take the church out of the PC(USA).

During the ReImagining controversy in 1994 (see Glossary), Bell led a conservative "tall steeple" church revolt. Bell called for the resignation of General Assembly Council (GAC) executive director James Brown, and his church withheld $1 million in contributions from the denomination. On the eve of an important GAC meeting during the controversy, Bell preached a topical sermon on the limits of tolerance, invoking Old Testament battles against foreign deities.[394]

Highland Park Church is a member of the Mission America network, whose chair and CEO is Rev. Paul Cedar, a pastor in the Evangelical Free Church, and a central figure in the conservative evangelical revival movement. Mission America brings together a wide variety of evangelical organizations, including Bob Weiner Ministries (a key structure in the right-wing charismatic shepherding movement), Focus on the Family, Pat Robertson's Regent University School of Divinity, as well as Ralph Winter's U.S. Center for World Mission. This network has recently focused on mounting a major national evangelism initiative called Celebrate Jesus 2000.[395]

Bell's involvement in the parachurch revival movement goes back to at least 1980, when he endorsed Bill Bright's Here's Life World initiative, a global evangelization campaign—the executive committee of which included Nelson Bunker Hunt, who personally contributed at least $10 million to the effort.[396] Billy Graham, Bell's brother-in-law, withdrew his support for Bright's predecessor initiative, Here's Life America, because he felt that Bright's Campus Crusade for Christ was competing with the churches, and had "become almost a denomination by itself." [397]

Rev. Dr. John A. Huffman Jr., was a founder and early member of the board of directors of PFR, and in 1993 he helped start the Presbyterian Coalition as a member of its incorporating board of directors. A nationally known preacher, Huffman has been pastor of the 4,500-member St. Andrew's Presbyterian Church in Newport Beach, California, since 1978. He was educated at Wheaton College, the University of Tulsa, and Princeton Theological Seminary,[398] and from 1967 to 1973 was pastor of Key Biscayne Presbyterian Church, where Richard Nixon was a parishioner.[399]

Key Biscayne's first pastor, Rev. Lane Adams, is currently the national minister-at-large for the Christian Reconstructionist-oriented Plymouth Rock Foundation.[400] Huffman's immediate predecessor was Rev. Ben Haden, a longtime member of the Council for National Policy. Huffman himself successfully kept Key Biscayne Church from leaving the PCUS for the Presbyterian Church in America (PCA) in 1973.[401] Key Biscayne finally left for the PCA in 1978, under Rev. Stephen Brown, who has been the keynote preacher at several Presbyterian Lay Committee events, including chapter meetings and annual conventions.[402]

Huffman was one of the four drafters of the definitive guidance statement against gay ordination at the PC(USA)'s General Assembly in 1978.[403] Nearly two decades later, Huffman's St. Andrew's Church spearheaded the "Fidelity and Chastity" amendment (Amendment B), which Huffman himself helped to write.[404] Twice elected moderator of Los Ranchos Presbytery, he was a candidate for

PC(USA) national moderator in 1991. He has served on the boards of Gordon-Conwell Theological Seminary, *Christianity Today*, and World Vision.[405]

Rev. Joseph Rightmyer, executive director of Presbyterians for Renewal since 1995, previously pastored Covenant Presbyterian Church in Jackson, Mississippi, for ten years. Raised in southern Georgia, Rightmyer emphasizes the example of his father, a pastor who suffered for his stance against racial segregation in the church. Rightmyer was educated at Georgia Southwestern College, Columbia Theological Seminary, and Fuller Theological Seminary, and was ordained by the Atlanta Presbytery in 1972. He has served as youth director at Chapel Woods Presbyterian Church in Decatur, Georgia, as organizing pastor of First Presbyterian Church in Church Hill, Tennessee, as pastor of Memorial Presbyterian Church in Elizabethton, Tennessee, and as associate pastor for evangelism and family nurture at St. Andrew's Presbyterian Church in Houston, Texas.[406] While in Jackson, Mississippi, he served as a trustee of Belhaven College.[407] He also served as presbytery moderator and was a member of the southeast regional board of PFR. In 1997 he simultaneously served as executive director of PFR and the Presbyterian Coalition.

In 1997, Rev. Joseph Rightmyer simultaneously served as executive director of PFR and the Presbyterian Coalition.

Rev. Kathy Goodrich, a founding member of Presbyterians for Renewal, is president of PFR's Network of Presbyterian Women in Leadership. She lives in Wyomissing, Pennsylvania, and has held numerous denominational positions, including membership on her presbytery's Permanent Judicial Commission. She previously served as vice president of Presbyterians United for Biblical Concerns and has served on the steering committee of Presbyterians for Democracy and Religious Freedom.[408]

Rev. Henry Greene has served as chair of PFR's issues and strategy task force[409] and directed PFR's strategic effort at the 1999 General Assembly in Fort Worth. PFR's 25-member General Assembly resource team, a key component of the overall renewal effort at Fort Worth, provided resources, counsel, and pastoral care for commissioners.[410] Greene is a Western regional board member of PFR and pastor of Dinuba Presbyterian Church in central California.

PFR's 25-member General Assembly resource team provided resources, counsel, and pastoral care for commissioners.

V. Funding

PFR funding comes from a combination of program fees and contributions from churches and individuals. The highest single contribution between 1991 and 1997 was $50,000.[411] The ratio of program fees to contributions is about two to one respectively, with a total funding stream of more than $11 million between 1989 and 1995. An initial $225,000 donation pool got things started in 1989. In 1990, PFR revenues rose fivefold and since then have risen at a steady 10–15 percent rate.[412] Executive director Joe Rightmyer has predicted a revenue stream of $5 million for 1999.[413]

CHAPTER 4

THE PRESBYTERIAN COALITION

I. Significance

For 30 years, the renewal movement has operated in sectors, according to a loose division of labor grounded in a spectrum of historical traditions, theological, political, and otherwise, as well as in distinct issue areas and demographic patterns. Seen as a whole, this loose association of like-minded renewal groups has built multiple fronts of conservative attack and mobilization against denominational leadership and the broader tradition of mainline social commitment. This political agenda developed along with certain pastoral and parachurch tendencies as represented in Presbyterians for Renewal and its predecessors.

REVOLUTION IN THE 21ST CENTURY?

The Presbyterian Coalition represents an historic reorganization of the conservative networks and an effort to redirect the movement beyond greater unity in pursuit of renewal, toward a united struggle for conservative evangelical control over the church. The structure and vision of this reorganization was spelled out in the Coalition's bold and confrontational *Declaration and Strategy Paper*, which was ratified at its national Gathering III in the fall of 1998.

"While the word 'revolution' may be extreme," then-Coalition moderator Jack Haberer said at the time, "we believe that the Gathering III will mark the launch of a movement that will shape the Presbyterian Church well into the next century."[414]

"While the word 'revolution' may be extreme," then-Coalition moderator Jack Haberer said at the time, "we believe that the Gathering III will mark the launch of a movement that will shape the Presbyterian Church well into the next century."

The Presbyterian Coalition is a political framework for uniting the various renewal groups under a holistic vision and strategy of denominational transformation. The Coalition's board consists of representatives of most of the major renewal groups, including the Presbyterian Lay Committee, Presbyterians Pro-Life, Presbyterians for Renewal, the Genevans (see below), and Presbyterian Action (see Glossary). The Coalition's *Declaration and Strategy Paper* is probably the most comprehensive confessional document ever to emerge from the conservative renewal movement. It is significant in part because of the breadth of the movement that created it. This vision is backed by a strategic political plan for transforming the church in its most important capacities and functions. The capacity of the interests bent on implementing this formidable plan is also growing. This is epitomized by the sophisticated institutional focus of the Presbyterian Forum, which has emerged from within the Coalition to take the lead in coordinating the renewal movement's policy efforts at the church's annual General Assembly.

II. Background

THE ANTI-GAY NINETIES   In 1993, a powerful movement for gay and lesbian rights in the church arose in response to a decision by the Permanent Judicial Commission to prohibit the installation of openly lesbian Jane Spahr as a minister at Downtown United Presbyterian Church in Rochester, New York. The campaign, with which outgoing PC(USA) moderator John Fife was clearly allied, was described by *The Presbyterian Outlook* as a "full-scale effort to overturn the national standard which forbids ordination of self-affirming, practicing homosexuals as ministers, elders, and deacons."[415]

Coupled with the election of conservative evangelical David Dobler as General Assembly moderator, the passing of a right-leaning compromise solution to the debate on ordination standards—upholding the anti-gay ban but commissioning further study of the issue—provoked a militant 30-minute demonstration on the floor of the General Assembly mounted by supporters of gay rights within the church.[416] In the aftermath of the 1993 General Assembly, the Coalition was formed for the purpose of defending the church's existing policy guidelines from increasing pressure within the church for gay ordination.[417]

THE ROLE OF PFR   The Coalition was formally incorporated in November of 1993 and has enjoyed federal tax-exempt status since 1994. Presbyterians for Renewal and its leadership played an important role in getting the Coalition started. The Coalition's official incorporating agent was Jackie Holland, who is an administrator for PFR. The Coalition's official address for tax purposes was for many years the same Louisville building in which PFR is housed.[418] As of the summer of 1999, the Coalition telephone contact was housed in the PFR office. PFR executive director Joseph Rightmyer served simultaneously as the executive director of the Presbyterian Coalition in 1997.[419] PFR founders Clayton Bell and John Huffman were also members of the incorporating board of the Presbyterian Coalition, and Betty Moore, PFR's executive director from 1989–1995, was the first treasurer of the Coalition and was its coordinator from 1996–1998.[420]

Rounding out the Coalition's incorporating board were Daryl Fisher-Ogden of Fuller Seminary, as well as William Giles and Robert Taylor, both southern presbytery executives. Two other important renewal leaders served as early board members of the Coalition: Rev. Robert Dooling of Loveland, Colorado, who would go on to found the Presbyterian Forum, and Parker Williamson, editor of *The Presbyterian Layman*.[421] The Coalition recently hired William Giles as executive director, and has moved its headquarters to Birmingham, Alabama.

THE ROLE OF THE GENEVANS

The founding of the Genevans in the spring of 1993 is an important reference point for the Presbyterian Coalition. The Coalition's first president and secretary, William Giles and Daryl Fisher-Ogden, respectively, as well as five out of eleven early Coalition board members, were also Genevans. All of the Genevans on the initial Coalition board in 1994 (except Fisher-Ogden and Al Ruth, a presbytery executive from Western Colorado) were southern presbytery executives: David Snellgrove (Mississippi), William Stewart (Tennessee), Robert Taylor (South Carolina), Barry Van Deventer (South Carolina), and William Giles (Alabama).[422]

The Genevans group is an association of Presbyterian leaders that, under the banner of ensuring "fair process," has sought to alter the institutional structure of the church in the service of conservative renewal. The group has also been targeting General Assembly committees on such issues as the PC(USA)'s involvement in the Consultation on Church Union (see Glossary), the chief mainline ecumenical initiative.[423] In 1995, Daryl Fisher-Ogden opened the Los Angeles office of the Genevans.[424]

Originally called The Gamaliel Society, the Genevans was formed in February 1993, after an initial meeting of 13 in Charlotte, North Carolina, where a statement of purpose highlighting issues of denominational process was drafted. The first general meeting was called by David Snellgrove (executive presbyter from St. Andrew Presbytery in Mississippi) and held in Atlanta in April 1993.[425] Two years earlier, Snellgrove organized a national strategy meeting, held in Hilton Head, South Carolina, for the purpose of defeating the church's sexuality report, *Keeping Body and Soul Together*.[426]

The original Genevans mailing list of 42 included several activists who have gone on to play pivotal roles in church politics. Among these is John Sloop, who, as a commissioner from the Shenandoah Presbytery, proposed an amendment from the floor to raise the existing definitive guidance against gay ordination (passed in 1978) to the status of a constitutional ban at the 1993 General Assembly. The Sloop

Amendment, which lost with 37 percent of the vote, was a precursor to Amendment B.[427] Also on the list was Mississippi GOP power broker Clarke Reed, who would serve as treasurer of the Genevans and as a behind-the-scenes mover of the Presbyterian Forum.

III. Structure, Activities, Agenda

1994–1998:

VERY PROACTIVE

MEASURES

An early Presbyterian Coalition letterhead indicates that the organization initially served as an umbrella group for key renewal organizations, including the Genevans, Presbyterians for Democracy and Religious Freedom, Presbyterian Elders in Prayer, PC(USA) Evangelical Pastors' Fellowship, Presbyterian Frontier Fellowship, the Presbyterian Lay Committee, Presbyterians Pro-Life, Presbyterians for Renewal, and Presbyterian and Reformed Renewal Ministries International. The letter that listed these groups was a general appeal for the mobilization of commissioners at the 1994 General Assembly in Wichita, a central focus of which was the controversy over the Christian feminist ReImagining movement.[428] The Coalition's early activity was apparently limited to twice-yearly meetings of a small group of renewal leaders and friends.[429]

The focus of the Coalition's first national event in Chicago in the fall of 1996 was the ratification process for the anti-gay Amendment B, passed in Albuquerque, New Mexico, the previous June.[430] David Dobler chaired the planning committee for this event.[431]

In 1996, the Coalition also elected a new steering committee. Daryl Fisher-Ogden, John Huffman, and Barry Van Deventer were retained from the old board of directors. New leadership included:

- Rev. David Dobler, former PC(USA) moderator (1993).
- Rev. Don Elliott, pastor of First Presbyterian Church in Corinth, Mississippi, and current president of Presbyterians Pro-Life.
- .Rev. Jack Haberer, pastor of Clear Lake Presbyterian Church in Houston, Texas.
- Wichita lawyer Robert Howard, board member and current chairman of the Presbyterian Lay Committee.
- Rev. James H. Logan, PFR board member and pastor of South Tryon Presbyterian Church in Charlotte, North Carolina.
- Nancy Maffett, former PFR president from First Presbyterian Church in Colorado Springs, Colorado.[432]

In both 1996 and 1997, the Presbyterian Coalition devoted resources to General Assembly activities and an "amendment project," apparently focusing on the Amendment B and Amendment A ratification struggles. The Coalition joined with the Genevans, the Presbyterian Forum, and other renewal groups to organize a strategy suite or "war room" at the 1998 General Assembly, a project that advanced significantly at the 1999 General Assembly.[433] But the focus in these transitional years was the Coalition's national Gatherings.[434]

Gathering II in the fall of 1997 drew about a thousand people to Dallas. The central issue was the ratification process for the pro-gay ordination Amendment A, passed at the 1997 General Assembly much to the dismay of conservatives who were caught off-guard. Gathering II marked an escalation in conservative opposition to the advancement of inclusiveness in the church,[435] coupled with the emergence of an agenda for a major transformation of the church, including a call for a new evangelical confessional statement.[436] Coalition moderator Jack Haberer said that Gathering II "called for very pro-active measures to influence the whole direction of the denomination." [437]

This call was ultimately answered in the form of the *Declaration and Strategy Paper,* which was ratified at Gathering III, the Coalition's third annual conference in 1998. This theological and strategic charter for transformation of the church was the product of a 16-member "visioning team." This group was chaired by Rev. James Singleton, then-pastor of Whitworth Community Church in Spokane, Washington, and included Joseph Rightmyer (PFR), Parker Williamson (PLC), Terry Schlossberg (Presbyterians Pro-Life), and Barry Van Deventer (Genevans). A follow-up "refinement team," commissioned to revise the Coalition's *Declaration and Strategy Paper* after circulation among its constituency, included Clayton Bell (PFR), Daryl Fisher-Ogden (Genevans), and Don Hofmann (PLC).[438]

Even as the Coalition was gathering momentum towards unity, however, it also faced continuing divisions.

A report in the *The Layman* on the visioning team's final editorial meeting in the spring of 1998 was strongly supportive of the proposed document's "radical" agenda.[439] This important reconfiguration of the Coalition was partly spurred by an upsurge in membership involvement at the 1997 Coalition meeting.[440]

Even as the Coalition was gathering momentum towards unity, however, it also faced continuing divisions. For example, in the final plenary session of Gathering II, a survey delineating possible strategies was taken. Several options were presented:

AGENDA AND IDEOLOGY: THE TROOPS OF THE LORD

- Defend (keep fighting and working for renewal).
- Withdraw (let renewal take its own course).

- Mobilize (redirect every entity back to the biblical Reformed faith).
- Confess (create a foundational statement with church endorsements).
- Separate (leave the denomination).
- Reinvent ("find partners in other faith traditions and reinvent the church; find a whole new way to be a church").

The survey results were as follows: Mobilize, 66 percent; Confess, 64 percent; Reinvent, 35 percent; Separate, 21 percent.[441]

This survey indicated that about one fifth, comprising the Coalition's activist constituency, was ready for schism, while two thirds wanted to mobilize to transform the church.

This survey indicated that about one fifth, comprising the Coalition's activist constituency, was ready for schism, while two thirds wanted to mobilize to transform the church. Perhaps most interesting is that 35 percent wanted to "reinvent" the church, aligning with other, presumably more conservative, reformed or evangelical organizations. A key arena for this type of reinvention is international missions, where evangelicals have historically been a significant presence. In fact, this type of reinvention is already well underway. The PC(USA) was the first mainline church, in 1995, to join the AD 2000 and Beyond movement, the most ambitious and comprehensive coalition of evangelical mission organizations ever developed.[442]

The notion of reinventing the church may also indicate a desire for greater public impact. While the Coalition's leading theologian, Andrew Purves (Pittsburgh Theological Seminary), advocates purifying the church of what he deems to be the negative influences of the prevailing culture,[443] there are also "dominionist" strains influencing the direction of the movement. Dominionists generally and Christian Reconstructionists in particular seek to theocratically purify society through the church, and the purification of the church is, for them, but a first step in the church's progress toward worldly dominion.[444] Parker Williamson's call for the church to be a "front" in the "culture war"[445] places the church's internal conflicts over ordination standards, for example, in a different light. The line between a rightist view of the church's "constitutional standard," on the one hand, and the authoritarian vision it carries into the rest of society, on the other, becomes blurred. This takes on an even more disturbing character when conservative leaders frame their viewpoints on church issues in military terms. Regarding the conflict over gay ordination, for instance, Andrew Purves claims that "troops loyal to the Lord of Hosts must defend the Kingdom where it is under attack." "We must remember," he continues, "that peace at the price of disobedience is surrender."[446]

While the Coalition's plans to purify the church seem to stop short of dominionism, these agendas are not necessarily mutually exclusive. Among the church purifiers, only the strain of apolitical pietism, which strictly separates the church as an institution from societal structures, stands as an obstacle to further political development. Nevertheless, Christian Reconstructionism and the renewal movement share a fundamental premise in their rejection of what Purves calls "the present and evolving values of left-wing American culture."[447] Both view things that commit the church to systemic social change on grounds of civil or human rights as incompatible with church doctrine and the word of God.

OUT FROM BEHIND CLOSED DOORS: A FIVE-YEAR PLAN FOR TAKEOVER

The assertion of a more comprehensive right-wing agenda for the renewal movement is consistent with the general advance of right-wing politics in recent years. Sexuality-based wedge issues are at the forefront of the drive for institutional hegemony in the PC(USA) and in the country generally. While gay ordination and the ReImagining controversy are the primary wedges in the PC(USA), the Coalition's *Declaration and Strategy Paper* made the group's wider goals clear: "We were directed to consider the broad range of possibilities, including options which, until now, have only been spoken of behind closed doors."[448] An "action plan" included in an early draft of the Coalition's paper highlighted the role of "strategic planning . . . to prepare participants for participation in a five-year program of denominational renewal."[449]

An early draft of the Coalition's paper highlighted a five-year program of denominational renewal.

THE CHURCH IN THE BALANCE

The game plan for conservative evangelical ascendancy as outlined in the *Declaration and Strategy Paper* focuses on key arenas within the church: mission, polity, worship, theological education, educational ministries, and church discipline.

One revealing example of the direction that the Coalition would like the church to take is its proposal for the development of "strategic partnerships . . . with parachurch mission organizations, such as the AD 2000 and Beyond movement."[450] Christian Right leaders Bill Bright and Ralph Winter, both Presbyterians, were among the organizers of the founding meeting of AD 2000 and Beyond, which was called the Global Consultation on World Evangelization and was held in Singapore in January 1989. Winter dubbed it the "meeting of the century," and contrasted it to the efforts of the older Lausanne Committee. He described the event as a meeting of church "generals" as distinct from the Lausanne Committee's "congressmen." "[The] congressmen's vote will count," he said, "but it's the generals who command troops that must really make a difference."[451] Organizer Jay Gary attributes the inspiration for this effort to Winter, whose leadership gave shape to the "prophetic watchword" of "A Church for Every People by the Year 2000." Bright has served on the advisory board of AD 2000 and Beyond's strategic mobilization task force.[452]

One component of the AD 2000 and Beyond program is "spiritual warfare," an extreme theological movement focusing on combating demonic powers thought to be blocking the global victory of evangelical Christianity.[453] PC(USA) support for this movement would be significant, since the church's global vision has been primarily aligned with social justice-based ecumenical institutions, such as the World Council of Churches, since the late 1940s.

The Coalition's goals in the area of polity essentially seek to end the mainline leadership tradition of the church.

The Coalition's goals in the area of polity essentially seek to end the mainline leadership tradition of the church.[454] This agenda includes:

- Assessment of polity structures for the purpose of eliminating what is "unwieldy" and "biblically unfaithful."
- The development of an "overall coordinating strategy" for General Assembly campaigns.
- A long-range plan for "biblically faithful" leadership recruitment at every level of church governance.
- Development of programs for the "recruitment and training of elder and pastor commissioners for effective service in the governing bodies of the church."

IN SEARCH OF ALIENS The Coalition's rightist polity analysis is partly masked by the rhetoric of decentralization of power and accountability. This is not, however, a progressive, populist effort to bring the church back to majority rule. Rather, the agenda is authoritarian and aimed at purgation and control.

The Coalition's intentions in the area of theological education provide an excellent example. The Coalition proposes to address the obstacles to its goal of controlling theological education by seeking to defund or undermine seminaries that do not conform to its view of doctrine. They propose to do this by attempting to redirect financial resources, as well as prospective students, away from seminaries historically affiliated with mainline churches and towards evangelical seminaries more in keeping with their views.[455] Indeed, PFR's Robert T. Henderson, who is a key organizer of the renewal movement's efforts to regain control of theological education, makes no bones about the extra-denominational thrust of the renewal agenda: "We evangelicals in the Presbyterian Church have much more in common with evangelicals in all of the other traditions than we have with those within our own tradition who reject the evangelical stance."[456]

In setting the historical context for its *Declaration and Strategy*

Paper, the Coalition acknowledges "good people can in good conscience disagree on many theological matters." Yet it offers no examples, and goes on to attack what it vaguely calls "theological and moral pluralism" and to characterize those ideas with which it disagrees as "alien to the faith of the church." [457] This phrase is used specifically to characterize the theological education presented in the church's historically affiliated seminaries, which the Coalition claims are "responsive to the interests and agendas of academic guilds rather than to the mission of the church." [458] This pitting of academic study against the mission of the church is of course a hallmark of fundamentalism, the main agenda of which is to marginalize interpretive methods that threaten to undermine conservative control of biblical authority in the life of the church.

The Coalition characterizes those ideas with which it disagrees as "alien to the faith of the church."

LIBERALS NEED NOT APPLY

As noted above, PFR is actively working to develop evangelical caucuses in PC(USA) seminaries as well as several conservative nondenominational seminaries. This agenda, which coincides with the Coalition's plan for theological education, is designed to help expand the conservative movement's pastoral power base in the wider church. This is significant in light of the fact that a key element in the right-wing strategy for taking over the Southern Baptist Convention was gaining control of the seminaries. Control of the seminaries meant that conservatives established themselves as gatekeepers of the future leadership of the church, controlling not only what will be taught, but who will teach it, and ultimately who will preach it.

One unusual component of the Coalition's agenda for church discipline is a proposal for the development of a network of "covenant groups" that will "practice confession" and "mutual accountability." The "obstacle" to be overcome by such groups is "an understanding of personal privacy which undermines" such accountability. [459] Such structures of small group inquisition and disclosure are proposed alongside efforts to revitalize the judicial machinery of the church.

The proposal to form these accountability groups bears certain marks of the "shepherding" movement (see Glossary, and the more detailed discussion in chapter 5). Shepherding is the system of authoritarian religious control that shapes the social base of some of the Christian Right. One of the main points of entry for shepherding within the mainline churches is clergy participation in Promise Keepers. [460]

Beyond the realm of small-group shepherding, the Coalition plans to encourage "more faithful and effective exercise" of church members' "vows and responsibilities as presbyters of the church, including the examination of candidates for church office." [461]

This focus on church members as "presbyters" reflects the Coalition's orientation toward purgative institutional power. Corroborating this heightened interest in the "vows and responsibilities" of church "presbyters," *Theology Matters*, the publication of Presbyterians for Faith, Family and Ministry, published what amounts to a 13-page training manual for keeping liberals out of Presbyterian pulpits, titled "A Theological Guide for Pastoral Nominating Committees."[462] The Coalition has posted a similar piece on its web site, titled "How to Examine a Candidate's Theology," which focuses on the need to probe a candidate's use of language in order to identify any deep-seated liberal beliefs.[463]

GATHERING III: THE SHAPE OF THINGS TO COME

In its broad, quasi-confessional scope, the Presbyterian Coalition's *Declaration and Strategy Paper* essentially announced the existence of a church within the Church. In any case, it is probably the most ambitious vision of conservative evangelical transformation of the church in the history of the renewal movement.

In its broad, quasi-confessional scope, the Presbyterian Coalition's Declaration and Strategy Paper essentially announced the existence of a church within the Church.

The document was ratified at the Coalition's Gathering III in Dallas in the fall of 1998. Small group sessions on key aspects of the plan were led by Fuller Theological Seminary professor Daryl Fisher-Ogden, Presbyterians Pro-Life executive director Terry Schlossberg, Pittsburgh Theological Seminary professor Charles Partee, and others.[464]

The Coalition introduced a new leadership plan at the same time, which included an expanded board of directors charged with overseeing the development of six strategy task forces to implement the areas of institutional transformation set out in the strategy paper. Daryl Fisher-Ogden chaired the nominating committee for the development of this leadership structure.[465] The structure was finalized at the December 1998 meeting of the Coalition's board. An executive committee, which included as moderator B. Clayton Bell, vice moderator David Dobler, and secretary-treasurer Don Elliott, led the new 24-member board. Strategy task force leaders were appointed as follows:[466]

- **Mission:** Rev. Howard Edington, pastor, First Presbyterian Church in Orlando, Florida.
- **Worship:** Rev. Daryl Fisher-Ogden, Fuller Theological Seminary, Pasadena, California.
- **Theological Education:** Rev. James Singleton, Whitworth Presbyterian Church, Spokane, Washington.
- **Educational Ministries:** Bettie Ann Stepp of West Palm Beach, Florida.
- **Church Discipline:** Julius Poppinga, elder, Grace Presbyterian

Church, Montclair, New Jersey.
- **Polity:** Rev. Jerry Andrews, pastor of First Presbyterian Church in Glen Ellyn, Illinois.
- **Communications and Development:** Robert Howard, chairman of the Presbyterian Lay Committee.

THE CHURCH AS ENEMY TERRITORY

The Coalition's Gathering IV held in Dallas, Texas, in September 1999, revealed a movement partially divided on issues of overall strategy, as well as certain emerging strategic currents aimed at paving the way for broader gains.

Rev. James Logan set the tone for Gathering IV with a ten-point opening sermon based on *I Samuel 30*. Logan's discussion of King David's conflict with the Amalekites presented a stark military analogy for the work of the renewal movement. In a communiqué posted on his web site, Presbyterian Forum leader Bob Davis enumerated Logan's points, including: "Sometimes God will give you a place in the midst of enemy territory," and, "When fighting the enemy, know that the enemy will retaliate."[467] It should be noted in this regard that, in addition to being on the board of the Coalition, Logan was also president of the charismatic Presbyterian-Reformed Ministries International (PRMI) in the mid-1990s. In the summer of 1999, PRMI initiated an intensive spiritual warfare campaign against church agencies deemed to be in the grip of Satan due to their support for feminist theology and the ordination of gays and lesbians.[468]

In the summer of 1999, PRMI initiated an intensive spiritual warfare campaign against church agencies deemed to be in the grip of Satan due to their support for feminist theology and the ordination of gays and lesbians.

In 1999, the Coalition struggled with its internal difference over how best to achieve its goals. Three distinct approaches were debated at the Coalition's Gathering IV:

1) A reformist, "common ground" approach based on further dialogue with the other side, represented by Rev. Jerry Andrews, then chair of the Coalition's task force on polity.
2) A mutual schism model, represented by Rev. Mark Toone, of Chapel Hill Presbyterian church in Gig Harbor, Washington.
3) A denominational conflict and takeover model, represented by Parker Williamson of the Presbyterian Lay Committee. Williamson's vision particularly roused the crowd. Williamson rejected both the common ground and the mutual schism approaches and called for a "bloody battle" for control of the church.[469]

Divisions over strategy not withstanding, certain activities are proceeding apace, notably the prosecution of Amendment B-related cases, supported and partly financed by the Coalition's task force on church discipline (see Chapter 6). Critical to the Coalition's strategy is the use of ecclesiastical judicial power to neutralize and eliminate unwanted groups and individuals.

Meanwhile, Parker Williamson's belligerent vision of denominational conflict and control is likely to remain well represented on the Coalition board, since Williamson is a member of the nominating committee that controls the board's development.[470]

The Coalition's 1999 board of directors contained a significant cross section of renewal leaders, including the three top officers of the Presbyterian Lay Committee (PLC). Robert Howard, PLC chairman, was elected to the Coalition's executive committee. Elected to the Coalition board were PLC vice chair Don Hofmann, PLC secretary Rebecca McElroy, and PLC board member John Boone. The Coalition's secretary-treasurer, Don Elliott, is also president of Presbyterians Pro-Life. Clayton Bell, David Dobler, and Jack Haberer, among others, have represented the PFR strain on the Coalition board. Jerry Andrews and Daryl Fisher-Ogden reflect the Genevans' emphasis on polity reform.[471]

Meanwhile the Coalition's agenda remains unchanged and it has continued to implement the action plans of the Declaration and Strategy Paper.

Andrews, who served as chair of the Genevans, was elected moderator of the Coalition for 2000. With the exception of Anita Bell, who replaced David Dobler as vice moderator, the Coalition's executive committee remained the same. Also continuing on the executive committee for 2000 were PPL president Don Elliott, PLC chair Robert Howard, Peter Barnes, Howard Edington, Daryl Fisher-Ogden, Julius Poppinga, and Bettie Ann Stepp.[472] Meanwhile the Coalition's agenda remains unchanged and it has continued to implement the action plans of the *Declaration and Strategy Paper.* In January 2000, Anita Bell announced that the Coalition's fifth national conference, Gathering V, "seeks to equip you and your church to uphold Biblical witness in a pluralistic world."[473]

IV. Key Leaders

Rev. J. Howard Edington is a member of the executive committee of the Presbyterian Coalition and chairs its task force on mission. Edington is senior minister of First Presbyterian Church in Orlando, Florida, the fifth largest church in the PC(USA) with 5,000 members. First Presbyterian's 150 ministries occupy an entire city block, the result of a $21 million expansion begun in 1993. In 1997, Edington established a corporation with Orlando businessman Bob Poe to finance a multimillion dollar film version of Adela Rogers St. John's 1996 novel, *Tell No Man,* with proceeds going in part to First Presbyterian's missionary and outreach programs. The effort was inspired by the commercial success of *The*

Spitfire Grill, a religious film financed by the Mississippi-based Catholic charity The Sacred Heart League.[474]

Edington was born in Monroeville, Alabama, and educated at Rhodes College in Memphis, Tennessee, and Louisville Presbyterian Theological Seminary. He has held many church offices and is currently president of the board of trustees of Montreat College in Montreat, North Carolina, as well as a trustee of the Outreach Foundation, which is an evangelical mission organization affiliated with the PC(USA) and a member of the Presbyterian Renewal Network.[475] He joined the board of reference of Presbyterians Pro-Life in 1999.[476] In 1991, Edington was nominated for moderator of the PC(USA) from the floor of the General Assembly, receiving 35 percent of the vote.[477]

Edington is a powerful figure in the central Florida evangelical community, which rivals Colorado Springs, Colorado, as a center for right-wing evangelical institutions.[478] Orlando is home to the evangelical parachurch agency Campus Crusade for Christ, headed by Christian Right leader Bill Bright. Campus Crusade for Christ moved to Orlando from California in 1991 and recently constructed a $45 million World Center for Discipleship and Evangelism. Bright is a member of Edington's church. Edington recommended his prominent parishioner for the lucrative Templeton Prize for Progress in Religion, which he won in 1996.[479] John Templeton, for whom the prize is named, is a former member of the Presbyterian Lay Committee board. Another prominent member of First Presbyterian Orlando is Robert Vander Weide, CEO of the Orlando Magic basketball team and son-in-law of Amway Corporation founder Richard DeVos.[480]

Edington is a powerful figure in the central Florida evangelical community, which rivals Colorado Springs, Colorado, as a center for right-wing evangelical institutions. Orlando is home to the evangelical parachurch agency Campus Crusade for Christ, headed by Christian Right leader Bill Bright.

Edington's national profile seems to be rising. In 1997, he participated in the National Day of Prayer, one of the most successful mainstreaming initiatives of the Christian Right, headed by Shirley Dobson, wife of James Dobson of Focus on the Family.[481] Edington was also listed on the speakers' roster for Bright's annual Fasting & Prayer rally. Founded in 1994, the Fasting & Prayer rally has become a major annual public evangelism event. The 1999 event was held in Houston in November and was simulcast to some 2,000 satellite sites.[482] The executive committee of Fasting & Prayer includes Christian Right leaders Pat Robertson and Promise Keepers founder Bill McCartney.[483] Other speakers at Fasting & Prayer '99 (in addition to Edington) were E. Brandt Gustavson, president of the National Religious Broadcasters, Michael Little, president of Pat Robertson's Christian Broadcasting Network, and Luder Whitlock, president of Reformed Theological Seminary.[484]

Rev. Dr. Daryl Fisher-Ogden was appointed chair of the Coalition's task force on worship in 1999 and is a member of the Coalition's executive committee. She is also on the steering committee of PFR's Network of Presbyterian Women in Leadership. She has worked as an instructor in historical theology and Presbyterian studies at Fuller Theological Seminary, where she was also formerly the director of the Office of Presbyterian Ministries. An expert in ecclesiastical law, Fisher-Ogden has a J.D. from Hastings College of Law in San Francisco, an M.A. and Ph.D. from the University of Notre Dame, and an M.Div. from Fuller Theological Seminary.

In 1998, Fisher-Ogden was pastor of adult education and fellowship at Bel-Air Presbyterian Church in Los Angeles. Bel-Air Presbyterian, the church of Ronald and Nancy Reagan, has a membership of 2,400 and recently underwent a $13.5 million expansion. The church's current head pastor, Rev. Michael Wenning, has been a leader in the Love L.A. clergy coalition, an intercessory prayer movement (see Glossary) co-founded by right-wing Pentecostal leader Rev. Jack Hayford, along with Rev. Lloyd Ogilvie, current U.S. Senate chaplain and previously pastor of First Presbyterian Church of Hollywood.[485] Ogilvie is a key Presbyterian link to the religious right, serving on the board of reference of the Christian Film and Television Commission, among other involvements.[486] He was an early board member of Presbyterians for Renewal.

Fisher-Ogden's leadership in the renewal movement is indicated by her role as an incorporating board member of the Presbyterian Coalition and as a driving force in the Genevans' proposals for right-wing polity reforms. One such Genevans campaign was waged against COCU (The Church of Christ Uniting, see Glossary) at the 1996 General Assembly in Albuquerque, New Mexico. In the campaign, the Genevans used the traditional Presbyterian opposition to the office of Bishop (an office that some Protestant denominations maintain) to argue for severing ties to COCU. Evangelicals have long opposed the PC(USA)'s ongoing dialogue within COCU, an agency that coordinates efforts to deepen the ecumenical alliance of mainline Protestantism.[487]

Julius Poppinga is a member of the Coalition's executive committee and was appointed chair of its task force on church discipline in 1999.

Julius (Jay) Poppinga, an elder at Grace Presbyterian Church in Montclair, New Jersey,[488] is a member of the Coalition's executive committee and was appointed chair of its task force on church discipline in 1999. He is a former senior partner and now of counsel for the Newark-based McCarter & English, the largest law firm in New Jersey.[489] Poppinga is well known for his role as counsel for the ten Rochester, New York area churches that took Downtown United Presbyterian Church to ecclesiastical court over its installation of openly lesbian Jane Spahr as a minister in 1992.[490]

Poppinga has also served widely in the internal governance of the PC(USA). He was the chair of the General Assembly's Quadrennial Review Committee that presented its report to the 1996 General Assembly in Albuquerque, New Mexico. The previous year, he chaired the General Assembly Polity Committee, which recommended a polity reform proposal influenced by the Genevans.[491] Passed by the General Assembly, this proposal would have radically decentralized the PC(USA) power structure on behalf of conservative forces in the name of "representation."[492] However, when remitted to Poppinga's Quadrennial Review Committee for implementation, it was severely curtailed in the Committee's final report, which was approved by the 1996 General Assembly.[493] That spring, the Christian Legal Society called for intercessory prayer in support of Poppinga's work on the Quadrennial Review Committee.[494]

In addition to his leadership role in the Presbyterian Coalition, Poppinga has devoted significant time to policy analysis on behalf of the renewal movement. Among other things, he prepared a 12-page "Digest and Commentary" on issues facing the 1999 General Assembly in Fort Worth.[495]

Conservative religious authority in society depends significantly on the disestablishment of the positions taken by the mainline churches that have so powerfully wielded cultural authority on behalf of social justice in the 20th century.

The significance of Poppinga's leadership role in the renewal movement lies partly in the history and activities of the conservative evangelical Christian Legal Society (CLS), of which he has been a longtime leader. CLS is a leading legal advocacy organization of the Christian Right with regional networks of several thousand lawyers. From 1978 to 1981, Poppinga served as CLS president.[496] He succeeded Herbert Ellingwood, who went on to become a key liaison to the Christian Right in the Reagan administration.[497] Following his tenure as CLS president, Poppinga continued to serve as a board member, once as interim executive director, and as vice chairman of its trend-setting litigation arm, the Center for Law and Religious Freedom.[498]

LURCHING TOWARD THEOCRACY?

Poppinga's leadership in the Christian Right legal movement has informed his leadership of the conservative drive to enforce church discipline in the PC(USA). Indeed, conservative religious authority in society depends significantly on the disestablishment of the positions taken by the mainline churches that have so powerfully wielded cultural authority on behalf of social justice in the 20th century.

A detailed understanding of Poppinga's Christian Right legal career may help illuminate his current role in the PC(USA). In October 1980, the CLS board, under Poppinga's leadership, recruited and mentored three young lawyers who would become prominent in right-wing legal circles:[499]

- Thomas Brandon of the legal staff of Bill Bright's Campus Crusade for Christ.
- Lawrence Eck, a prominent trial lawyer, member of the steering committee of the Coalition on Revival in 1986, and a signer of the 1986 COR manifesto calling for biblical government.[500]
- Samuel Ericsson opened the CLS Washington office[501] and became special counsel to the CLS's Center for Law and Religious Freedom.[502] Ericsson went on to become president of Advocates International, a Virginia-based group that promotes right-wing legal principles and interests in Eastern Europe[503] and elsewhere.[504]

Lynn Buzzard, executive director of CLS from 1971 to 1985, is now director of Legal Education and of counsel at Advocates International.[505] Curran Tiffany, brought in as director of CLS's Jurisprudence Project under Poppinga,[506] has been a leader in the theocratic Coalition on Revival[507] and is a consultant to the National Association of Evangelicals.

CLS is part of the broader legal movement of the Christian Right. The main goal of this movement is to build a framework of legal protection, legislative initiative, and religious support for the advancement of evangelical Christian views and practices within the public sphere. Despite the interfaith appearance of this sprawling legal movement in defense of "religious liberty," at its core it is a creature of the Christian Right, epitomized by the work of Pat Robertson's American Center for Law and Justice and John Whitehead's Rutherford Institute.[508] CLS has a reputation for strategic moderation compared to those groups. CLS is also unique in having incorporated a pastoral counseling component designed to resolve conflict prior to court proceedings. This initiative, called the Christian Conciliation Service, was launched in 1979.

CLS's Center for Law and Religious Freedom, founded in 1975, was one of the first Christian Right legal advocacy organizations. It has filed *amicus* briefs in every major church-state case to come before the Supreme Court since 1980 and helped draft and lobby for the passage of two of the most important legislative initiatives of the Christian Right legal movement: the Equal Access Act (1984), guaranteeing religious parties certain forms of access to public venues, and the Religious Freedom Restoration Act (1993).[509]

The Religious Freedom Restoration Act was eventually found unconstitutional but has laid the groundwork for an ongoing political agenda to limit the public accountability of religious institutions. The most significant CLS-backed initiative in this area is the Religious Liberty Protection Act (RLPA), which has passed in the House of Representatives but was still pending in the Senate as of

March 2000.[510] According to attorney Kristian D. Whitten, "the bill would require courts to overturn federal, state and local regulations that burden the exercise of religion, unless the government promulgating the regulation could show that it had a 'compelling state interest.'"[511] Among other things, this doctrine could be used to exempt religious institutions and practices from civil rights regulations. Professor Marci Hamilton of Cardozo Law School has asserted that the RLPA "is a bald-faced attempt to transform the subject matter of the First Amendment (the free exercise of religion), which is a limitation on Congress, into an enumerated power."[512]

More recently, CLS has played a major role in the development of "charitable choice" legislation, originally sponsored by Sen. John Ashcroft (R-MO). Ashcroft was an early favorite of the Christian Right in the 2000 presidential race before dropping out.[513] The first charitable choice provisions were included as part of the 1996 Welfare Reform Act and have been included in or proposed for other pieces of federal legislation since. Charitable choice provisions seek to allow what critics call "pervasively sectarian" institutions to receive federal funds to administer social services and public health benefits on behalf of the government.[514] This would, according to CLS member and Ashcroft aide Annie Billings, who helped draft the legislation, allow churches to receive federal funds without "having to compromise their religious character." Other CLS representatives involved in drafting and lobbying for the charitable choice legislation included board member Carl Esbeck, Center for Law and Religious Freedom director Steve McFarland, and the Center's chief litigator Gregory S. Baylor.[515] In 1997, CLS co-published *A Guide to Charitable Choice* with the Center for Public Justice, a conservative think tank in Washington, D.C. Charitable choice is a legislative framework considered by many to be dangerously unconstitutional, even as it is a central component of George W. Bush's 2000 presidential campaign platform and has been more cautiously endorsed by President Clinton as well as Vice President Albert Gore. The Presbyterian Church (USA) opposes charitable choice legislation.

Ashcroft says he wants to enact "a comprehensive expansion of Charitable Choice to all federally funded social services."[516] Troubled by the growing mainstream interest in this decisively right-wing agenda, Rev. Charles Moore, pastor of Grace United Methodist Church in Austin, Texas, characterizes charitable choice as an agenda that "opens the door more than anything that I have seen in my lifetime to the church being able to take over the state and turn this nation into a theocracy."[517]

CLS works closely with the Alliance Defense Fund (ADF), a key coordinating arm of the Christian Right legal movement.[518] Together with its affiliate, the Western Center for Law and Religious

Freedom, CLS and ADF jointly sponsor the National Legal Resource Center, which facilitates litigation work with an electronic database and resource distribution network.[519] ADF provided seed money for this project[520] and has also been a funder of the Western Center for Law and Religious Freedom as well as CLS's litigation arm, the Center for Law and Religious Freedom.[521] Julius Poppinga joined the board of directors of the Western Center when it became a CLS affiliate in 1995.[522] Its client list includes notable Christian Right organizations such as Focus on the Family, Operation Rescue, Concerned Women of America, Campus Crusade for Christ, and the Traditional Values Coalition.[523] One of Poppinga's fellow board members at the Western Center was the late William Bentley Ball, a constitutional lawyer who played an important role in church-state legal history from the mid-1960s forward, beginning with his opposition to the Kennedy and Johnson administrations' policy of denying federal funds to parochial institutions.[524]

V. Funding

The Presbyterian Coalition reported only $5,000 income in its first year, 1993. 1994 saw an increase to $63,320 in contributions, followed by a decline to $15,350 in 1995. In 1996, the year of Amendment B and the first national Gathering, contributions jumped to $159,486; and in 1997, the year of Amendment A, contributions totaled $206,588.[525] Projecting a budget of approximately $350,000 to $500,000 in 1999, the Coalition states that most of its money comes from a "handful of large churches."[526] Clayton Bell's Highland Park Church in Dallas is a major contributor to the Coalition.[527]

CHAPTER 5

THE PRESBYTERIAN FORUM

I. Significance

The emergence of the Presbyterian Coalition in the last few years epitomizes the reorientation of the renewal movement away from single-issue politics and toward comprehensive institutional transformation and control. It is not alone. Another leading organization in the reorientation of renewal is the Presbyterian Forum and Review, generally referred to as the Forum.

The Forum is a driving force behind the conservative renewal movement's growing political power at PC(USA) General Assemblies—most prominently displayed at the 1999 General Assembly in Fort Worth.[528] The Forum is also a central player in the Presbyterian Renewal Network, which functions as a coordinating brain trust for the movement across its many parts. Rev. Kennedy McGowan, a close observer of the renewal movement, asserts that "over a fairly brief amount of time, they [the leaders of the Forum] have helped bring together the many groups on the right side of the aisle including the Coalition into a united and highly effective presence at General Assemblies."[529]

The Forum's practical focus on political information and knowledge of political processes filled a void.

The Forum's practical focus on political information and knowledge of political processes also filled a void, largely unfilled by the Coalition. Perhaps indicative of the direction of this wing of the movement, Forum founder Robert Dooling was an early board member of the Coalition, while today no Forum leaders are on the Coalition board. It remains unclear whether the Presbyterian Coalition will effectively mobilize the full range of theological and political opinion in its ranks and thus become the encompassing vehicle of renewal politics. [530] The Forum, however, is poised to be a potent political force. It is staking out ground to the right of the Coalition, emphasizing a theology of "discipling" the nations and waging a prophetic "battle" against, among other things, what it calls a church "leadership [that] has been inclined to extend tolerance under the guise of grace."[531]

While the Forum is primarily engaged in the mechanics of conservative political change, it stands with the PLC at the more conservative, institutionally-oriented end of the renewal spectrum, emphasizing "stewardship responsibility to preserve the church historic; entrusted to us by those who have already borne witness to the God revealed in Scripture."[532] PLC leader Parker Williamson's call for a "bloody battle" for control of the church is similarly grounded in a sense of historic, fiduciary responsibility for Presbyterian heritage.

While the Forum is primarily engaged in the mechanics of conservative political change, it stands with the PLC at the more conservative, institutionally-oriented end of the renewal spectrum.

The Forum emphasizes the role of conservative presbyteries in shaping institutional change through the development of "visionary" legislation up to the General Assembly level.[533] In this way, renewal leaders want to go beyond the traditional conservative pattern of reactive politics in response to denominational staff initiatives. Thus, the Forum's plan coincides with the sweeping institutional agenda of the Presbyterian Coalition's *Declaration and Strategy Paper*.

II. Background

The details of the origins of the Forum are not a matter of public record. It is well known, however, that the Forum arose in response to the failure of conservatives, particularly the Presbyterian Coalition, to effectively advance the renewal agenda.[534] This political tension apparently culminated around the 1997 General Assembly in Syracuse, New York—one of the most controversial Assemblies ever.[535] The Forum was organized in late May 1997, just prior to the General Assembly,[536] by Rev. Robert Dooling, senior pastor at Mountain View Presbyterian Church in Loveland, Colorado; Bob Davis, then a student at Fuller Theological Seminary; and Clarke Reed of Mississippi, who has served as treasurer of the Genevans and is a longtime Republican Party leader.

III. Structure, Activities, and Agenda

The Forum is registered with the federal government as a tax-exempt public charity.[537] Called the Presbyterian Forum Foundation, it is based in Greenville, Mississippi, Clarke Reed's hometown, but headquartered in Pasadena, California, and run day-to-day by Bob Davis.

The Forum is officially a trust. The trustees are Clarke Reed, Robert Dooling, and Rev. Douglas Brandt, senior pastor at Lancaster Presbyterian Church outside Buffalo, New York. Clarke Reed is the "donor of the trust."[538] A board of directors that has not been made public oversees the Forum's activities.[539] The board includes Reed and Douglas Brandt,[540] and Bob Davis is the executive director.[541] The Forum's internet publication, *The Presbyterian Review*, is probably the most important source of continuous political information for the renewal movement. The Forum is also the official contact point (i.e., phone and e-mail) for the Presbyterian Renewal Network.

The Forum has three roles at the General Assembly: 1) to provide technical infrastructure for renewal resources; 2) to help coordinate the General Assembly campaigns of different renewal groups; and 3) to help implement political efforts through a network called The Shepherds, which is described as "a fellowship of Presbyterian Pastors and Elders who have organized to support General Assembly commissioners." This network, to be discussed in more detail below, has evolved since the 1993 General Assembly and was made public for the first time at the 1999 General Assembly.[542]

According to Forum executive director Bob Davis, the Forum developed out of the campaign to mobilize presbytery votes in support of Amendment B in the fall and winter of 1996–97.[543] The Forum has emphasized the development of a more "visionary" agenda for renewal presence in the General Assembly political process since the pivotal 1997 General Assembly,[544] where it ran the first renewal movement "war room," now a fixture of conservative power at the General Assembly level.[545]

The Forum provides resources and advisory assistance to renewal forces throughout the church.[546] Its notion of "resourcing" renewal is essentially a political education and mobilization process aimed at shaping the voting membership of the church.[547] This takes the form of providing timely political information, strategic advisory training and input, and pastoral mediation of institutional engagement. Clarke Reed claims that the Forum has the "ability and resources to respond to many of the crises and problems that members and congregations face throughout the year."[548]

FROM THE WAR ROOM TO THE WAR

The Forum organized its first war room at the 1997 General Assembly in Syracuse, New York.[549] With the passage of Amendment A (see Glossary) in Syracuse, the Forum organized a campaign to mobilize the presbytery vote against it—a difficult task, according to Davis, because many of the people he had previously organized in favor of Amendment B were dispirited and threatening to leave the church at this apparent reversal.[550] The Forum collaborated with the Presbyterian Coalition, the Genevans, Presbyterians Pro-Life, and other groups, in assembling the renewal war room at the 1998 General Assembly in Charlotte, North Carolina.[551]

The Forum organized its first war room at the 1997 General Assembly in Syracuse, New York.

The political influence and power of renewal forces were displayed at the 1999 General Assembly in Fort Worth, Texas. The Forum played a central role in planning and implementing the renewal strategy, based in a suite of rooms procured from an "influential connection" at the Texas Wesleyan Law School across the street from the Fort Worth Convention Center.[552] The Forum brought to the General Assembly professional convention management techniques reminiscent of a major political party convention.

The Forum brought to the General Assembly professional convention management techniques reminiscent of a major political party convention.

In addition to technical infrastructure for the generation and distribution of text and information—the Forum's specialty—a high-powered leadership team was put in place to control the implementation of renewal strategies on key issues. This leadership team was drawn mainly from the Presbyterian Coalition, including executive committee members Daryl Fisher-Ogden and Jerry Andrews, as well as former Coalition moderator Jack Haberer. Henry Greene, former Presbyterians for Renewal president and chair of its issues task force, was also a key strategist. The impact of this effort was evident on the plenary floor, where much of the core renewal agenda was ratified, due in large part to a combination of effective parliamentary engagement, carefully scripted rhetoric, and relative political moderation on sensitive issues.

The success of this major effort reflected months of planning and a significant commitment of resources. The Forum, in conjunction with the Presbyterian Renewal Network, organized the first pre-Assembly training for commissioners, in Fort Worth in May 1999.[553] This was accompanied by the distribution of a comprehensive manual of General Assembly procedures put together by the Forum and now posted on the Presbyterian Renewal Network web site. The manual also includes sections on plenary procedures, nominations from the floor, and committee work, with flow charts illustrating the development of both majority and minority reports. It also includes information on key issues such as ordination standards, inclusive language, the National Network of Presbyterian College Women (NNPCW), and the sexuality curriculum.[554] With the possible exception of NNPCW, the renewal movement subsequently won in all these areas at the General Assembly.[555]

THE AUTHORITY FACTOR: GIVING SHEPHERDS AND SHEEP A WHOLE NEW MEANING

One unusual aspect of the Forum's General Assembly tactics and strategy is the project called The Shepherds. According to Forum leader Rev. Doug Pride,[556] The Shepherds network was created in the wake of the 1993 General Assembly in Orlando, where commissioners expressed frustration at the opacity and fast pace of the parliamentary procedures. To help guide and direct the conservative bloc of commissioners, The Shepherds work to provide commissioners with "pastoral care and support," "timely and accurate information," and "linkages to a variety of experts"[557]—with an emphasis on prayer. Forum moderator Robert Dooling describes his General Assembly involvement in terms of "taking with him a team of 40–50 pastors from all across the nation who offer a ministry of support and empowerment to commissioners."[558]

The Shepherds network was created in the wake of the 1993 General Assembly in Orlando.

The Forum's shepherds operated quietly behind the scenes at subsequent General Assemblies until publicly emerging prior to the 1999 General Assembly in Fort Worth. *The Presbyterian Layman* published an article promoting the Forum's recruiting campaign for shepherds for the 1999 General Assembly.[559]

The role of The Shepherds again places the politics and culture of the renewal movement in the context of the wider Christian Right. Shepherding is a concept and term with a controversial history in recent American evangelicalism.[560] Shepherding is also one of the least understood undercurrents in the political development of the Christian Right since the 1970s.

Generally, the various strains of shepherding are marked by a system of hierarchical and authoritarian social control, with an emphasis on "accountability" and "covenant relationships," sometimes bordering on the cultic.[561]

The most extreme and authoritarian versions of shepherding arose in the 1970s, particularly among charismatic nondenominational churches and parachurch organizations such as Maranatha Campus Ministries. While the excesses and abuses of the time were modified, such principles as submission, authority, accountability, and manipulation of group dynamics, have continued as tools of church growth and of the development of political projects of the Christian Right.

The Forum's shepherds operated quietly behind the scenes at subsequent General Assemblies until publicly emerging prior to the 1999 General Assembly in Fort Worth.

One contemporary parachurch organization with roots in the shepherding movement is the evangelical men's movement organization, Promise Keepers (PK). One of the most sophisticated mobilizations of the Christian Right in the 1990s, PK exemplifies the way in which right-wing evangelical programs, with shepherding techniques as a central component, have taken aim at the center of American culture at a time of both greater acceptance and resistance to gender and racial diversity. As noted above (see page 60), PK is one of the chief forums for evangelical "racial reconciliation." While sometimes providing a platform for genuine efforts at racial healing at a personal level, in certain contexts, such as The Christian Coalition, racial reconciliation serves to undermine public policy approaches to racial issues while presenting a public relations image of opposition to racism.

PK has made significant inroads into the clergy and membership of the PC(USA). In 1996, 400 to 500 PC(USA) pastors attended a PK Clergy Conference held in Atlanta, Georgia, where the focus was shepherding.[562] This is significant not simply because PK founder Bill McCartney has a long history in the Catholic shepherding network known as Word of God, based in Ann Arbor, Michigan,[563] but because it reflects PK's agenda of mainline infiltration. Shepherding structures such as accountability groups, coupled with group control through disclosure of highly personal information on sexuality and finances, are an integral part of the PK program.

One contemporary parachurch organization with roots in the shepherding movement is Promise Keepers.

A commissioner's resolution for denominational endorsement of PK at the 1999 General Assembly lost, but received 40 percent of the vote. Speaking for the resolution, Commissioner Rick Porter of Southern New England Presbytery asserted, "ten times as many of our men are involved in Promise Keepers as they are in Presbyterian Men."[564]

The Presbyterian Forum's "Shepherds" ministry suggests the influence of the broader shepherding movement. It is well known that General Assembly commissioners, and especially youth advisory delegates, are often "coached" in their plenary participation. Whatever the ethical boundaries of such coaching, the most important issue is the emergence of a distinct institutional capacity for pastoral intercession in political processes, the very charter of the Forum's Shepherds ministry.

The extent of the Forum's shepherding activity beyond the General Assembly is not clear; the Forum's year-round political coverage and build-up toward the General Assembly, however, suggests a potentially broad framework for shepherding activity and an authoritarian guidance of the membership franchise.

Among the publicly identified shepherding contacts for the 1999 General Assembly were Sylvia Dooling of Voices of Orthodox Women, former Presbyterian Coalition moderator Jack Haberer, and Ted Nissen—who, among other things, was associate pastor of Bel-Air Presbyterian Church in Los Angeles in the early 1960s. Bel-Air is part of a group of Southern California churches with roots in the post-WWII right-wing evangelical revival epitomized by Rev. Billy Graham.[565]

PK has made significant inroads into the clergy and membership of the PC(USA).

Another Forum Shepherd is Russ Stevenson, a PFR board member and senior pastor of First Presbyterian Church in Baton Rouge, Louisiana. Parker Williamson's father, rightist political philosopher Rene de Visme Williamson, was a ruling elder at First Presbyterian until his death in 1998. This church was an early supporter of the Covenant Marriage Act[566] and hosted a statewide

Covenant Marriage event for 150 ministers and their spouses in 1998.[567] The Covenant Marriage Act uses "the vehicle of the state to promote a religious doctrine," according to Joe Cook, executive director of the American Civil Liberties Union of Louisiana.[568] Already under consideration in 22 other states, the Covenant Marriage Act takes aim at the concept of no-fault divorce. It requires both premarital and predivorce counseling, as well as a two-year wait before a no-fault divorce may be granted.[569]

The Covenant Marriage Act is a bellwether effort by the Christian Right to transform religious doctrine into civil law. While it is binding only to those who choose to be married under it, there is a clear possibility of pastoral coercion, where shepherding techniques may come into play and seriously undermine the voluntary character of the act. Russ Stevenson emphasizes that "covenant marriage needs to be required by pastors."[570]

The Covenant Marriage Act is a bellwether effort by the Christian Right to transform religious doctrine into civil law.

In 1999, Voices of Orthodox Women posted a "Commissioner's Report to the Presbytery" (Muskingum Valley) from minister commissioner Gary W. Miller, describing his "stewardship" at the Fort Worth General Assembly. Miller's prostrate appeal for forgiveness and plan for public repentance suggests the influence of the shepherding movement:

> On nearly every question, I sought the Lord's guidance from His holy word, the Bible, and before His throne I desired only His pleasure. I weakened my resolve and betrayed my integrity on two votes. For that lapse I am deeply sorry. I will repent of this sin publicly through my confession to this body and to the General Assembly through its Stated Clerk.

Miller goes on to denounce what he considers the prioritization of "individual rights" in what has become a "church of victims." He thinks this is something that "might have started with the abolitionist movement." Specifically, Miller focuses on the General Assembly vote to continue denominational support for the National Network of Presbyterian College Women, where he says, "Reformed doctrine is utterly missing, or, when addressed, dismissed as the central cause of pain and the father of all victims." Miller concludes, "Until we regain our love of biblical truth and our fear of displeasing God, we shall remain hopelessly conflicted . . . I've begged for our Lord's forgiveness, now I ask for yours." [571]

The emergence of such shepherding-style activities in the church suggests a profound new dimension to the nature of the political wing of renewal.

The emergence of such shepherding-style activities in the church suggests a profound new dimension to the nature of the political wing of renewal.

IV. Key Leaders

Rev. Robert Dooling is a founder and moderator of the Forum. A PC(USA) pastor since the late 1960s, Dooling is from the San Fernando Valley, where his family owns Dooling Manufacturing, a niche manufacturer of small engine components.[572] He was educated at the University of Redlands and California State College Northridge and received his M.Div. from Fuller Theological Seminary, followed by additional work at San Francisco Theological Seminary.[573]

His pastoral history includes four years at First Church Sherman Oaks (southern California) and 12 years at First Church Woodland (northern California). He has been at Mountain View Presbyterian Church in Loveland, Colorado, for 12 years and is currently senior pastor.[574] Dooling was on the board of directors of the Presbyterian Coalition in 1994, but has not played a prominent role in subsequent years.[575]

He is married to Sylvia Ross Dooling, president of Voices of Orthodox Women, the main women's organization of the renewal movement. Her father is Dick Ross, founder and CEO of World Wide Pictures, the film and television arm of the Billy Graham Evangelistic Association.[576] Based in Minneapolis, World Wide Pictures has financed, produced, and distributed more than 125 films since the mid-1950s.[577]

Bob Davis is executive director of the Forum. A recent graduate of Fuller Theological Seminary, with plans to enter the ministry, he was previously a medical malpractice lawyer in Indianapolis.[578]

Clarke Reed, a Greenville, Mississippi-based businessman and conservative political leader, is "donor of the trust," as well as a trustee, of the Presbyterian Forum Foundation, the title under which the Forum is registered as a tax-exempt entity based in Greenville. Rev. Kennedy McGowan credits Reed with providing significant financial support for the Forum.[579]

Reed has also served as treasurer of the Genevans, the right-leaning polity reform movement started by a network of southern presbytery executives in 1993.[580] Previously, he served as a board member (1988–1991)[581] and as treasurer (1990–1991)[582] of Presbyterians for Democracy and Religious Freedom, now called Presbyterian Action, a project of IRD. IRD, as has been previously mentioned, is an agency which has mounted nationally and internationally significant campaigns against the mainline denominations and their social justice initiatives since the early 1980s.

Largely operating behind the scenes, Reed is a pivotal figure in the Presbyterian renewal movement. It is not well known within the church, however, that he is a major political figure in recent U.S. history. A self-described right-winger,[583] Reed played a key role in the development of Richard Nixon's "southern strategy" in 1972. The Republican southern strategy was based on racial mobilization veiled in law-and-order politics and was built on Barry Goldwater's anti-civil rights electoral sweep of the Deep South in his failed 1964 presidential bid[584] and on Alabama Gov. George Wallace's capture of four southern states as a third-party candidate in 1968. Reed was the founder of the Southern Republican Leadership Conference in 1969 and was the longtime chairman of the Mississippi Republican Party. Between 1968 and 1972, Richard Nixon's Mississippi vote increased from the smallest percentage of any state to the largest (78.2 percent).[585]

Largely operating behind the scenes, Reed is a pivotal figure in the Presbyterian renewal movement.

The GOP southern strategy has been a cornerstone in the political foundation of the New Right, whose agenda has included the elimination of affirmative action, the repeal of abortion rights, the re-enfranchisement of conservative Christianity as an institutional force in public life, and white male cultural control in intellectual life. With the election of Reagan in 1980, the South became central not only to conservative and Republican politics of this sort, but has increasingly informed the center of American politics. [586]

Some Republicans view Reed as a source of resistance to the rise of women and African Americans in the Party.[587] Perhaps Reed's most important political protégé is fellow Mississippian Haley Barbour, who as chairman of the Republican National Committee was a chief architect of the Republican congressional takeover in 1994.[588]

Reed was campaign finance chairman for Mississippi Governor Kirk Fordice's successful re-election bid in 1996.

Reed was campaign finance chairman for Mississippi Governor Kirk Fordice's successful re-election bid in 1996, and is considered to be a "friend and adviser" to Fordice.[589] Fordice's first term was notable for wooly episodes such as supporting corporal punishment modeled on Singapore's policy of public flogging and calling on the legislature to make Mississippi the "capital of capital punishment."[590] Clyde Woods, historian of the century-long political reinvention of plantation control in the Mississippi Delta, summarizes the Fordice agenda as follows:

> Fordice immediately sent shock waves through the African-American community when he expressed his desire to bring the "Reagan Revolution" to Mississippi, cut educational spending, repeal the Voting Rights Act of 1965, veto legislation designed to increase the penalties for crimes motivated by racial, ethnic, or religious hatred, and to call out the

National Guard rather than implement a federal court order to equalize funding between black and white state universities.[591]

When federally mandated redistricting resulted in the election of a record number of black state legislators in 1993, Fordice attempted to "downsize" the legislature. Though the plan was defeated, it would have resulted in a reduction of black representation from 42 seats to 7. "This sounds like 1894 instead of 1994," said state Rep. Ed Blackmon, referring to the dismantling of Reconstruction and the inauguration of the Jim Crow regime of white supremacy in the south.[592]

Fordice also implemented one of the most draconian versions of welfare reform under the Personal Responsibility and Work Opportunity Act of 1996. According to columnist Robert Sheer, Fordice's program "seizes food stamp and welfare money from recipients and uses it to subsidize a mandatory work program:"

> A welfare mother must accept a minimum wage job in the private sector mostly paid for with federal funds. In what may herald a return to the plantation economy, this time around, subsidized with federal funds, the private employers put up only a dollar an hour of their own money. . . .[593]

Fordice has also endorsed the Council of Conservative Citizens, the ascendant far-right segregationist network that made national news in 1999 after revelations about the involvement of Senate majority leader Trent Lott (R-MS).[594] Former Rep. Webb Franklin (R-MS, 1982–1986), a recipient of campaign cash from Reed,[595] has also endorsed the Council of Conservative Citizens.[596]

Reed has contributed to many conservative candidates since the early 1980s, including former Sen. Paula Hawkins (R-FL) and, more recently, Donald Devine (R-MD), as well as Mississippi senators Trent Lott and Thad Cochran. Reed is also a contributor to the Conservative National Committee, a political action committee that has supported the candidacies of Oliver North, Jesse Helms, and Ron Paul, among others.[597]

A prominent landowner and businessman, Reed has been deeply involved in environmental politics around land-use issues, forming the Delta Wildlife Foundation to advocate private conservation practices as opposed to public ownership and regulation.[598] Recent scholarship on land-use in the Mississippi Delta points to entrenched patterns of government-subsidized growth and control benefiting landowners at public expense.[599]

Clarke Reed has informed and shaped the revolutionary renewal movement currently taking aim at the PC(USA), much as he did in the political "revolution" founded on southern Republicanism. His involvement reflects the scale of what is at stake in the current crisis in the church, and should elicit a certain historical perspective on this crisis.

Because the mainline churches are significant institutions and wield considerable cultural authority on a national level, the neutralization and realignment of the mainline churches has been one of the most unifying objectives of right-wing politics in the 20th century.[600] Reed's earlier role as a leader of the IRD-affiliated Presbyterians for Democracy and Religious Freedom places him in the long tradition of anti-mainline attack agencies dating back to the 1940s, and underscores the broad political purpose he brings to the work of the Forum.

At the current crossroads, a conservative realignment of the church—what the renewal movement is aiming at with the support of people like Reed—will deepen the hold of right-wing politics in a time of political volatility and transition. Reed's involvement in the renewal movement should signal the nature, not simply of the movement itself, but of what is at stake if the movement wins.

V. Funding

The Forum's 1997 Form 990 shows that it received $56,320 in contributions in its first year of operation. The Forum's tax-exempt status filings on Form 1023 show annual contributions of $48,320 in 1997, $52,000 in 1998, and $56,000 in 1999.[601] According to *The Washington Times* (Sept. 21, 1999), Clarke Reed "helps raise the $130,000 budget for the Forum to educate church members."

CHAPTER 6

THE REVIVAL OF CHURCH DISCIPLINE

I. Significance

While the Presbyterian Forum has emerged as a catalyst for organizing conservative political power in church policy, this political focus is coupled with a drive to utilize the judicial mechanisms of the church to enforce conservative policies passed by the General Assembly and the presbyteries, notably the 1996 constitutional ban on gay ordination known as Amendment B.

Four cases tried by the Permanent Judicial Commission of the Synod of the Northeast in the fall of 1999 mark the first stage in the conservative movement's "judicial track" toward power in the church.[602] As of the completion of this report, three of the four cases have been appealed to the Permanent Judicial Commission of the General Assembly, the highest court in the church. Not since the modernist-fundamentalist battles of the 1920s and 1930s has the role of judicial power been so central to the future of mainline Presbyterianism.

Not since the modernist-fundamentalist battles of the 1920s and 1930s has the role of judicial power been so central to the future of mainline Presbyterianism.

The use of judicial power as a mechanism of enforcement and control within the structure of the church has arisen out of the Presbyterian Coalition's confessional emphasis on church discipline, as specified in its *Declaration & Strategy Paper* of 1998. The Coalition's task force on church discipline has made this a reality through its legal and financial support for the complainants in the four ecclesiastical trials of 1999–2000. These cases signal the possibility that, as church policy increasingly reflects the views of the conservative renewal movement, an era of ecclesiastical trials and purges may follow. Moreover, the controversy surrounding judicial enforcement is a catalyst for the movement's bid to recapture the church as an institutional whole. *The Presbyterian Layman* reports that the Coalition's task force on church discipline is, according to PLC leader and task force member Peggy Hedden, "considering recommendations that would make it easier for Presbyterians to understand and work within the denomination's judicial system." What's more, the task force may also develop a network of Presbyterian attorneys to provide *pro bono* services for judicial cases.[603]

The Coalition's strategy for church discipline is centered in the concepts of authority and accountability. The goal is to purify the church of practices and people deemed to have, among other things, a "distorted understanding of grace," an "understanding of privacy which undermines practices of self-examination," and an aversion to living "under the authority of the biblical and constitutional standards of the church."[604] The Coalition's vision of church discipline is based in a network of disciplinary "covenant groups," along with so-called restoration ministries,[605] a primary reference here being to gay conversion.[606]

Such purification efforts require, of course, increased control of church leadership capacities. Therefore, the Coalition is developing a polity plan for "recruiting and equipping biblically faithful and effective leaders for service at every level of church governance."[607]

SYNOD OF THE NORTHEAST TAKES CENTER STAGE

Julius Poppinga, the Coalition's point man on church discipline, has said that if the complainants in the four major cases of 1999–2000 do not prevail, then a special session of the General Assembly may be warranted to address what he would consider to be a constitutional crisis in the church. He says that the purpose of the special session would not be "to reverse the individual cases," but rather "to address constitutionally the distortion that these cases will have foisted upon us."[608]

THE FOUR CASES

• *Hair and McCallum v. the Session of First Presbyterian Church of Stamford, Connecticut*

A remedial case brought against the Session of First Presbyterian Church Stamford for its vote to install an openly gay man as an elder in the church.

• *The Session of Londonderry Presbyterian Church, N.H., et al. v. the Presbytery of Northern New England*

A remedial case brought against the Presbytery of Northern New England for its refusal to bring Christ Presbyterian Church (Burlington, Vermont) into compliance with Amendment B, against which the church has taken a formal position of dissent.

• *The Session of Bethlehem Presbyterian Church, et al. v. Hudson River Presbytery*

A group of churches led by Bethlehem Presbyterian Church brought this remedial case against the Hudson River Presbytery because of its vote to allow for local discretion in the performing of "holy unions," that is, religious ceremonies of same-sex partnership commitment.

- *The Session of Merchantville Presbyterian Church, et al. v. West Jersey Presbytery*

A remedial case brought against the Presbytery of West Jersey by a group of churches led by Rev. John S. Sheldon, pastor of First Presbyterian Church of Ocean City, New Jersey. At issue was the Presbytery's acceptance of an openly gay man into candidacy for ordination.

Of the four cases, all but the Stamford case were appealed to the Permanent Judicial Commission of the General Assembly. In both the Hudson River and West Jersey cases, the complaints were denied at the synod level. In the Northern New England case, the complaint was upheld. In the Stamford case, the complaint was upheld in part, requiring First Presbyterian Stamford to reexamine the elder in question in regard to his sexuality.

THE POLITICS OF THE TRIALS OF 1999

A Coalition fundraising letter dated October 1999 states that the Presbyterian Coalition's task force on church discipline "has provided expert legal advice, and some financial assistance, to those who have been prosecuting the four complaints currently being considered by the Permanent Judicial Commission of the Synod of the Northeast." In fact, task force members have played a direct or indirect role in the litigation process in all four cases.

The Presbyterian Coalition's task force on church discipline "has provided expert legal advice, and some financial assistance, to those who have been prosecuting the four complaints."

Julius Poppinga, chair of the Coalition's task force on church discipline, states that his group is "not out on a hunt," but it has been "assigned a task." He has compared the Northeast Synod cases to "clusters of cancer" which have been discovered in the region.[609] Among those assigned to the task force are several leaders of the Presbyterian Lay Committee, an organization with a long track record of inquisitorial campaigns. PLC participants on the task force have included board members Don Hofman,[610] Peggy Hedden, an attorney from Ohio, and Robert Fish, who chairs the Republican Party in Wood County, West Virginia, and is a research associate for E.I. du Pont de Nemours & Co., Inc.[611]

Poppinga was counsel for the complainants in the Northern New England and Hudson River cases. He and fellow task force member Rev. James Tony of Palos Park, Illinois, also assisted Gary Griffith in preparing legal materials in the West Jersey case.[612] Coalition task force member Walter E. Baker was lead counsel in the Stamford case.[613]

William Prey, complainants' co-counsel in the Stamford case, represented One By One, a gay conversion ministry, at a meeting of the Presbyterian Renewal Network, held in February 1999 in Louisville, Kentucky.[614] Prey endorsed a statement by the Presbyterian Renewal Network calling for funding limits and greater oversight of the National Network of Presbyterian College Women.[615] Baker and Prey are both elders at the Presbyterian Church of Old Greenwich, in Old Greenwich, Connecticut. Their pastor, Rev. Arthur Chartier, joined the board of Presbyterians Pro-Life in 1996.[616]

Walter E. Baker has been a member of the Coalition's task force on church discipline since May 1999.[617] A prominent businessman, he was, among other things, senior vice president of Salomon, Inc., and a director of its subsidiary, Philipp Brothers, Inc., in the 1980s.[618] Before its merger with Salomon in 1981, Philipp Brothers was one of the largest commodities brokerage firms in the world, with historic ties to Harry Oppenheimer's Anglo-American Corporation, the diamond and metals empire at the heart of the South African apartheid regime.[619] Baker is currently president of Philipp Brothers, Inc.[620]

The role of prominent members of the Presbyterian Church of Old Greenwich in the trials of 1999–2000 highlights a local and historical continuity in the renewal movement. Nearby Noroton Presbyterian Church was home to three of the key founders of the Presbyterian Lay Committee in 1965: George Champion, chairman of Chase Manhattan Bank; Roger Hull, then-president of Mutual Life Insurance of New York; and Hugh MacMillan, then-senior vice president of Coca-Cola Exports.

SPIRITUAL WARFARE The charismatic wing of the renewal movement, as represented by Presbyterian-Reformed Ministries International (PRMI), is also linked to the recent conservative judicial campaign. Rev. Samuel Schreiner, chief complainant in the case against the Presbytery of Northern New England, has worked closely with Brad Long, executive director of PRMI. Long invited Schreiner to be part of a PRMI revival in Taiwan in the fall of 1992. At one point during the Taiwan revival, Schreiner "collapsed in the Spirit" and had a vision of the church as a bubbling fountain toward which emaciated people were crawling from four directions.[621] Subsequently, Schreiner's Londonderry Presbyterian Church has moved in a charismatic direction, and Schreiner has continued to work with PRMI.[622]

PRMI has attacked women's ministries and the gay and lesbian movement in the church with particular vehemence.

PRMI has attacked women's ministries and the gay and lesbian movement in the church with particular vehemence. Responding to the church's 1999 Women of Faith awards, which honored lesbian church leader Jane Spahr, PRMI has called for spiritual warfare against the "demonic stronghold" which it asserts has "taken root in the PC(USA) women's work."[623]   Specifically, PRMI states, "We believe strongly that we have been led by the Holy Spirit to spend the money and time to call all the intercessors of [PRMI] to also engage in this spiritual battle."[624]   Schreiner's alliance with this spiritual warfare movement in many ways epitomizes both the purgative political agenda of the conservative movement and the use of the judicial processes of the church to carry it out.

PRMI has called for spiritual warfare against the "demonic stronghold" which it asserts has "taken root in the PC(USA) women's work."

Leaders of Presbyterians Pro-Life, which emphasizes the importance of church discipline in its literature,[625] are also involved in the judicial crisis that has gripped the church. Rev. John S. Sheldon, pastor of First Presbyterian Church of Ocean City, New Jersey, and the chief complainant in the West Jersey Case, has served on the board and as vice president of Presbyterians Pro-Life.[626]   As previously noted, John Sheldon is the son of Benjamin Sheldon, the longtime president of PPL. Church discipline task force member James Tony has served on the PPL board.[627]

Gary Griffith, a lawyer from Ocean City, New Jersey, is attorney for the complainants in the West Jersey case. Griffith has also been a member of the Christian Legal Society (CLS), a conservative evangelical legal advocacy and litigation network.[628]   Julius Poppinga, who assisted Griffith in bringing this case, is a longtime CLS leader.

THE MAN BEHIND THE TASK

Julius (Jay) Poppinga was appointed chair of the Coalition's task force on church discipline in early 1999, although his reputation as a church litigator dates to 1992 when he served as counsel for the ten Rochester-area churches who took Downtown United Presbyterian Church to ecclesiastical court over its installation of openly lesbian Jane Spahr as pastor.[629]   Poppinga's leadership in the conservative judicial movement in the PC(USA) is a logical extension of his long-time leadership of a network of conservative evangelical attorneys called the Christian Legal Society[630] (see page 83).

Poppinga's leadership in the conservative judicial movement in the PC(USA) is a logical extension of his longtime leadership of a network of conservative evangelical attorneys called the Christian Legal Society.

Poppinga's sense of what is at stake is reflected in his characterization of the Northern New England case as a potential "full-blown constitutional crisis" in the church. He has also declared that if holy unions are not banned in the Hudson River case, "the reservoir of moral authority of our congregation to speak in matters of sexual morality will have been utterly exhausted." He describes holy unions as a pattern that is "totally out of sync with the created order," and maintains that if this practice is brought into the church, the result will be an "ecclesiastical crisis."[631]

This drive against gay and lesbian leadership and empowerment plays a dual role in the conservative movement's bid for power in the church.

HAMMERING HOME INJUSTICE: PRESBYTERIAN JUDICIAL POWER IN HISTORICAL PERSPECTIVE

Firstly, judicial proceedings are necessary to enforce conservative church policies passed by the General Assembly, so that the work of groups like the Forum does not go in vain. Secondly, the cases themselves help to define new vistas of conservative policy: shortly after the complaint seeking to overturn Hudson River Presbytery's affirmation of holy unions was rejected at the synod level,[632] an overture seeking a constitutional ban on holy unions was passed by the Presbytery of Tampa Bay for consideration at the 2000 General Assembly.

The judicial process is not happening in isolation from broader right-wing political developments, moreover. In certain respects, the judicial situation in the church mirrors the role the courts have played in shaping fundamental civil rights in the U.S. for 40 years, but in reverse: against civil rights, against social justice, and with sanction of God and the institutional church, rather than the constitution and the state. Given the cultural authority as well the historic institutional role of mainline Presbyterianism in supporting social progress for much of the century, the current judicial struggle in the church could set a regressive precedent in the context of ongoing challenges to civil rights more generally in our society. These challenges arguably represent the core agenda of resurgent right-wing politics since the mid-1970s.

Gary North's history of Presbyterian conflict, *Crossed Fingers: How the Liberals Captured the Presbyterian Church*, details the modernist defeat of conservative orthodoxy within Presbyterianism in the 1930s.[633] The key aspect of conservative failure in this period, according to North, was a loyalist refusal to use judicial power to sanction and eliminate liberal control. To reverse this victory, North suggests, purgative judicial power, this time exerted *against* modernism, is the key.[634] North's analysis is like a crystal ball onto the current situation in the PC(USA). Indeed, Poppinga's judicial thinking is clearly on the grand scale advocated by North.

North's detailed history is also testament to the deeper political legacy of rightist obsession with mainline social witness. That North has spent years studying the "liberal triumph" in mainline Presbyterianism illuminates the scale of what is at stake. His vision of the future of church history is one in which successive mainline denominations are recaptured using political strategy and judicial power. He celebrated the first of these reversals—the fall of the Southern Baptist Convention in the 1980s—as "the most remarkable ecclesiastical reversal of the past three centuries."[635] The conservative judicial movement in the PC(USA) is one sign that mainline Presbyterianism may be next.

CHAPTER 7

CONCLUSION

Twenty years ago, a committed group of conservative activists within the Southern Baptist Convention (SBC) set out to systematically target and gain control of the key institutions of that denomination of 14 million members.[636] Today the SBC has been transformed into a major bloc of conservative religious power in the public sphere. In 1998, the SBC adopted an official doctrine of women's submission to men, signaling a dramatic political realignment of Baptist power in the "culture wars" currently being waged against social progress on so many fronts.

IT CAN'T HAPPEN IN THE PC(USA)

Conservative evangelical power has been gaining ground in many of the mainline churches with similar effect. While the SBC takeover analogy is imprecise, it does demonstrate that mainstream institutions are not immune to a well-planned and sustained conservative insurgency.

In fact, mainstream institutions have never been more vulnerable to conservative power, whether through devolutionary strategies of elimination, as with public education, or through strategies of institutional control, as with the federal judiciary, higher education, and the mainline churches. It almost stretches the imagination to recall— or to learn for the first time—that the SBC was moderately pro-choice in the 1970s and a longtime staunch advocate of separation of church and state. It is hardly a matter of speculation that the mainline churches have been targeted for political realignment by conservative movements. Conservatives are quite frank about it.

Parker Williamson, for one, contends that the church is but one front in the "culture war."[637] The culture war, of course, is shorthand for right-wing mobilization against everything from feminism and gay and lesbian rights, to public education and the separation of church and state. A politically clearer version of Presbyterian renewal as a front in the culture war, and the church as a strategic target in that war, has been articulated by James R. Edwards, PFR board member and professor of religion at Whitworth College in Spokane, Washington. Writing in *Theology Matters*, the leading intellectual journal of conservative Presbyterian renewal, Edwards explicitly pits renewal in the church against democracy in society:

Mainline Protestantism has historically championed the ideals of liberal democracy, and in doing so it has comfortably regarded society as a social extension of the church. That accommodation is no longer possible—if it ever was. The pluralism of modern culture is not only not compatible with the great ends of the church, but increasingly inimical to them.[638]

He goes on to claim that liberal Protestant tradition, to the extent that it is premised on a social vision of the church, is akin to the political imperialism of Constantinian Christianity. Of course, any organized religion is both an extension and a reflection of the existing social order. Thus, the question is not whether the church is an extension of social order, but rather what kind of social order the church legitimates. Thus, Edwards' pitting of the "great ends" of the church against liberal democracy suggests a vision of the church intolerant of, and lacking in fundamental respect for, the needs and views of others. It is this, the culture war model of church renewal, that most threatens the integrity of Christian faith.

It may be only a small historical step from a religious movement that sets itself against liberal democracy in the name of confessional orthodoxy to a decimation of democracy undertaken in the name of a purified church.

It may be only a small historical step from a religious movement that sets itself against liberal democracy in the name of confessional orthodoxy as Edwards describes the Presbyterian renewal movement—to a decimation of democracy undertaken in the name of a purified church.[639] Moreover, the use of democratic means—in this case Presbyterian polity—to achieve anti-democratic ends is a paramount issue in coping with the conservative bid for power in the church. Christian Right theorist Gary North makes precisely this point in frankly explaining how to exploit what he calls the "dilemma of democratic pluralism," in which anti-democratic agendas can gain power by recognizing that pluralists by definition must tolerate even those who would eliminate pluralism.[640]

Views as severe as those of James Edwards often sustain a long-term determination that ought not be taken lightly by anyone unfortunate enough to be set in their sights. This is part of the challenge facing mainline Christianity as the renewal movement in its various parts continues its efforts to destabilize and replace the vision, leadership, and institutions of 20th century Protestantism.

THE REST OF THE STORY

This report presents a broad overview of the key groupings of the Presbyterian renewal movement. The focus has been on historical background, organizational development, political agenda, and leadership profiles. But there is more to the story than can be presented here. In addition to other major groups, certain other renewal currents have generally received less attention than the more overtly political organizations. For example, several conservative evangelical mission groups—Presbyterian Frontier Fellowship, Presbyterian Outreach Foundation, and the Presbyterian Center for Mission Studies—have had a significant impact on the direction of PC(USA)'s global missions. This development augurs a profound realignment in the global perspective of the PC(USA) and warrants an in-depth study in its own right.

Also deserving close attention is the role of seminaries. The Presbyterian renewal movement (especially the Coalition and PFR) is focused on transforming seminary education into a training ground for conservative evangelical leadership. This is likely to be played out through increasing influence over curricula, faculty hiring, appointments to boards of trustees, and more. To begin with, the Coalition's task force on theological education has declared its intent to establish a series of consultations with seminary presidents.[641]

The Presbyterian renewal movement is focused on transforming seminary education into a training ground for conservative evangelical leadership.

This report is but a first step in the effort to describe and understand the politics of the ascendant Presbyterian renewal movement. The possibility that the PC(USA) may become the first fully mainline church to be transformed into a conservative evangelical institution is as disturbing to some as it is exciting and profoundly motivating to others. Those who take these facts seriously may well determine the direction and identity of the church.

Amendment A: A 1997 PC(USA) General Assembly revision of Amendment B, subsequently defeated in the presbyteries, which would have overturned its effective prohibition of gay ordination.

Amendment B: A 1996 amendment to the PC(USA)'s *Book of Order* (part of the constitution of the church), which effectively banned gay ordination in the church.

Book of Order: Part of the constitution of the church. Contains the structure of church government, the rules of discipline and conflict resolution, and the guidelines for worship.

Charismatic: A Christian of any denomination who believes that, through the operation of the Holy Spirit, God's power can be directly manifested in the human body or in a person's life. Some charismatics claim to be able to perform supernatural acts, such as miraculous healings, under the influence of the holy spirit, while others emphasize God's power to holistically possess and guide a person's entire life—behavior, decision making, consumption patterns, etc. The charismatic style of worship is marked by emotional activities such as shouting and weeping, and sometimes more specialized supra-rational activities, such as "speaking in tongues." Charismatics include old-fashioned Pentecostals, some Catholics, and both denominational and nondenominational Protestants. Many also accept a literal interpretation of the Bible.

Christian Reconstructionism: A theocratic, politically oriented theological movement that arose out of conservative Presbyterianism, asserting that contemporary application of the laws of Old Testament Israel is the basis for reconstructing society as the kingdom of God on earth. Reconstructionism is controversial in part for its advocacy of capital punishment for a long list of "offenses," including such sexually oriented crimes as adultery and homosexuality and such religious crimes as propagation of false doctrines, heresy, blasphemy and apostasy. The movement's seminal text is *Institutes of Biblical Law,* by Rousas John Rushdoony, published in 1973. Other prominent Reconstructionists mentioned in this report include Gary North, Rev. George Grant, Rev. Joseph Morecraft, and the late Rus Walton.

Christian Right: The political movement of Christian conservatives in the U.S., epitomized by Pat Robertson's Christian Coalition and such leaders as D. James Kennedy of Coral Ridge Ministries, Gary Bauer of the Family Research Council, and James Dobson of Focus on the Family.

The Church of Christ Uniting (COCU): An ongoing ecumenical dialogue among a number of mainline Protestant denominations, including the PC(USA), which are seeking mutual recognition of ministries and cooperation in their activities; formerly known as The Consultation on Church Union.

Coalition on Revival: Founded in 1982 as a successor organization to the International Council on Biblical Inerrancy, COR brokered a series of theological compromises among competing religious factions and evangelical leaders. The apparent goal was to forge a trans-denominational evangelical theology and to reduce theological divisions that impeded the political progress of the Christian Right. The leadership of this movement included conservative evangelical theologians, Christian Right leaders, prominent televangelists, and notably, leaders of the Christian Reconstructionist movement. COR founder and leader Dr. Jay Grimstead was a member of the United Presbyterian Church until at least the early 1970s before leaving to join a series of evangelical churches. He was also an area director of Young Life. He published an article entitled "Cancer of Materialism—Our Subtle Enemy," in *The Layman* in January 1972.

Commissioner: A voting member elected to the annual PC(USA) General Assembly by a presbytery.

Confession of 1967 (C-67): The first new confession adopted by the Presbyterian Church since the 19th century, C-67 was ratified by the presbyteries of the United Presbyterian Church and added to the church's Book of Confessions along with several other historic Reformed confessions. C-67 was notable for its recognition of the church's obligation to engage the pressing social issues of the day.

Confessional Statement: In the Reformation period and since, a church's affirmation of its faith. Confessional statements summarize doctrine and interpret scripture, sometimes in question and answer form, as in a catechism.

Confessionalism: A church's posture of loyalty to its confessions or historic statements of faith.

The Consultation on Church Union (COCU): An ongoing ecumenical dialogue among a number of mainline Protestant denominations, including the PC(USA), which are seeking mutual recognition of ministries and cooperation in their activities; since renamed The Church of Christ Uniting.

Council for National Policy (CNP): A secretive, conservative leadership and strategy organization, headquartered in Alexandria, Virginia. The CNP is composed of several hundred top conservative funders and political and religious leaders.

Covenant Fellowship of Presbyterians: Predecessor to Presbyterians for Renewal, CFP was a conservative evangelical organization originating in the former southern Presbyterian Church.

Definitive Guidance: Unofficial term for a denominational policy prohibiting gay ordination adopted at the 1978 General Assembly of the United Presbyterian Church.

Dispensationalism: An interpretive approach to the Bible that became a movement within American evangelicalism after the 1870s. Dispensationalism essentially involves the dividing of all time into separate dispensations, or different stages in God's revelation. Dispensational views spread into conservative evangelicalism through the Bible and prophetic conference movement, the Bible institutes (e.g., the Moody Institute in Chicago), and the influence of the Scofield Reference Bible (published in 1909 and revised thereafter). By the 1920s, it had eclipsed other forms of premillennialist beliefs and was subsequently taken up by what became known as the fundamentalist movement.

Dominionism: Dominionism consists of a number of different tendencies, but all adhere to the notion that the Scriptures have given dominion over the earth to Christians, who thus owe it to God to seize the reins of secular society. The leading dominionist grouping is Christian Reconstructionism.

Ecclesiology: Theological doctrine about the church.

Elder (and ruling elder): A member elected by a Presbyterian congregation and ordained to serve on the congregational session with other members of the government of the session and assist in the administration of the sacraments.

Gay Conversion Therapy: A controversial practice, advocated by Christian Right organizations, which presumes that homosexuality is not an innate orientation, but a choice, a confusion, or a demonic possession, and therefore subject to a therapeutic change or a change in sexual orientation based on religious conversion. Groups often referred to as "ex-gay ministries" advocate conversion therapy.

General Assembly: The highest governing body of the PC(USA).

General Assembly Council: A body elected by the General Assembly to carry out the policy and programs as set by the General Assembly.

Holy Union: A celebration of a committed, same-sex relationship performed in a marriage-like ceremony; the subject of one of the 1999 ecclesiastical trials in the Presbyterian Church (USA).

Institute on Religion and Democracy: Washington, D.C.-based organization that has, since its founding in the early 1980s, sought to undermine the social justice work of the mainline denominations. Among its projects are the Ecumenical Coalition on Women and Society (ECWS) and the Association for Church Renewal (ACR). The IRD maintains committees that work for "reform" in the mainline denominations, including Presbyterian Action for Faith and Freedom (formerly Presbyterians for Democracy and Religious Freedom), Episcopal Action, and United Methodist Action.

Intercessor (and intercessory prayer): One who engages in intercession—"prayer, petition, or entreaty in favor of another." Within the Christian Right, intercession is often utilized as a pastoral method intertwined with engagement in politics.

John Birch Society (JBS): A far-right organization founded in 1958 by Robert Welch, and named after a young fundamentalist Baptist U.S. Army captain killed by Chinese Communist forces in China in 1945. Before forming the JBS, Welch, a Unitarian, was vice president of a candy company. He was also a director and vice president of the National Association of Manufacturers. In the 1960s, the JBS was one of the most prominent organizations of the far right, and is credited with helping Barry Goldwater get the 1964 GOP presidential nomination. Given to conspiracy theory, the JBS once accused President Dwight Eisenhower of being a "dedicated, conscious agent of the Communist conspiracy." Its members have opposed Medicare, Social Security, farm subsidies, pro-union legislation, foreign aid, nuclear disarmament, and participation in the United Nations. Headquartered in Appleton, Wisconsin, the JBS publishes books, produces audio and video programs, sponsors speakers, and maintains an elaborate web site. Its nationally distributed magazine is *The New American*. Several members of Congress have close relationships with the JBS, including Rep. Bob Barr (R-GA), Rep. Helen Chenoweth (R-ID), and Rep. Ron Paul (R-TX), who taped an interview for a JBS video designed to expose, according to *The New American*, the United Nations' "funding of abortion plus pressure to abolish anti-abortion laws wherever they still exist."

Moderator: In the PC(USA), a presiding officer of a committee, youth group, or a governing body such as a presbytery or the General Assembly.

Neo-Confederate Movement: A modern movement rooted in Southern pride and nostalgia, and wedded to extreme right-wing politics in pursuit of these cultural agendas. Some neo-Confederates are also slavery apologists. The neo-Confederates think of themselves as the South rising again. Among the organizations generally associated with the movement is the League of the South, which advocates secession. The

League held a Southern Independence Day Rally in Montgomery, Alabama, the birthplace of the Confederacy, in January 2000.

New Right: Historically rooted in the movement surrounding the presidential campaign of Barry Goldwater in 1964, the New Right organized itself and came to power in the Carter years. Ronald Reagan's failure to win the Republican presidential nomination in 1976 proved decisive in galvanizing the network of political operatives that would constitute the New Right. Among the hallmarks of this movement was the rise of conservative think tanks such as the Heritage Foundation, which played a major role in helping shape the policies of the Reagan administration. Also important was a unique sociopolitical convergence of evangelical Christianity with the more traditional national security and free-market currents of the conservative movement. The hallmark of this convergence was the emergence of Rev. Jerry Falwell's Moral Majority in the early 1980s.

Old Right: A loosely organized movement, largely backed by conservative manufacturing leaders, which arose during the 1930s and especially after WWII to combat the development of public policy as well as social movements oriented toward civil rights, greater social equality, and international peace. Old Right trends such as isolationism and anti-immigrant sentiment remain current, notably in the populist politics of Pat Buchanan. But these are only part of a spectrum that included libertarianism as well as traditional social conservatism.

Overture: A request for action by the General Assembly.

Orthodox Presbyterian Church: A small denomination organized in 1936 in protest against modernist trends in the northern Presbyterian Church. Conservative protestors led by J. Gresham Machen were suspended from the church after refusing to disband a foreign mission society they had formed.

Paleo-conservatism: A conscious reaction to neoconservatism, paleo-conservatism combines traditional business and property rights libertarianism with extreme cultural traditionalism and a streak of nativism and racism.

Parachurch: A kind of organization, common in the evangelical Christian community, that delivers religious services outside of traditional denominational structures, sometimes in strategic circumvention of, or opposition to, those structures. One of the best-known parachurch organizations is Campus Crusade for Christ.

Permanent Judicial Commission: An ecclesiastical court responsible for hearing remedial and disciplinary cases at the presbytery, synod, and General Assembly levels of the PC(USA).

Presbyterian Action for Faith and Freedom: Generally called Presbyterian Action, a project of the right-wing Institute on Religion and Democracy in Washington, D.C. since 1990; formerly known as Presbyterians for Democracy and Religious Freedom.

Presbyterian Church in America (PCA): Formed in 1973 in a schism with the southern Presbyterian Church (PCUS) over issues of social and theological liberalism, membership in the National Council of Churches and World Council of Churches, ordination of women, and the then-prospective merger with the more liberal northern church. Among the leadership of the schism was unsuccessful 1971 candidate for moderator of PCUS D. James Kennedy, now a prominent televangelist based in Ft. Lauderdale, Florida. The PCA is home to many leaders of the Christian Right, including Rev. Lou Sheldon of the Traditional Values Coalition, Operation Rescue activist Rev. Joe Foreman, and theocratic author George Grant.

Presbyterian Church in the United States (PCUS): The former "southern church" of Presbyterianism after a split during the Civil War; existed until the 1983 reunion with the northern church.

Presbyterian Church (USA) or PC(USA): The name of the mainline Presbyterian Church following the reunion of the northern and southern churches in 1983.

Presbyterians for Democracy and Religious Freedom: A project of the right-wing Institute on Religion and Democracy in Washington, D.C., since 1990; renamed Presbyterian Action for Faith and Freedom in 1999.

Presbyterian Health, Education, and Welfare Association (PHEWA): A network of denominational social service organizations including Presbyterians Affirming Reproductive Options (PARO), a pro-choice entity often targeted by right-wing elements in the church.

Presbyterians United for Biblical Concerns: Previously called Presbyterians United for a Biblical Confession (both had the acronym PUBC).

Presbytery: A regional governing body.

ReImagining: Name of a controversial 1993 ecumenical conference on feminist theology held in Minneapolis, Minnesota. After the conference, and partly in response to furious accusations from right-wing organizations in the mainline denominations that the conference was dominated by neo-pagan and heretical elements, an explicitly Christian and reformist membership organization, The ReImagining Community, was formed to provide information and support to conference participants and the wider public. The wider ReImagining movement is quite heterogeneous; different currents within it emphasize to varying degrees traditionalism, the radical reinterpretation of prevailing spiritual and liturgical practices in the churches, and the Christian validity of feminist theologies and feminist biblical hermeneutics.

Religious Coalition for Reproductive Choice: Founded in 1973 as the Religious Coalition for Abortion Rights (RCAR), this Washington D.C.-based organization of pro-choice people of faith in the United States comprises more than 40 national organizations from major denominations and faith groups, and addresses public policy concerns such as the spread of HIV/AIDS and adequate health care and economic opportunities for women and families.

Religious Right: The political movement of religious conservatives, usually but not necessarily Christian.

Renewal: The renewal movement in the Presbyterian Church (USA) is a network of groups which, while diverse in their methods and their areas of focus, share the common objective of renewing the church through the introduction of conservative evangelical agendas often defined in contrast to the liberal leadership and social witness traditions that have shaped mainline Presbyterianism for much of this century.

Reunion: The 1983 merger of the northern and southern branches of mainline Presbyterianism, which had separated at the time of the Civil War. The reunited church is called the Presbyterian Church (USA).

Sanctuary movement: A national effort in the 1980s to shield refugees from the wars in Central America from deportation by the U.S. government. This often involved hiding illegal aliens who feared for their lives if they were forced to return.

Secular Humanism: A small, nonreligious philosophical movement. However, the religious right has seized on and stigmatized the term as the supposed obstacle to evangelical Christian advancement, arguing that it is a competing religious system that is taught in public schools and dominates the culture. The federal courts have found this allegation to be groundless. In religious right circles, secular humanism is often equated with atheism, demonism, or even Satan.

Schism: A formal division in or separation from a church or religious body. The Presbyterian Church experienced a number of major schisms in the 20th century, most recently the 1973 split that led to the formation of the conservative Presbyterian Church in America (PCA).

Session: The ruling body of a Presbyterian congregation consisting of the elders in active service and the minister, who is moderator.

Shepherding: An authoritarian pastoral methodology utilized in creating hierarchical parachurch networks, generally charismatic in their theology and often wedded to extreme right-wing politics. Beginning in the late 1960s, the shepherding movement united thousands of churches under the authority of a network of Ft. Lauderdale-based rightist ministers clustered around Rev. Bob Mumford. The Word of God and Sword of the Spirit communities, led by Ralph Martin and Stephen Clarke, respectively, and based in Ann Arbor, Michigan, formed the leadership core of a parallel and sometimes overlapping Catholic shepherding movement during the same period.

Spiritual Warfare: A form of intense prayer—often accompanied by charismatic practices such as speaking in tongues—intended to change either a material or supernatural situation. Practitioners consider it to be a direct confrontation with the source of all evil, Satan. Spiritual warfare is often used in groups where the desired goal is political, such as when "prayer warriors" focus on a particular public figure or piece of legislation or an entire nation believed to be under attack by Satan. More broadly, it is a theological movement focusing on the role of demonic powers in blocking the global victory of evangelical Christianity.

Synod: In the PC(USA), a regional governing body between the presbyteries and the General Assembly.

United Presbyterian Church: The former "northern church" of Presbyterianism. Following the union of the PC(USA) and the United Presbyterians in 1958, it reunited with the southern church (PCUS) in 1983 to form the PC(USA).

U.S. Taxpayers Party: A nationally organized third party, founded in 1992 from elements of the former American Independent Party (which fielded Alabama Gov. George Wallace as a candidate for president in 1968 and 1972, and former Georgia governor Lester Maddox in 1976), and the far right Populist Party (best known for fielding David Duke for president in the 1980s). The party comprises many factions of the farther reaches of the American right, from the militant wing of the anti-abortion movement to the theocratic Christian Reconstructionist camp, of which party founder and presidential candidate Howard Phillips is an adherent. Other Reconstructionists in the party and mentioned in this report include George Grant, R.J. Rushdoony, the late Rus Walton, and Joseph Morecraft. In 1999, it changed its name to the Constitution Party.

1   James R. Edwards, "What Ever Happened to the Great Ends of the Church?" *Theology Matters,* vol. 4, no. 3, May/June 1998, p. 10. NOTES

2   Presbyterian Coalition Gathering IV, conference tape, September 20, 1999.

3   Institute for Religion and Democracy web site, January 25, 2000, www.ird-renew.org.

4   Gary North, *Crossed Fingers: How the Liberals Captured the Presbyterian Church,* Tyler, Texas: Institute for Christian Economics, 1996, p. xvi. For a detailed discussion of Christian Reconstructionism and its influence on the contemporary Christian Right, see Frederick Clarkson, *Eternal Hostility: The Struggle Between Theocracy and Democracy,* Monroe, Me.: Common Courage Press, 1997.

5   North, *ibid.,* pp. 1–31; ch. 12. North states that "[without] the willingness and the ability to impose negative sanctions on specific ordained ministers . . . [all] that the conservatives had was rhetoric against modernist ideas in general, Church boards taken as collectives, and trends. The trends were all against them, as Machen well knew, and had known since his 1912 Seminary lecture on 'Christianity and Culture'" (p. 734).

6   *The Presbyterian Layman's* coverage of the church's largely symbolic support for black activists James Forman and Angela Davis, reviewed in more detail in chapter 1, reflected the broader conservative backlash of the Nixon years. This backlash was framed largely in terms of "law and order." A classic statement of the conservative evangelical contribution to this backlash was provided by PLC board member John Jenks in an editorial in *The Layman* (May 1968, p. 6). Jenks attacked the church's social-justice commitments as an evasion of the "fundamental" problem—"the disease of unregenerate human nature itself."

7   See the editorial in *The Layman* calling for greater loyalty to the state, March 1970, p. 8.

8   See the Witherspoon Society's review of the controversy surrounding the church's support for the J. P. Stevens textile boycott of the mid-1970s in "Scrutiny of the Layman [sic]," *Witherspoon Society* newsletter, vol. XI, no. 2, February–March, 1978.

9   See *The Presbyterian Layman,* November/December 1985, pp. 8–9.

10 Early on, the PLC distributed materials from the rightist American Security Council in order to challenge the church's position against the development of a national Anti-Ballistic Missile system (*The Presbyterian Layman,* July–August 1969).

11 In the 1990s in particular, the PLC challenged feminist theological exploration in its campaigns against the ReImagining movement and the closely related National Network of Presbyterian College Women, which was nearly defunded in 1998.

12 See the Witherspoon Society's review of the PLC's attack on World Council of Churches' support for the anti-colonial movement in Zimbabwe: "Scrutiny of the Layman [sic]," *Witherspoon Society* newsletter, vol. XI, no. 6, September 1978. More recently, the PLC has challenged the partially faith-based movement to close down the School of the Americas in Fort Benning, Georgia. Dubbed the "School of the Assassins," this international military training center has a well-documented record of credentialing Latin American military personnel who have gone on to become notorious human rights violators. In 1994, the PC(USA) voted to call for the closure of the School of the Americas (See "Assembly's Call to Close School of the Americas Challenged," *The Presbyterian Layman,* September/October 1994, p. 14).

13 "An Heir to the Kingdom," *The Presbyterian Layman,* January/February 1988, p. 5.

14 *Ibid.,* p. 5.

15 Paul Cupp, "Lay Committee President Addresses National Convention," *The Presbyterian Layman,* August 1973, p. 4.

16 *Ibid.*, p. 5.

17 "Profile," *The Presbyterian Layman*, November/December 1976, p. 7.

18 David Cay Johnston, "Ketchum, Inc. Has Plan to Close Later This Year," *The New York Times*, February 9, 1995, p. D2.

19 "Carlton Ketchum is Dead," *The New York Times*, July 25, 1984, p. D23.

20 "Minutes of the Meeting Called by Governor Arthur B. Langlie and Roger Hull," January 29, 1965. The recollections of the founding meeting that Cupp highlights are not fully corroborated in the minutes of this meeting, copies of which have survived. Since Cupp does not date his version, it is unclear if the January 29th meeting was the same meeting, remembered incorrectly by Cupp, or a different meeting.

21 Stephen Miles, letter to "Mr. William C. Mullendore," November 27, 1965. A declaration named "A Call to Every United Presbyterian," which focused on opposing the Confession of 1967, was published in national newspapers in 1966 (cf. *The Presbyterian Layman*, January/February 1998, p. 12).

22 "Minutes of the Meeting called by Governor Arthur B. Langlie and Roger Hull," *op. cit.* On Humphrey, see Sharon Morgan, "John Humphrey was retired Carey official," *The Cincinnati Enquirer*, October 4, 1995, p. B6.

23 Certificate of Incorporation of Presbyterian Lay Committee, Inc., State of New York, Department of State, July 8, 1965.

24 William C. Mullendore, letter to "Mr. Stephen B. Miles," August 1, 1966.

25 Paul Cupp, "Lay Committee President Addresses National Convention," *The Presbyterian Layman*, August 1973, p. 4.

26 See Elizabeth A. Fones-Wolf, *Selling Free Enterprise: The Business Assault on Labor and Liberalism* 1945–1960, Urbana: University of Illinois Press, 1994, ch. 1, for a general introduction to what she calls "the postwar employer counteroffensive."

27 In *Roads to Dominion: Right-Wing Movements and Political Power in the United States,* New York: The Guilford Press, 1995, Sara Diamond emphasizes the role of anti-communism in unifying traditionalist and libertarian trends throughout the 1950s. By the mid-1950s, such major national efforts as the Intercollegiate Studies Institute and the *National Review*—reflected the fusionist turn—bringing together Burkean arch-traditionalists like Russell Kirk with Misesian libertarians like Leonard Read. While ideological differences were debated in publications and on the lecture circuit, shared antipathy to New Deal liberalism and general envelopment in the anti-communist movement held the different trends together in the 1950s. From the mid-60s forward, a resurgent racist right, the John Birch Society, and an anti-statist radicalization among younger libertarians, among other things, would significantly complicate the fusionist mix of the 1950s.

28 Pew opposed federal aid to education as well. Speaking about the staff at Grove City College, his alma mater and a major beneficiary of his philanthropy, Pew asserted that "Men like that don't believe in government planning for the other fellow. They spurn all social measures designed to carry us into a collectivist state and know that one of the most vicious of these measures is federal aid to education . . . . Like most of you here today, I deplore the headlong plunge that our country is taking toward a totalitarian state. Most of my time, energy, and money is devoted to devising ways and means by which this trend can be arrested and reversed, because I realize that life in such a state would not be worth living. All history teaches us that." (Grove City College web site, December 1, 1998, www.gcc.edu). Pew's rage at Truman's "Fair Deal" defeat of Thomas Dewey in the presidential election of 1948 may be reflected in this speech. Pew heavily financed Dewey's campaigns in 1944 and 1948.

29 Characteristic of the NAM right-wing was a rejection of collective bargaining rights manifested through opposition to the Wagner Act, as well as an ideolog-

ical commitment to laissez-faire economics, much deepened, to be sure, in reaction to the egalitarian threat posed by New Deal interventionist policy. The Pews' Sun Shipbuilding, which implemented a segregated production system to handicap labor organizing, was characteristic of the NAM right wing in its use of violence to break organizing drives. See George Seldes, *In Fact*, vol. 3, no. 11, December 20, 1943. On the American Liberty League, see George Wolfskill, *The Revolt of the Conservatives: A History of the American Liberty League, 1934–1940*, Boston: Houghton Mifflin Company, 1962.

30 George Wolfskill, *The Revolt of the Conservatives, op. cit.*, pp. 231–233, 240–242.

31 George Seldes, *Facts and Fascism*, New York: In Fact, Inc., 1948, p. 97.

32 Andrew A. Workman, "Manufacturing Power: The Organizational Revival of the National Association of Manufacturers, 1941–1945," *Business History Review*, vol. 72, no. 2, Summer 1998, pp. 279–317.

33 Elizabeth Fones-Wolf, *Selling Free Enterprise: the Business Assault on Labor and Liberalism 1945–1960*, Urbana, Ill.: University of Illinois Press, 1994, p. 220. Crane was also a financial supporter of the National Education Program. See Arnold Foster and Benjamin R. Epstein, *Danger on the Right*, New York: Random House, 1964, p. 94. The National Education Program originated at the Churches of Christ-affiliated Harding College in Searcy, Arkansas and was directed by Harding College president George Benson from 1936 to 1954. Benson was one of the major figures in the anti-communist movement that so influenced mainstream culture during the Cold War. In the early 1960s, millions of people saw NEP propaganda films, such as *Communism on the Map* narrated by Herbert Philbrick and *The Truth About Communism* narrated by Ronald Reagan. See L. Edward Hicks, *"Sometimes in the Wrong, but Never in Doubt": George S. Benson and the Education of the New Religious Right*, Knoxville, Tenn.: University of Tennessee Press, 1994, ch. 4, *passim*.

34 Elizabeth Fones-Wolf, *Selling Free Enterprise, op. cit.*, p. 221.

35 *Ibid.*, p. 223.

36 Historian Carey McWilliams quoted Fifield in an article in *The Nation:* Fifield opposed "the efforts of minorities to push in where they are not wanted." "We do not intend to turn the town over to Jews, Mexicans and Negroes," Fifield said. See Ralph Lord Roy, *Apostles of Discord: A Study of Organized Bigotry and Disruption on the Fringes of Protestantism*, Boston: The Beacon Press, 1953, pp. 286, 290–291.

37 Eckard Vance Toy Jr., *Ideology and Conflict in American Ultraconservatism, 1945–1960*, University of Oregon, Doctoral Thesis, 1965, p. 191.

38 Pew helped finance the purchase of the estate housing the Foundation for Economic Education (FEE) in Irvington, NY. See Margit von Mises, *My Years with Ludwig von Mises*, Cedar Falls, Iowa: Center for Futures Education, Inc., 1984, p. 94. Subsequently, the J. Howard Pew Freedom Trust provided regular grants to the FEE, and Pew himself served as a trustee.

39 J. Howard Pew Freedom Trust, grant list; Roy, *Apostles of Discord, op. cit.*, p. 294.

40 Donald Meyer, *The Protestant Search for Political Realism, 1919–1941*, Middletown, Conn.: Wesleyan University Press, 1988 [1960], p. 46.

41 *Ibid.*, chs. 2–4.

42 *Ibid.*, p. 314.

43 On the FCC conference, see Fones-Wolf, *op. cit.*, pp. 235–236.

44 Besides Spiritual Mobilization and the Christian Freedom Foundation, in the 1940s Pew contributed to groups such as Vernon Kaub's American Council of Christian Laymen, as well as Carl McIntire's ultra-fundamentalist American Council of Christian Churches—both vehement opponents of the mainline ecumenical movement. See Ralph Lord Roy, *Apostles of Discord, op. cit.*, p. 304.

45 Fones-Wolf, *op. cit.*, p. 218.

46 For a detailed review of the National Lay Committee, see Fones-Wolf, *op. cit.*, ch. 8.

47 *The Presbyterian Layman*, January 1968.

48 On Hook, see George Seldes, *In Fact*, vol. 5, no. 5, May 11, 1942, p. 4. It was later revealed that the Committee to Uphold Constitutional Government was run by a German foreign agent and early Nazi Party member named Edward Rumely. See Charles Higham, *Trading With the Enemy: An Expose of the Nazi-American Money Plot*, New York: Delacorte Press, 1983, pp. 142–143.

49 Arnold Forster and Benjamin R. Epstein, *Danger On the Right*, New York: Random House, 1964, pp. 181–182. These executives included Fred C. Koch of Rock Island Oil and Refining Company, and J. Howard Pew of Sun Oil. Moreell was also a member of the national strategy committee of the private American Security Council, which developed into the main vehicle of far-right "roll-back" foreign-policy advocacy in the mid-1970s.

50 Margit von Mises, *My Years with Ludwig von Mises*, Cedar Falls, Iowa: Center for Futures Education, 1984, p. 94.

51 Ralph Lord Roy, *Apostles of Discord, op. cit.*, p. 223.

52 William Holtz, *The Ghost in the Little House: A Life of Rose Wilder Lane*, Columbia: Univ. of Missouri Press, 1993, p. 331. One of Hart's financial backers was the extreme racial-nationalist oil magnate George W. Armstrong. See Arnold Forster and Benjamin R. Epstein, *The Trouble Makers*, Westport: Negro Universities Press, 1970, p. 204. On Armstrong's racial views, see Ralph Lord Roy, *Apostles of Discord, op. cit.*, p. 80. For example: "This is a Christian country and a white man's country...and we do not need the Ishmaelites and negroes to help us run it."

53 Hagley Museum & Library, Jasper E. Crane Papers, introductory notes.

54 On McGowan, see Charles Higham, *Trading With the Enemy: An Expose of the Nazi-American Money Plot 1933–1949*, New York: Delacorte Press, 1983, pp. 179, 182. Crane described Lammot du Pont in a letter to Rose Wilder Lane. See Roger Lea MacBride, *The Lady and the Tycoon: Letters of Rose Wilder Lane and Jasper Crane*, Caldwell, Id.: The Caxton Printers, Ltd., 1973, p. 128. On Bedaux, see Higham, *Trading With the Enemy, op. cit.*, ch. 10.

55 Roger Lea MacBride, ed., *The Lady and the Tycoon: op. cit.*

56 For the right-wing southern Presbyterian take on this, see G. Aiken Taylor, "Power Blocs, Power Politics and The National Council of Churches," *Your Church, Their Target*, Arlington,Va.: Better Books, 1966, ch. 8. G. Aiken Taylor was editor of the *Presbyterian Journal*, the voice of southern Presbyterian conservativism founded by L. Nelson Bell, father of former Presbyterian Coalition moderator Clayton Bell. The *Presbyterian Journal* was called the *Southern Presbyterian Journal* until 1959, when Taylor became editor.

57 This summary of the conflict draws primarily on Elizabeth A. Fones-Wolf, *Selling Free Enterprise*, Urbana: Univ. of Illinois Press, 1994, ch. 8.

58 Frank E. Holman, a Seattle attorney and member of the National Lay Committee, wrote the Bricker Amendment. Among other things, Holman feared that the United Nations would intervene against racial segregation in the United States. See Justus D. Doenecke, *Not to the Swift: The Old Isolationists in the Cold War Era*, Lewisburg: Bucknell Univ. Press, 1979, n. 22, pp. 236, 249.

59 Fones-Wolf, *op. cit.*, p. 243.

60 "What We Stand For," *The Presbyterian Layman*, April 1968, p. 6. This editorial also established a principle of institutional engagement, as distinct from boycott, as the most important tool of conservative power in the church.

61 Pew was a member of the editorial advisory committee of the John Birch Society's main publication, *American Opinion.* He was reputedly a close friend of JBS founder Robert Welch, and held stock in Robert Welch, Inc., the entity under which JBS publishing activities were incorporated. See Bernard Lefkowitz, Sidney Zion, and Marvin Smilon, "Far Right & Far Left: The Birch Society," *New York Post,* April 2, 1964, p. 25. Pew's turn toward the John Birch Society coincided with his establishment of the J. Howard Pew Freedom Trust in 1957.

62 "Thirty years of speaking to, and for, Presbyterians," *The Presbyterian Layman,* supplement, November/December 1995, p. 1.

63 J. Howard Pew Freedom Trust, grant list. The PLC is a "memorial legacy" of the Pew Freedom Trust, receiving approximately $4.4 million between 1968 and 1995.

64 George Morris, "Telling the News: Former Baton Rouge resident heads major conservative Presbyterian paper," *The Advocate,* April 18, 1998, p. 1E.

65 *The Presbyterian Layman,* November 1971, p. 6.

66 The July/August 1969 issue of *The Presbyterian Layman* provided extensive coverage of the Forman controversy.

67 Angela Davis, now a professor at the University of California, Santa Cruz, faced prosecution at the time as an accomplice to a dramatic escape attempt staged at the Marin County hall of justice by black activists seeking to free several men considered to be political prisoners. Though she was ultimately acquitted by an all-white jury, the surrounding political circumstances of her prosecution, which were seen by many as a threat to her right to a fair trial, led to the development of a legal defense fund on her behalf. In the PC(USA), a letter of concern from St. Andrew's church in Marin County, California, prompted the denominational grant at issue in this major controversy.

68 "$85,000 World Council of Churches Grant to Terrorists Infuriates Church Members," *The Presbyterian Layman,* October/November 1978, p. 1.

69 See front page articles in July/August and September 1968 issues of *The Presbyterian Layman.*

70 *The Presbyterian Layman,* June/July 1975, pp. 12–13; January 1976, p. 1.

71 "The Chronology of the Study of Sexuality by the Church," *The Presbyterian Layman,* June/July 1978, p. 5.

72 Presbyterians Pro-Life, *Presbyterians and Abortion: A Look at Our Church's Past* (brochure), received spring 1999.

73 See John Fry's analysis in *The Trivialization of the Presbyterian Church,* New York: Harper & Row, 1975, pp. 38–52.

74 "A Resolution Approved by the Board of Directors of the Lay Committee," *The Presbyterian Layman,* August 1978, p. 1.

75 *The Presbyterian Layman,* June/July 1978, provided extensive coverage of this General Assembly decision.

76 PDRF letterhead, July 4, 1990.

77 Rockford Institute, annual reports, 1991, 1997.

78 See Leon Howell's profile in *Funding the War of Ideas,* Cleveland: United Church Board for Homeland Ministries, 1995, pp. 33–40.

79 *The Presbyterian Layman,* September/October 1985. This article was reprinted from *West Watch,* published by the Council for Inter-American Security (CIS). CIS was set up in the late 1970s to support South American military regimes, notably those of Chile and Argentina. In 1980, this Washington D.C.-based lobbying operation published a key statement of the Reagan-era counter-insurgency doctrine called *A New Inter-American Policy for the Eighties,* drafted by a group of right-wing national security experts who called themselves the Committee of Santa Fe. CIS founder L. Francis Bouchey formerly worked for Mar-

vin Liebman's American Chilean Council, the main American lobbying arm of the Pinochet regime, which came to power in 1973 through a military coup against democratically elected Chilean president Salvador Allende [On CIS and Bouchey, see Sara Diamond, *Roads to Dominion, op. cit.*, 1995, pp. 215, 379].

80 "Ptacek Joins Staff," *The Presbyterian Layman*, November/December 1985, p. 11.

81 "The Presbytery Liaison Network," *The Presbyterian Layman*, January/February 1988, p. 11.

82 "Training Institute Held in Charlotte, N.C.," *The Presbyterian Layman*, May/June 1988, p. 11.

83 The PLC campaign against the peacemaking initiative began with the September/October 1986 issue of *The Layman*, which included an article by right-wing political philosopher Rene Williamson (Parker's father) and a statement of protest signed by such national security figures as former National Security Advisor Robert C. McFarlane, who was indicted for his role in the Iran-Contra scandal. Other signers included such right-wing evangelicals as Mark Amstutz, political science chair at Wheaton College, and John Jefferson Davis, a Gordon-Conwell seminary professor and leading theologian of the Presbyterian renewal movement.

84 Paul F. Scotchmer, *Peace in the World and Peace in the Church: A Response to "Christian Obedience in a Nuclear Age"* (Presbyterians for Democracy and Religious Freedom, 1988). See also "Peacemakers Bite the Bullet," *The Presbyterian Layman*, July/August 1988, p. 11.

85 "Another Voice on South African Conditions," *The Presbyterian Layman*, November/December 1985, p. 8.

86 "An Interview with Jonas Savimbi," *The Presbyterian Layman*, May/June 1986, p. 9. The American Security Council, the main organization of the far right in national security circles, sponsored Savimbi's efforts to secure American support for his movement against the Angolan government. This campaign culminated in 1985, with the repeal of the Clark Amendment banning aid to UNITA. See Russ Bellant, *Old Nazis, the New Right, and the Republican Party: Domestic fascist networks and their effect on U.S. cold war politics*, Cambridge, Mass.: South End Press, 1991, pp. 81–83. The interview in *The Layman* focuses on Savimbi's evangelical roots and the "communist threat" in Africa. However, among Savimbi's advisors in his now decades-long attempt to take control of Angola was Stefano Delle Chiaie, the Italian terrorist who engineered the 1980 Bolivian cocaine coup along with Nazi war-criminal Klaus Barbie. See Alexander Cockburn and Jeffrey St. Clair, *Whiteout: the CIA, Drugs,* and the Press, London: Verso, 1998, p. 183.

87 "Meet Clayton Bell," *reNews*, June 1998, p. 14. 1991 was the cut-off point for former PCUS churches to leave with their property intact, a provision of the 1983 reunion. This provision of the reunion agreement was in part the work of the Covenant Fellowship of Presbyterians.

88 "Human Sexuality Report Rejected," *The Presbyterian Layman*, July/August 1991, p. 1.

89 George Grant and Mark Horne, *Unnatural Affections: The Impuritan Ethic of Homosexuality and the Modern Church*, Franklin, Tenn.: Legacy Communications, 1991, p. 70.

90 *Ibid.*, back cover.

91 *Ibid.*, pp. 69–70.

92 George Grant and Mark A. Horne, *Legislating Immorality: The Homosexual Movement Comes Out of the Closet*, Franklin, Tenn.: Legacy Communications and Chicago, Ill.: Moody Press, 1993, p. 186.

93   *Ibid.*, p.1.

94   Regarding the PLC, the authors declare in the acknowledgments to *Legislating Immorality:* "The stalwart men and women at the Presbyterian Lay Committee stayed the course and shared our concerns and our sense of urgency, all the while giving unselfishly of their time, energy, and expertise." Grant is also a leader in the far-right U.S. Taxpayers Party (renamed the Constitution Party in 1999), in which the Christian Reconstructionist movement plays a major role. See Frederick Clarkson, *Eternal Hostility, op. cit.*, p. 105.

95   "Philosophy of the RE-Imagining Community [sic]," *The Re-Imagining Community,* at members.aol.com/reimaginin/re00004.htm.

96   Stewart M. Hoover and Lynn Schofield Clark, "Event and Publicity as Social Drama: A Case Study of the RE-Imagining Conference 1995 [sic]," *Review of Religious Studies,* vol. 39, no. 2, December 1997, p. 153.

97   Leon Howell, *Funding the War of Ideas, op. cit.*, p. 56.

98   *Ibid.*, p. 36.

99   A member of the Presbyterian Renewal Network, PFFM publishes materials advancing a Reformed worldview and focuses on questions of heresy. A 1999 issue of *Theology Matters* featured an article by Phillip E. Johnson, leader of The Wedge, a movement seeking to discredit the theory of evolution (See "The Wedge in Evolutionary Ideology: Its History, Strategy, and Agenda," *Theology Matters,* vol. 5, no. 2, March/April 1999, p. 1). Johnson is a law professor at the University of California-Berkeley, and an elder at First Presbyterian Church in Berkeley. FPC Berkeley was long the pulpit of Rev. Robert Munger, the conservative evangelical leader who brought PLC founder Robert Stover to Christ in the late 1940s. Responding to the decision by the Kansas Board of Education to cut evolution from the state curriculum, Johnson was quoted as saying that defending evolution is becoming the "science educators' Vietnam" (Pam Belluck, "Board for Kansas Deletes Evolution from Curriculum," *The New York Times,* August 12, 1999, p. A15).

100 Parker Williamson, *Standing Firm: Reclaiming Christian Faith in Times of Controversy,* Lenoir, NC: PLC Publications, 1996, p. 20.

101 North labels those in the broad middle "pietists." See *Crossed Fingers, op. cit.,* pp. 15–31.

102 Judy Theriault, "Woman leader calls denomination to return to first love," *The Presbyterian Layman,* May/June 1995, p. 18. See also Judy Theriault, "Evangelical feminism has come a long way, but where is it?" The Presbyterian Layman, March/April 1995, pp. 18-19. For more on the antifeminist movement, see Lee Cokorinos, *Antifeminist Organizations: Institutionalizing the Backlash,* New York: Institute for Democracy Studies, April 2000.

103 See the web site of Voices of Sophia, www.execware.com/vos/index/html.

104 See Parker T. Williamson, "Demonstration disrupts General Assembly meeting," *The Presbyterian Layman,* July/August 1998, p. 1.

105 See Parker Williamson's summary presentation, "To the Task Force investigating the National Network of Presbyterian College Women," January 11, 1999, www.layman.org/layman/news/national-network-college-women/nnpcs-presentation.htm.

106 "College women's network provided links to pornographic material," *The Presbyterian Layman,* press release, July 8, 1998.

107 Edward E. Plowman, "Web of Heresy," *World* on the web, February 24, 2000, www.worldmag.com/world/issue/10-17-98/national_1.asp.

108 See Williamson's report to the "General Assembly Council Special Committee to Evaluate the National Network of Presbyterian College Women," July 8, 1998, www.layman.org/layman/news/national-network-collegewomen/nnpcw-cover-letter.htm.

109 Barbara Kellam-Scott, "NNPCW hearings today in Louisville," January 12, 1999.

110 For a history of this controversy, see Michael Kruse, "Lessons from 'Building Community among Strangers,'" *The Presbyterian Review*, www.pforum.org/resources/kruse.htm. Kruse recounts how he worked with Alan Wisdom, vice president of the Institute for Religion and Democracy, and the Presbyterian Forum, to significantly modify the report at Fort Worth. The final sentence of the document originally read: "...together we might strive for a community bonded by its faith in Jesus Christ to build a different kind of community in society." Instead it now reads, "Together we might strive to build a different kind of community in society, always pointing toward the ultimate human community centered around Christ as Savior. We long for the day, anticipated in Revelation, when it will be proclaimed, 'the kingdom of the world has become the kingdom of our Lord and his Christ, and he will reign forever and ever (Revelation 11:15).'" In anticipation of the 1999 General Assembly vote on the revised version of this paper, Presbyterians for Renewal affirmed that "All references to the 'Community Banquet Table,' offensive to many, have been removed. . . . and the Lordship of Jesus Christ has been upheld and made central to the paper" (see *reNews*, insert, June 1999, p. 4).

111 Rockford's influential publication *Chronicles* runs regular articles by its contributing editor Samuel Francis, whom political scientist Jean Hardisty characterizes as a notorious racial nationalist. On Rockford and Francis, see Jean Hardisty, *Mobilizing Resentment: Conservative Resurgence from the John Birch Society to the Promise Keepers,* Boston: Beacon Press, 1999, pp. 170–175. One *Chronicles* article by Francis lends support to the movement generated by former Ku Klux Klan leader David Duke's recent electoral efforts, questioning Duke's leadership potential merely in terms of "persistent rumors about irregularities in his personal life." He encourages Duke to "institutionalize the movement he has started in a nationwide organization that could exert cultural and indirect political power and radicalize Middle American consciousness still further" (January 1991, p. 10). In another *Chronicles* article, Francis claims that, in the context of immigration, such measures as hate crime laws, racial sensitivity courses, and "anti-Western Third World curricula" threaten to "[plow] under Euro-American patterns of culture on behalf of the nation's new populace" (March 1990, p. 9). The Rockford paleo-conservatives distinguish themselves from contemporary neoconservatives, whom Rockford views as having substantially taken over the conservative movement with a secular and global agenda inimical to the preservation of American cultural heritage. In March 1989, an historic split took place between the paleo- and the neocons over issues of immigration and support for the state of Israel. The result was the ousting of neoconservative Richard John Neuhaus from Rockford. Neuhaus accused Rockford's Thomas Fleming and the paleo-cons of reviving "forbidden bigotry," including "nativism, racism, anti-Semitism, xenophobia, a penchant for authoritarian politics and related diseases of the *ressentiment* that flourishes on the marginalia of American life." See John B. Judis, "The War at Home," *In These Times*, March 14–20, 1990.

112 William A. Rusher, *The Rise of the Right*, New York: National Review Books, 1993, p. 243.

113 The Rockford Institute, annual reports, 1995, 1997. The Rockford Advisory Board is also called The Main Street Committee.

114 The Rockford Institute, annual report, 1993.

115 The Rockford Institute, annual report, 1990, p. 19. Other Main Street Committee members have included such far-right luminaries as Murray Rothbard, Samuel Francis, Lew Rockwell, Tom Pauken, Charles Rice, Otto Scott, and Howard Phillips.

116 Telephone interview with Rus Walton, spring 1999.

117 "Welcome Aboard, Lane Adams!!," CComCor *Memorandum,* vol. 7, no. 1, February 1997, p. 1.

118 See Russ Bellant, "Secretive Rightwing Group: The Council for National Policy," *Covert Action Information Bulletin,* Number 34, Summer 1990, pp. 17–20.

119 CNP "Member Directory," Institute for First Amendment Studies, IFAS web site, December 1, 1998, www.ifas.org/cnp/contents2.html.

120 Sara Diamond, *Roads to Dominion, op. cit.,* pp. 98–99.

121 On the Constitution Party, see Sara Diamond, *Roads To Dominion, op. cit.,* pp. 87–88. On Greaves' involvement with the Constitution Party and Liberty Lobby, see *ibid.,* p. 99. On Liberty Lobby, see David Cantor, *The Religious Right: The Assault on Tolerance and Pluralism in America,* New York: Anti-Defamation League, 1994. p. 14. A *Christian Economics* editorial accused both Democrats and Republicans of promoting socialism during the 1952 presidential election and instead hailed General Douglas MacArthur as a "statesman of the highest order" (see Ralph Lord Roy, *Apostles of Discord, op. cit.,* p. 296).

122 See Russ Bellant, *Old Nazis, the New Right and the Republican Party: Domestic fascist networks and their effect on U.S. cold war politics,* Boston: South End Press, 1991, p. 38.

123 See Bernard Lefkowitz, Sidney Zion, and Marvin Smilon, "Far Right and Far Left," *The New York Post,* Sunday, April 5, 1964, p. 24

124 John S. Saloma III, *Ominous Politics: The New Conservative Labyrinth,* New York: Hill and Wang, 1984, p. 54; J. Howard Pew Freedom Trust, grant list.

125 John S. Saloma III, *Ominous Politics, op. cit.,* p. 54.

126 Rus Walton, *One Nation Under God,* Marlborough, N.H.: Plymouth Rock Foundation, 1993 [reprint], back cover. "The Plan to Save America," a detailed report on this early convergence of the new Christian Right, was published by Jim Wallis and Wes Michaelson in *Sojourners,* vol. 5, no. 4, April 1976.

127 See Flo Conway and Jim Siegelman, *Holy Terror: The Fundamentalist War on America's Freedoms in Religion, Politics and Our Private Lives,* Garden City: Doubleday & Company, 1982, p. 92, 142.

128 Sara Diamond, *Roads to Dominion, op. cit.,* p. 368, n57.

129 John B. Conlan, "Christians Needed in Politics," *The Presbyterian Layman,* November/December 1975, p. 12.

130 In 1976, GCC refused to file its Title IX compliance form with the Department of Education. Title IX (of the Education Amendments of 1972) extended the race-based anti-discrimination protections of the 1964 Civil Rights Act to women, barring federal aid to schools that discriminate against women. The case went to the Supreme Court, which upheld an initial federal district court decision ruling in favor of GCC on the grounds that Title IX did not mandate coverage institution-wide, but only in the areas where federal aid was directly given. In the case of GCC, the school could have discriminated in all areas except the financial aid office, according to the logic of the ruling. The decision thus opened loopholes in the enforcement of Title IX. As of 1988, when legislation overturning the GCC ruling was finally passed by Congress, 834 Title IX cases had been shelved as a result of the decision [see "Editorial," *The Washington Post,* January 27, 1988, p. A18; for a general analysis, see Veronica M. Gillespie and Gregory L. McClinton, "The Civil Rights Restoration Act of 1987— A Defeat for Judicial Conservatism," *National Black Law Journal,* vol. 12, no. 1, Spring 1990, pp. 62–72].

131 Gary North, "The Beacon Factor," in *A Man of Principle: Essays in Honor of Hans F. Sennholz,* ed. John W. Robbins and Mark Spangler, Grove City, Pa.: Grove City College Press, 1992, p. 12.

132 *Ibid.,* p. 1.

133 *Ibid.*, ch. 2, *passim.*

134 *The Presbyterian Layman,* inset, March/April, 1995, p. 23.

135 Reformed Theological Seminary, "Dr. Luder Whitlock," Reformed Theological Seminary web site, July 30, 1999, www.rts.edu/faculty/whitlock. For more on the Council on Biblical Manhood and Womanhood, see Lee Cokorinos, *Antifeminist Organizations: Institutionalizing the Backlash, op. cit.*

136 *The Education Liberator,* vol. 4, no. 1, September 1988.

137 Separation of School and State Alliance, endorsement list, December 20, 1999, www.sepschool.org. See *The Education Liberator,* vol. 4, no. 1, September 1988.

138 Separation of School and State Alliance, member list, December 20, 1999, www. sepschool.org.

139 W. Robert Stover, *The Complete Marquis Who's Who Biographies,* 1996.

140 "Member directory," Institute for First Amendment Studies web site, December 1, 1998, www.ifas.org/cnp/contents2.html.

141 Parker T. Williamson, "Two Ministers, One Ministry: Kari McClellan and Robert Munger proclaim the gospel," *The Presbyterian Layman,* September/October 1995, p. 13.

142 W. Robert Stover, *The Complete Marquis Who's Who Biographies,* 1999.

143 *Ibid.*

144 *Ibid.* For information on Latin America Mission and its targeting of progressive social currents in Nicaragua and Guatemala, among other countries, see Sara Diamond, *Spiritual Warfare: The Politics of the Christian Right,* Boston: South End Press, 1989, pp. 208–211.

145 "Parker T. Williamson: Slain missionaries defining moment for Layman editor," *The Presbyterian Layman,* January/February 1998, p. 14.

146 Langdon Strong Flowers, *The Complete Marquis Who's Who Biographies,* 1998.

147 As reported in *Freedom Writer,* January 1995, www.ifas.org/fw/9501/100per cent.html.

148 Federal Election Commission records of political contributions can be found at FECInfo, www.tray.com/fecinfo/.

149 For more on the U.S. Taxpayers Party, see Frederick Clarkson, *Eternal Hostility, op. cit., passim.*

150 *Ibid.* p. 126.

151 FECInfo, www.tray.com/cgi-win/_allindiv.exe.

152 Carlos Campos, "Legal group's action stirs concern," *The Atlanta Journal and Constitution,* July 11, 1999, p. 2D.

153 Pam Easton, "Flowers chief resigns from Southeastern Legal Foundation board," *Associated Press,* July 22, 1999.

154 Patricia J. Mays, "Conservative legal group trying to dismantle affirmative action," *Associated Press,* August 8, 1999.

155 "Blackburn's Joke," *Newsweek,* November 24, 1975, p. 95.

156 *Ibid.* Blackburn later claimed the comment was a joke, but the Senate Banking Committee nonetheless decided to reject President Ford's nomination of Blackburn as chair of the Federal Home Loan Bank board.

157 Carlos Campos, "Legal group's action stirs concern," *op. cit.,* p. 2D. The connections of men like Blackburn and Maddox are significant. While the legal campaign against affirmative action has attempted to cast itself as holding libertarian concern about excessive and unconstitutional government regulation, there is some justification for characterizing it (as Atlanta Mayor Bill Campbell has) as a political repackaging of the legacy of racist opposition to civil rights. See "Southeastern Legal Foundation and Atlanta Face Off Over Affirmative Action," *Morning Show* transcript, National Public Radio, July 28, 1999. See

also Vern E. Smith, "Showdown: Mayor Bill Campbell is fighting the right-wing attack on the city's affirmative action program—but much more is at stake," *Emerge*, November 1999.

158 "Regional News," *United Press International*, August 30, 1983.

159 Carlos Campos, "Boycotted Firm Has Diverse Work Force," *The Atlanta Journal and Constitution*, October 3, 1999, p. 1C.

160 Carlos Campos, "Affirming His Actions: Flowers CEO Calls for Education, Not Preferences," *The Atlanta Journal and Constitution*, October 3, 1999, p. 6C.

161 See entry for Chapman Beecher Cox, *The Complete Marquis Who's Who Biographies*, 1999. On his Defense Department work, see "Former Diplomat Chosen for Defense Dept. Post," *Los Angeles Times*, May 4, 1988, pt. 1, p. 16. Cox was a spokesman for the Reagan Administration policy of increasing U.S. military support for supply-oriented drug eradication efforts in places such as Bolivia. The Reagan Administration opposed Congress's prioritization of a police-style border interdiction role for the military (see James Gerstenzang, "Pentagon Opposes Wider Drug War Role," *Los Angeles Times*, September 17, 1986, pt. 1, p. 4).

162 *The Complete Marquis Who's Who Biographies*, 1999.

163 Derk Arend Wilcox, ed., *The Right Guide: A Guide to Conservative and Right-of-Center Organizations*, Ann Arbor, Mich.: Economics America, Inc., 1997, p. 157. On Edison's ties to the Old Right, which generally overlap with J. Howard Pew's, see Arnold Forster and Benjamin R. Epstein, *Danger on the Right, op. cit.*, index.

164 Derk Arend Wilcox, *The Right Guide, op. cit.*, p. 157.

165 "Highland Park pastor named moderator of the Coalition," *The Presbyterian Layman*, January/February 1999, p. 22.

166 "Robert L. Howard," *The Presbyterian Layman*, October 14, 1999, www.layman.org/ layman/the-layman/1998/january-feb/bob-howard.htm.

167 Bob Cox, "Outcome of Koch Industries Trial to be Decided by a Dozen Kansans," *The Wichita Eagle*, April 5, 1998; Leslie Wayne, "Zero is the Verdict in $2 Billion Koch Family Feud," *The New York Times*, June 20, 1998, p. D1.

168 As of 1997, Charles G. Koch was listed as director of the Charles G. Koch Charitable Foundation and David Koch was listed as president of the David H. Koch Charitable Foundation. See Derk Arend Wilcox, ed., *The Right Guide, op. cit.*, pp. 90–91, 121–122.

169 Leslie Wayne, "Pulling Wraps off Koch Industries," *The New York Times*, November 20, 1994, p. 3:1.

170 Arnold Forster and Benjamin R. Epstein, *Danger on the Right, op. cit.*, p. 270.

171 "Robert L. Howard," *The Presbyterian Layman, op. cit.*

172 "Lay Committee's President Campbell Retires," *The Presbyterian Layman*, November/December 1993, p. 4.

173 See "Robert L. Howard: Lay Committee Chair Optimistic About its Expanded Mission," *The Presbyterian Layman*, January/February, 1998, p. 13.

174 Federal Election Commission, itemized receipts, February 20, 1992.

175 "Dr. Frank N. Kik," Reformed Theological Seminary web site, July 30, 1999, www.rts.edu/faculty/kik.

176 "World Impact's National Advisory Board," World Impact web site, October 20, 1997, www.worldimpact.org/aboutus/boards.html.

177 Charles Sherrard MacKenzie, *The Complete Marquis Who's Who Biographies*, 1999.

178 "PLC adds new board member," *The Presbyterian Layman*, March/April 1995, p. 8.

179 See www.womenlegislators.org/campcollege/ayres.html, January 18, 1999. See also Kevin Sack, "Georgian Makes a Bold Stand on Abortion," *The New York Times,* June 16, 1996, p. 1:18; On Coverdell, see Jeanne Cummings, "Christian Coalition Softens Image to Gain GOP Influence," *The Atlanta Journal and Constitution,* January 27, 1993, p. A5.

180 Q. Whitfield Ayres, "Civil Rights Bill Could be Boon to GOP," *The Atlanta Journal and Constitution,* June 9, 1991, p. G3.

181 "Williamson Named Editor," *The Presbyterian Layman,* November/December 1987, p. 1.

182 See "Department History," Louisiana State University web site, April 19, 1999, www.lsu.edu/guests/poli/public_html/depthis.html. Right wing anti-modernist political philosopher Eric Voegelin left a strong imprint on the department during his tenure from 1945 to 1958.

183 "Parker T. Williamson: Slain missionaries defining moment for Layman editor," *The Presbyterian Layman,* January/February 1998, p. 14.

184 The funding in question, from the WCC's Fund to Combat Racism, was devoted to humanitarian aid for the Patriotic Front, the leading political force in the anti-colonial movement against Ian Smith's Rhodesia in the 1970s. In the introduction to his collection of essays on the recent 50th anniversary meeting of the WCC held in Harare, Zimbabwe, Williamson reviews an internal PLC controversy regarding his posting of essays critical of Zimbabwean president Robert Mugabe directly from Harare. PLC board member Lloyd Lunceford, chairman of the publications committee of the PLC, feared that the Zimbabwean government would monitor *The Layman* Online and that Williamson's life would be in danger because, as Williamson put it, "people who oppose Mugabe often wind up dead." Williamson convinced Lunceford to relent in the service of his journalistic mission. See Parker T. Williamson, *Essays from Zimbabwe,* Lenoir, N.C.: PLC Publications, 1999, p. 1.

185 Parker T. Williamson, "Another Voice on South African Conditions," *The Presbyterian Layman,* November/December, 1985, p. 8.

186 "A Reply by Rev. Parker T. Williamson, September 20, 1995," *The Presbyterian Layman,* November/December, 1985, p. 8.

187 *Ibid.,* p. 9.

188 For example, an editorial in *The Layman* states, "In their moral pronouncements [regarding South Africa] national church leaders in this country play the role of the Pharisee. One can expect this kind of behavior from politicians who cater to the emotions of black constituencies. That's politics. But the church should do better than politics." *The Presbyterian Layman,* November/December 1986, p. 12.

189 Leon Howell, *Funding the War of Ideas, op. cit.,* pp. 55–56.

190 Parker T. Williamson, "Returning to Zimbabwe," *The Presbyterian Layman* web site, December 8, 1998, www.layman.org/layman/news/news-around-church/wcc-returning-to-zimbabwe.htm. This was essentially the same argument used by the white Rhodesian minority trying to maintain power during a bi-racial transition government as the Ian Smith regime crumbled. The Patriotic Front subsequently won the internationally supervised elections in 1980.

191 Association for Church Renewal, *Proclaim Liberty: A Jubilee Appeal,* p. 39. Williamson's fellow PC(USA) members involved in ACR include Susan Cyre, Kari McClellan, Sylvia Dooling, and Terry Schlossberg.

192 The Rockford Institute, 1992 annual report, p. 18.

193 John A. Howard, "Making Virtue Respectable Again," *The Presbyterian Layman,* September/October 1991, pp. 6–7.

194 The Rockford Institute, 1992 annual report, p. 24; League of the South web site, November 12, 1999, www.dixienet.org/1s-natl-conf/lsc98-fleming.htm.

195 Parker T. Williamson, "Who Are Our People?" [text of presentation, April 13, 1999, Carnegie Hall, New York City], *The Presbyterian Layman*, April 16, 1999, www.layman. org/layman/news/news-from-PC(USA)/who-are-ourpeople.htm.

196 The Rockford Institute, annual report, 1997, p. 10.

197 The Howard Center, annual report, 1998.

198 See the World Congress of Families web site, www.worldcongress.org.

199 Parker T. Williamson, *Standing Firm, op. cit.*, 1996.

200 *The Presbyterian Layman*, March/April 1987, p. 6.

201 Presbyterian Lay Committee, Inc., www.guidestar.org.

202 J. Howard Pew Freedom Trust, grant list, received January 22, 1999.

203 Howell, *Funding the War of Ideas, op. cit.*, p. 58. The PLC's 1994 Form 990, a public document, was unavailable for verification of this claim.

204 The Presbyterian Lay Committee, Form 990, Internal Revenue Service, 1995.

205 *Ibid.*, 1995, 1996, 1997.

206 Howell, *Funding the War of Ideas, op. cit.*, p. 59.

207 Form 990, Schedule A, Part IV, item 26b, requires tax-exempt organizations to file an anonymous list of individual contribution streams that exceed 2 percent of the total income (minus service/merchandise fees) for the previous three-year period.

208 Howell, *Funding the War of Ideas, op. cit.*, p. 59.

209 *Ibid.*

210 *Ibid.*

211 See the flow chart representing this campaign in *National Right to Life News*, vol. 26, no. 1 & 2, January 22, 1999, p. 16. The other historic mainline anti-abortion groups include Episcopalians for Life and Lutherans for Life. Anti-abortion groups in the United Methodist Church and the United Church of Christ emerged in the mid-1980s.

212 "Presbyterians and Abortion: A Look at Our Church's Past," Presbyterians Pro-Life, brochure, received April 1999.

213 Benjamin E. Sheldon, "A Brief History of the Development of P.P.L.," Presbyterians Pro-Life Research, Education and Care, Inc., articles of incorporation, secretary of state, Atlanta, Georgia, February 13, 1984.

214 J. Andrew White, letter to "All SPPL Members," November 1978.

215 Benjamin E. Sheldon, "A Brief History," *op. cit.* Blizard first got involved with the group after submitting a letter to the editor in the *Presbyterian Survey* that expressed the wish to see a pro-life witness within the PCUS.

216 "PPL Conference: Challenges, Ads, Overtures," *Presbyterians Pro-Life News*, June–July, 1980.

217 "Right People in Right Places of Major Importance," *Presbyterians Pro-Life News*, April 1981.

218 Gary Bauer, fundraising letter, Care Net, July 5, 1999.

219 *Ibid.* The Schaeffers co-founded and operated the L'Abri Fellowship, an international evangelical retreat center in Switzerland, for many years. See Marjorie Hyer, *The Washington Post*, May 19, 1984, p. C10.

220 Gary North, *Political Polytheism: The Myth of Pluralism*, Tyler, Tex.: Institute for Christian Economics, 1989, pp. 166–167.

221 Marjorie Hyer, *The Washington Post, op. cit.*, p. C10.

222 Frederick Clarkson, *Eternal Hostility, op. cit.*, p. 93. John Whitehead, president of the religious right legal group, The Rutherford Institute, names as his key influences both Francis Schaeffer and Rousas John Rushdoony, the founder of the Christian Reconstructionist movement.

223 Gary Bauer, fundraising letter, July 5, 1999.

224 See Tracy Jefferies-Renault and Jerry Sloan, *Without Justice for All: A Report on the Christian Right in Sacramento and Beyond*, Sacramento, Calif.: Planned Parenthood of Sacramento Valley Public Affairs Department, 1993, pp. 45–47. A CAC training manual from 1985 begins by stating, "Abortion is one of the greatest moral evils in America today." It also states that "[the] primary purpose of the CPC is to assist pregnant women to carry their children to term, not to educate people on the abortion issue." Care Net's president, Guy Condon, articulates the organization's anti-abortion agenda in his preface to a 1995 manual (*CareNet Volunteer Training Manual*): "Through the power and the leading of Jesus' spirit, you will be releasing those who are caught in the deathgrip of sin and the threat of abortion." According to the manual, volunteer staff "must have a solid understanding of what the Bible teaches about the sanctity of human life and a firm commitment to the pro-life position—even in the more difficult cases (e.g., rape, incest, suspected fetal deformity)."

225 On Americans United for Life, see Cynthia Gorney, *Articles of Faith: A Frontline History of the Abortion Wars*, New York: Simon & Shuster, 1998, pp. 435–442.

226 Gary Bauer, Care Net fundraising letter, undated (ca. August 1999).

227 "Local Chapter News," *Presbyterians Pro-Life News*, Winter 1998, p. 11.

228 J. Andrew White, letter to "Southern Presbyterians Pro-Life," June 3, 1977; J. Andrew White, "Newsletter Update," Southern Presbyterians Pro-Life, Spring 1978.

229 "Conventions Scheduled for May and June," *Presbyterians Pro-Life News*, May 1981.

230 "SOHLS set for Jan 20," *Presbyterians Pro-Life News*, November/December 1984.

231 "Stay Active to Maintain Victory, Dr. Brown Advises Conference," *Presbyterians Pro-Life News*, April 1981, and "The Hatch Amendment: Understanding the Controversy," *Presbyterians Pro-Life News*, March/April 1998, p. 2.

232 For example, First Presbyterian Church in Prestonburg, Kentucky, helped to found a CPC with support from the Christian Action Council as well as the Pearson Foundation, publisher of CPC manuals the deceptive tactics of which have been exposed by the National Abortion and Reproductive Rights Action League ("Deceptive Anti-Abortion Crisis Pregnancy Centers," NARAL Factsheet, January 28, 2000, www.naral.org/publications/facts/1999/crisis.html). See Tim Jessen, "Alternatives in Eastern Kentucky," *Presbyterians Pro-Life News*, Fall 1986. See also "Educating Your Church Family," *Presbyterians Pro-Life News*, November/December 1983; "'Something I Wish I Had Never Done,'" *Presbyterians Pro-Life News*, December 1981; Marilyn Fanning, "A New Mission Field," *Presbyterian Pro-Life News*, February/March 1983; "Christian Action Council Ministers in Japan," *Presbyterians Pro-Life News*, March 1984, p. 2; "Crisis Counseling: Presbyterians Pro-Life Offers Information and Expertise to Help Churches Establish Ministries to Pregnant Women," *Presbyterians Pro-Life News*, Summer 1985.

233 "PPL Board Members Active Pro-Life Speakers," *Presbyterians Pro-Life News*, August 1980.

234 "Come and Grow with Presbyterians Pro-Life," *Presbyterians Pro-Life News*, March 1984.

235 Harold O. J. Brown, "A Settlement," *Chicago Tribune*, December 17, 1989, p. C2. Among the more notable graduates of Trinity Evangelical Divinity School is rightwing activist and Christian Reconstructionist Paul Lindstrom. He is a leader in the Christian home-schooling movement, but best known as an anti-communist activist. Lindstrom was chairman of the Remember the Pueblo Committee and an activist in MIA and POW campaigns in Southeast Asia.

236 J. Andrew White, letter to "All SPPL Members," November 1978.

237 Julia Duin, "Rockford Institute Chief Leaves To Form His Own Think Tank," *The Washington Times*, December 10, 1997, p. A2. Presbyterian renewal leaders connected to Rockford include *The Presbyterian Layman* editor Parker Williamson and former president of Grove City College, Charles MacKenzie. The Center on Religion and Society was recently renamed the Religion & Society Studies Center and is now a part of the Howard Center for Family, Religion & Society, which was formed out of the Rockford Institute in 1997 [see Howard Center web site, www.profam.org].

238 Council on Biblical Manhood and Womanhood, "Board of Reference," CBMW web site, January 6, 1999, www.cbmw.org/html/board_of_refer ence.html.

239 Council on Biblical Manhood and Womanhood, *Danvers Statement*, CBMW web site, August 17, 1999, www.cbmw.org/html/RBMW%20Pages /rbmw_appendix_2.html.

240 "Presbyterians Pro-Life Meet in Atlanta," *Presbyterians Pro-Life News*, November/December 1983.

241 Benjamin E. Sheldon, "A Brief History," *op. cit.*

242 Rev. Donald A. Elliott, "PPL Board Expands; Greater Diversity Achieved," *Presbyterians Pro-Life News*, Spring 1986.

243 Presbyterians Pro-Life, "A Little History," Presbyterians Pro-Life web site, July 20, 1999, www.ppl.org/Chap_home.html.

244 "Come and Grow With Presbyterians Pro-Life," *Presbyterians Pro-Life News*, March 1984.

245 "Local Chapter Network Off to Quick Start; Information Available," *Presbyterians Pro-Life News*, Spring 1986.

246 PPL claims different numbers at different times. In 1997, it claimed about 90. In 1998, however, it reported about 70. The organization offered no explanation for the discrepancy. See "Local Chapter News," *Presbyterians Pro-Life News*, Winter 1997, p. 15; Presbyterians Pro-Life Chapters (list), October 21, 1998.

247 Presbyterians Pro-Life, Form 990, 1996.

248 "Presbyterians Pro-Life: A Voice for Renewal in the Presbyterian Church (USA)," Presbyterians Pro-Life, pamphlet.

249 See Terry Schlossberg, "Abortion is a Challenge to Christian Orthodoxy," presented to the Task Force on Problem Pregnancy and Abortion, February 2, 1991.

250 Presbyterians Pro-Life, "Position Statement on Abortion" (adopted June 1988; revised September 1993).

251 Presbyterians Pro-Life, "Statement of Purpose," Presbyterians Pro-Life web site, July 13, 1999, www.ppl.org/purpose.html.

252 Terry Schlossberg, "PHEWA's View of Inclusiveness and of Implementing General Assembly Policy," *Presbyterians Pro-Life News*, Spring/Summer 1999, p. 8.

253 "PHEWA Committed to Using Denominational Funds for Campaign Against Constitutional Standards," *Presbyterians Pro-Life News*, Winter 1999, p. 6.

254 Terry Schlossberg, "Woman to Woman: The Politics of the Spiritual Life," Voices of Orthodox Women web site, July 8, 1999, www.vow.org/woman-to-woman.html. See also chapter 7 of *Not My Own: Abortion & the Marks of the Church*, Grand Rapids, Mich.: Eerdmans Publishing Company, 1995, a book co-authored by Schlossberg and Elizabeth Achtemeier. Here a more detailed vision of disciplinary revival, centered on accountability and repentance, is presented. In its pastoral setting, this focus derives from trends broadly linked to the charismatic shepherding movement (see chapter 5 on the Presbyterian Forum above), but in its theological underpinnings it echoes Gary North's nos-

talgia for the early Puritan theocracy of the Massachusetts Bay Colony. North prefers rigorous church discipline systems to the increasingly "non-judicial" models of discipleship culminating in the revivalist, free-grace ethos of the Great Awakening (see Gary North, *Crossed Fingers, op. cit.*, pp. 99–115).

255 "Relief of Conscience on Abortion: How to Make It Work," *Presbyterians Pro-Life News*, Winter 1999, p. 8.

256 Terry Schlossberg, "G. A. Commissioners Hear Mother Theresa, Vote for New Study of Abortion," *Presbyterians Pro-Life News*, July/August/September 1988, p. 1.

257 "Assembly refers implementation of abortion policy to ACSWP," *Presbyterians Pro-Life News*, Winter 1999, p. 1.

258 "Minority Abortion Report Loses Vote, but Gains Solid Following at G.A.," *Presbyterians Pro-Life News*, Fall 1992; and "The Bottom Line of the Majority Report: No Change," *Presbyterians Pro-Life News*, Special Edition, Spring 1992.

259 "Lutherans (ELCA) and United Church of Christ (UCC) Join Other Mainline Denominations in Moving Away from Abortion Advocacy," *Presbyterians Pro-Life News,* July/August/September 1989, p. 3.

260 "General Assembly Expresses 'Grave Moral Concern' about Partial Birth Abortions," *Presbyterians Pro-Life News*, Fall 1997, p. 1.

261 Terry Schlossberg, "Reproductive Choice Ignores the Baby," Presbyterians Pro-Life *Daily Delivery*, 1999 General Assembly, June 21, 1999.

262 "Should an Interfaith Lobby Speak for Presbyterians in the Public Square?" *Presbyterians Pro-Life News*, Spring/Summer 1999, p. 7.

263 *Ibid.*, p. 7.

264 "Teaching our Children the Biblical Message about Their Sexuality," *Presbyterians Pro-Life News*, Spring/Summer 1999, p. 6.

265 *Ibid.*

266 Richard John Neuhaus, fundraising letter, November 1997.

267 See, for example, Terry Schlossberg, "Abortion is a Challenge to Christian Orthodoxy," presented to the Task Force on Problem Pregnancy and Abortion, February 2, 1991.

268 See Presbyterians Pro-Life, "Critiques of 'Do Justice, Love Mercy, Walk Humbly,' the Policy Document on Problem Pregnancies and Abortion of the Presbyterian Church (USA)," April 1992.

269 See *Presbyterians Pro-Life News*, Winter 1999.

270 Presbyterians Pro-Life, "Pastor to Pastor: The Pastoral Counseling of Those Involved with Abortion," pamphlet.

271 *Building a New Millennium,* National Right to Life Committee *1999 Yearbook*, p. 78.

272 *Ibid.*, pp. 30, 32.

273 See Kathleen Sweeney, "The Protestant Churches on Abortion: Complex, Contradictory, and Challenging," *National Right to Life News*, January 22, 1999, p. 16.

274 Walter M. Weber, "Swipe At Religion," *Chicago Tribune*, April 29, 1988, p. C26.

275 David G. Savage, "Justices To Rule On Abortion Protesters," *Los Angeles Times,* February 26, 1991, p. A24.

276 Other organizations represented by Weber include Catholics United for Life, National Organization of Episcopalians for Life, American Baptist Friends of Life, Baptists for Life, Southern Baptists For Life, Lutherans for Life, Moravians for Life, United Church of Christ Friends for Life, Task Force of United Methodists on Abortion and Sexuality, and the Christian Action Council. "*Webster v. Reproductive Health Services,* Taking Sides," *The National Law Journal,* May 1, 1989, p. 28.

277 "Supreme Court Deluged With Friend-of-Court Briefs in Abortion Case," _Associated Press_, April 19, 1992.

278 Terry Schlossberg, "Woman to Woman: Our Right to Choose," _Presbyterians Pro-Life News,_ July/August/September 1989, p. 6.

279 Terry Schlossberg, "Woman to Woman," _Presbyterians Pro-Life News,_ Winter 1991–1992, p. 8.

280 "IRD Coalition Speaks up for Faith, Freedom, and Family," _Faith & Freedom,_ Winter 1995–1996, p. 5.

281 Jennifer Caterini, "Three Years Later: Feminists Still 'Re-Imagining' God," _Faith & Freedom,_ Fall 1996, p. 6.

282 _Ibid._

283 George Archibald, "Groups Coalesce to Fight 'Gender' Agenda; UN Platform Called Divisive," _The Washington Times_, June 23, 1995, p. A6.

284 Glen Elsasser, "Bernardin's Anti-Abortion Plea; Cardinal, Clerics Urge Senate To Override Clinton Veto," _Chicago Tribune_, September 13, 1996, p. 10N; Charles Canady, "Strong Showing Of Support Reflects Public Sentiment," Congressional Press Releases, September 12, 1996.

285 "Right to Life sets Bend conference," _The Bulletin_, April 24, 1998, p. A2.

286 Matthew Marx, "Anti-Abortion Display Meant to Shock," _The Columbus Dispatch_, October 20, 1998, p. 7C.

287 Presbyterian Action for Faith and Freedom, leaflet, received September 21, 1999.

288 Herbert Schlossberg, _A Fragrance of Oppression: the Church and Its Persecutors,_ Wheaton, Ill.: Crossway Books, 1991, back cover.

289 Christians for Justice International, brochure, May 2, 1988.

290 Diamond's perspective is borne out by Donnan's claim concerning his work among Christians in Nicaragua that "We intend to use the current relaxed circumstances to beef up the evangelical church in biblical world and life view teachings which will give them the ability to discern between satanic 'liberation theology' and the true liberating Gospel." Liberation theology contributed to the popular movement that brought the Sandinistas to power in the late 1970s. On Caribbean Christian Ministries, see Sara Diamond, _Spiritual Warfare, op. cit.,_ p. 179–180. The organization was originally sponsored by Paul Lindstrom's Christian Liberty Academy, an historic hub of the Christian Reconstructionist wing of the home schooling movement. Lindstrom was also a promoter and participant in Randall Terry's militant Operation Rescue founded in 1988. See Dr. Paul D. Lindstrom, _4 Days in May . . . Storming the Gates of Hell,_ Arlington Heights, Ill.: Christian Liberty Press, 1988, p. 14.

291 Alive & Free, brochure, received July 27, 1986.

292 Sara Diamond, _Spiritual Warfare, op. cit.,_ pp. 127–128.

293 Coalition on Revival, _A Manifesto for the Christian Church,_ July 4, 1986.

294 "Schlossberg, Herbert," _The Complete Marquis Who's Who Biographies,_ 1991.

295 Herbert Schlossberg, _A Fragrance of Oppression: The Church and Its Persecutors,_ Wheaton, Ill.: Crossway Books, 1991.

296 On Ahmanson's role in California politics, see Tracy Jefferies-Renault and Jerry Sloan, _Without Justice for All, op. cit.,_ ch. 2.

297 Ralph Frammolino, "Ahmanson Heir Bankrolls Religious Right's Agenda," _The Los Angeles Times,_ October 19, 1992.

298 Trevor H.G. Smith, "Presbyterians Pro-Life Represented at National Right to Life Convention," _Presbyterians Pro-Life News,_ September 1982.

299 John Dart, "Anti-Abortionists Face Ethical Dilemmas," _Los Angeles Times_, January 26, 1985, p. II4.

300 "Pro-Life Religious Council Formed," _Presbyterians Pro-Life News,_ October/

November/December 1987.

301 "Presbyterians Pro-Life President Ben Sheldon Retires," *Presbyterians Pro-Life News,* Winter 1996.

302 See *Priests for Life: A New Era of Anti-Abortion Activism,* New York: Institute for Democracy Studies, October 1999.

303 *Choose Life,* National Right to Life Religious Outreach, May/June 1999.

304 "Guard Your Women," *The Washington Times,* May 7, 1998, p. A9.

305 "Lay Committee's President Campbell Retires," *The Presbyterian Layman,* November/December 1993.

306 *Presbyterians Pro-Life News,* November/December 1983.

307 "Presbyterians Pro-Life Board Expands; Greater Diversity Achieved," *Presbyterians Pro-Life News,* Spring 1986.

308 First Presbyterian Church of Corinth, "First Presbyterian Staff," FPC Corinth web site, July 15, 1999, www2.tsixroads.com/~1stpres/staff.htm.

309 *First National Bank v. Cities Service* (391 U. S. 253), The Villanova Center for Information and Policy web site, www.law.vill.edu/Fed-Ct/Supreme/Flite/opin ions/391US253.htm.

310 Presbyterians for Democracy and Religious Freedom, annual report, secretary of state, Nashville, Tenn., 1998.

311 *Presbyterians Pro-Life News,* October/November/December, 1987, p. 4.

312 Presbyterians Pro-Life, letterhead, 1999.

313 "Group Vows To Monitor Teaching About Aids," *The Columbus Dispatch,* February 15, 1994, p. 3C.

314 Lee Moriwaki, "Minister Assails Pornography—'Poison' Linked To Violence; Others Disagree," *The Seattle Times,* March 13, 1993. p. A14.

315 See profile of Kirk on the National Coalition's web site, January 24, 2000, www. nationalcoalition.org/kirk/htm.

316 *Ibid.*

317 Council for National Policy, "member biographies," May 1995.

318 *Presbyterians Pro-Life News,* Winter 1991/1992, p. 6.

319 Focus on the Family, Form 990, Internal Revenue Service, 1992.

320 Promise Keepers, conference document, February 13, 1996.

321 Presbyterians Pro-life, letterhead, 1997–1998.

322 Young Life, "Board of Trustees," Young Life web site, August 27, 1999, www.young life.org/pages/ylboard.html.

323 *Presbyterians Pro-Life News,* October/November/December 1987, p. 4.

324 *The Presbyterian Layman,* March/April 1987, p. 6.

325 Chip Berlet and Matthew N. Lyons, "Militia Nation," *The Progressive,* vol. 59, no. 6, June 1995, p. 22.

326 Massachusetts Citizens for Life, Inc. annual report, 1997, p. 1.

327 *Presbyterians Pro-Life News,* October/November/December 1987, p.4.

328 *reNews,* June 1999, p. 2.

329 The Institute on Religion and Democracy, letterhead, ca. 1986.

330 National Day of Prayer, brochure, ca. February 2, 1987.

331 "Leslie Newbigin joins Presbyterians Pro-Life Board of Reference: Board of Directors Elects Four New Members," *Presbyterians Pro-Life News,* Fall 1993, p. 6; "Presbyterians Pro-Life Elects Two New Board Members," *Presbyterians Pro-Life News,* Winter 1999, p. 7.

332 "New Abortion Policy: No Peace, But the Two Reports Sharpen the Lines of Division," *Presbyterians Pro-Life News,* Fall 1992, p. 2.

333 Presbyterians Pro-Life, "Building a Ministry for Life: A National Pastors' Con-

ference on Life Issues," Presbyterians Pro-Life web site, July 13, 1999, www.ppl.org/Buildlife. html.

334 Union Theological Seminary in Virginia and Presbyterian School of Christian Education, "Emeriti/ae Faculty," UTS web site, July 13, 1999, www.utsva.edu/copy/ fac/emeritus.shtml.

335 Terry Schlossberg and Elizabeth Achtemeier, *Not My Own: Abortion & the Marks of the Church,* Grand Rapids, Mich.: William B. Eerdmans Publishing Co., 1995.

336 "Elizabeth Achtemeier is 1998 Groneman Lecturer," July 13, 1999, www.methodists. net/cc980918.html.

337 Presbyterians Pro-Life, "Building a Ministry for Life: A National Pastors' Conference on Life Issues," Presbyterians Pro-Life web site, July 13, 1999, www.ppl.org/Buildlife. html. The conference was titled "Building a Ministry for Life: A National Pastors' Conference on Life Issues."

338 "CBMW Executive Director Challenges Fellow Pastors: Council unanimously Appointed Presbyterian Pastor to post in November," *CBMW News,* Council for Biblical Manhood and Womanhood web site, August 17, 1999, www.cbmw.org/html/vol2_no2 .html.

339 "Mother Teresa Pleads for Life," *The Presbyterian Layman,* July/August 1988, p. 3.

340 "CBMW Executive Director Challenges Fellow Pastors: Council Unanimously Appointed Presbyterian Pastor to Post in November," *CBMW News, op. cit.*

341 See Lee Cokorinos, *Antifeminist Organizations: Institutionalizing the Backlash, op. cit.*

342 Presbyterians Pro-Life Research, Education, and Care, Inc., Form 990, Internal Revenue Service, 1991.

343 Presbyterians Pro-Life Research, Education, and Care, Inc., Form 990, Internal Revenue Service, 1996.

344 *Ibid.*

345 See in particular former executive director Betty Moore's anniversary comments in "Recalling the Beginnings: An Interview with Betty Moore and Murray Marshall," *reNews,* June 1990, pp. 8–9.

346 Harry Sharp Hassall, *On Jordan's Stormy Banks I Stand: A Historical Commentary of the Life and Times of The Covenant Fellowship of Presbyterians 1969–1989,* Dallas: self-published, 1989, p. 100.

347 "Recalling the Beginnings" *reNews, op. cit.,* p. 8.

348 *reNews,* June 1999, insert, pp. 1–4.

349 *Ibid.,* insert, p. 3.

350 Ralph Reed, *Active Faith: How Christians are Changing the Soul of American Politics,* New York: The Free Press, 1996, pp. 56–68.

351 For three preceding paragraphs, see "History," Presbyterians for Renewal booklet, 1998.

352 Hassall, *On Jordan's Stormy Banks I Stand, op. cit.,* pp. 13–17.

353 Joel L. Alvis Jr., *Religion & Race: Southern Presbyterians, 1946–1983,* Tuscaloosa, Al.: University of Alabama Press, 1994, pp. 74–75.

354 Hassall, *On Jordan's Stormy Banks I Stand, op. cit.,* p. 15.

355 *Ibid.,* p. 10.

356 *Ibid.,* pp. 27–28. Significantly, future right-wing televangelist D. James Kennedy lost the moderator's race in 1971 by a historically narrow margin of 271-170.

357 For a more detailed list of issues, see Appendix F in Hassall's *On Jordan's Stormy Banks I Stand, op. cit.,* pp. 151–152.

358 For a discussion of how CFP provided a framework for retaining conservatives,

see Hassall, *On Jordan's Stormy Banks I Stand, op. cit.*, p. 15. Harry Hassall is himself a good example of this conservative retention factor, claiming that his own position was closer to that of ultraconservative L. Nelson Bell and *The Southern Presbyterian Journal (ibid.,* p. 77).

359 *Ibid.,* p. 108.

360 *The Presbyterian Layman,* January 1975, p. 1; March 1976, p. 5; April 1977, p. 2.

361 "PUBC-PLC Cooperation Stressed," *The Presbyterian Layman,* March 1975, p. 1.

362 *The Presbyterian Layman,* February/March 1978, p. 1.

363 See U. S. Center for World Mission web site, "History," December 8, 1999, www.uscwm.org.

364 Coalition on Revival, letterhead, April 4, 1991. COR's Church Council Steering Committee recently held its Los Angeles/Orange County organizing meeting at Winter's U.S. Center for World Mission.

365 "PC(USA) Evangelical Presbyterian Pastors' Conference," *reNews,* March 1991, p. 13.

366 "PFR Hosts Annual General Assembly Breakfast," *reConnect,* August 1999, p. 2. In his acceptance speech, Winter highlighted the failure of Christianity to rid itself of neo-Platonic strains that, in his view, soften believers on the existence of evil. He took the opportunity to announce a new project, the Institute for the Study of the Origins of Disease. "You cannot have a proper theology without a sound demonology," he asserted, admonishing participants for accepting "demonic cultural delusion" on top of the "demonic physical distortion" of disease. Winter's demonological framework is part of the conceptual armory of the religious right, especially in charismatic circles. The question is why PFR has aligned itself with a figure as integral to the Protestant far right as Ralph Winter. Moreover, the fact that Marian McClure, director of the PC(USA) World Wide Ministries division, introduced Winter, is indicative of the growing influence of PFR and its right-wing connections on the denominational leadership.

367 Hassall, *On Jordan's Stormy Banks I Stand, op. cit.*, pp. 100–110. Hassall also claims that the CFP was involved in organizing annual gatherings of renewal executives from all the mainline denominations, from 1976 to 1989 (p. 147).

368 *Ibid.,* p. 107.

369 *Ibid.,* pp. 100–101.

370 Joe Rightmyer, "Reflections: So Far, So Good," *reNews,* June, 1999, p. 3.

371 "A Covenant of Renewal," *reNews,* March 1999, back cover.

372 Priscilla Lasmarias Kelso, "PFR Board of Directors Meeting Focuses on Racial Reconciliation and Urban Renewal Ministries," *reNews,* May 1994.

373 Frederick Clarkson, *Eternal Hostility, op. cit.*, pp. 196–197, 111–114.

374 Coalition on Revival, *A Manifesto for the Christian Church,* July 4, 1986.

375 "1999 General Assembly," *reNews,* June 1990, insert, p. 12–13.

376 "Serving Faithfully for Ten Years Plus!" *reNews,* June 1999, p. 18.

377 Hassall, *On Jordan's Stormy Banks I Stand, op. cit.*, p. 90.

378 "Network of Presbyterian Women in Leadership (NPWL) Launched at General Assembly," *reNews,* August 1994, p. 13.

379 See Lee Cokorinos, *Antifeminist Organizations: Institutionalizing the Backlash, op. cit.*

380 "Lydia Fund Scholarship Under Care of NPWL," *reNews,* December 1997, p. 16. NPWL and Voices of Orthodox Women (VOW) are part of a growing women's antifeminist movement in the church, which is partly coordinated by the Institute on Religion and Democracy and its subsidiary Ecumenical Coalition on Women and Society.

381 David Moore, "Mars Hill Seminarian Conference: What Does It All Mean,"

September 13, 1999, www.pforum.org/wupdates/sept13. htm.

382 "PFR Seminary Ministry," *reNews*, December 1997, p. 16.

383 Hassall, *On Jordan's Stormy Banks I Stand, op. cit.*, p. 77. On his role in PFR, see Commonwealth of Kentucky, secretary of state, corporate record #0270949, May 28, 1996.

384 Hassall, *On Jordan's Stormy Banks I Stand, op. cit.*, pp. 90, 110.

385 "1999 General Assembly," *reNews,* insert, June 1999.

386 Jack Haberer, "'Don't Lower the Bar': An evangelical analysis of the 1999 General Assembly," The Presbyterian Coalition, July 27, 1999, www.presbycoalition.org/For YourReflection%20072199.htm.

387 Hassall, *On Jordan's Stormy Banks I Stand, op. cit.*, p. 125.

388 Pew financed the founding of *Christianity Today* as well as several years' worth of free subscriptions to build an evangelical readership. It was possibly Pew's ultraconservative influence (Pew opposed church involvement in social issues) that led to the firing of editor Carl F. H. Henry in 1967. See Marjorie Hyer, "A Theologian Confesses," *The Washington Post,* July 26, 1986, p. G12.

389 Joel L. Alvis Jr., *Religion & Race, op. cit.*, pp. 51–53.

390 Biographical data culled from profile and interview with Bell in *reNews,* June 1998, p. 13–15.

391 Bruce Buursma, "Presbyterians Meet to Get Back to Basics," *Chicago Tribune,* January 12, 1985, p. C10.

392 The Foundation Center records a Perot Foundation grant of $262,000 to Highland Park Presbyterian Church in 1995. Bunker Hunt and his siblings donated $3.5 million to Highland Park to finance a major expansion program. Hunt has been a major underwriter of Bill Bright's Campus Crusade for Christ, including a $5.5 million grant for the film *Jesus,* one of the most successful evangelizing projects ever mounted by the Christian Right (see Holly G. Miller, "Bunker Hunt's greatest investment," *Saturday Evening Post,* January 1985, p. 42).

393 Toby Nelson, "From church split and heart crisis to a joyful church," *The Presbyterian Layman,* September/October 1994, p. 23.

394 See coverage in "Tall Steeple Pastors Express 'No Confidence,'" *The Presbyterian Layman,* March/April 1994, p. 11.

395 See the Mission America web site, www.missionamerica.org/denominations.html.

396 Tad Bartimus, *Associated Press,* June 1, 1980; Tad Bartimus, "Part 1: A Billion Dollars to Save the World," *The Associated Press,* June 2, 1980.

397 Kenneth L. Woodward, "Politics From the Pulpit," *Newsweek,* September 6, 1976, p. 49.

398 See biographical profile and interview, "Meet John Huffman," in *reNews,* March 1991, pp. 14–16.

399 "History of Key Biscayne Presbyterian Church," undated.

400 "Welcome Aboard, Lane Adams!!," CComCor *Memorandum, op. cit.*

401 John Huffman, "Statement in Support of Los Ranchos Overture #96-41," undated.

402 "History of Key Biscayne Presbyterian Church," *op. cit.*

403 John Huffman, "Statement in Support of Los Ranchos Overture #96-41," *op. cit.*

404 John Dart, "Clergy Celibacy Ruling Seen as Anti-Gay," *Los Angeles Times,* March 22, 1997, p. B10.

405 "Meet John Huffman," *op. cit.*

406 See interview and profile in *reNews,* September 1995, pp. 3–5, 17.

407 Belhaven was the last Presbyterian college to desegregate (1967), over the protests of segregationists in the Synod of Mississippi. See Joel L. Alvis Jr., *Religion & Race, op. cit.*, pp. 90–91.

408 Presbyterians for Democracy and Religious Freedom, steering committee list, undated.

409 Greene's summary of the 1994 General Assembly, where ReImagining was the central issue, is instructive on the politicized nature of PFR. See "Responding to the Re-Imagining Conference [sic]," *reNews,* insert, August 1994, p. 12–15.

410 Henry Greene, "Reflections on the 1999 General Assembly," *reConnect,* August 1999, p. 1.

411 Presbyterians for Renewal, Form 990, Internal Revenue Service, 1997.

412 Presbyterians for Renewal, Form 1990s, Internal Revenue Service, 1991–1997.

413 Joe Rightmyer, "Reflections: So Far, So Good," *reNews,* June 1999, p. 3.

414 The Presbyterian Forum, "Presbyterian Coalition Moderator Jack Haberer Answers Questions About 'The Gathering III,'" *The Presbyterian Review,* July 20, 1999, www. pforum.org/Weekly/haberer.htm.

415 Parker T. Williamson, "Coalition Launches Full-Scale Assault," *The Presbyterian Layman,* March/April 1993, p. 1.

416 According to *The Presbyterian Layman,* Brad Long, leader of the charismatic Presbyterian and Reformed Renewal Ministries International, rose to implore commissioners to respond, shouting down the protest as an "abomination." Not even a chorus of "Onward Christian Soldiers" silenced the protestors. Future Coalition leader J. Howard Edington, whose First Presbyterian Church in Orlando was host to the General Assembly, retreated to the newsroom to call the police, while moderator Dobler ordered the sound system shut off and the lights dimmed. As Commissioners filed out, the demonstration split apart to send people off at the auditorium exits. For this account of the episode, see "Homosexual Activists Demonstrate at General Assembly," *The Presbyterian Layman,* July/August 1993, pp. 10–11.

417 The Presbyterian Coalition, "Why the Presbyterian Coalition," The Presbyterian Coalition web site, July 1, 1999, www. presbycoalition.org/WhytheCoalition.htm.

418 Articles of Incorporation of Presbyterian Coalition, Inc., Commonwealth of Kentucky, 1993.

419 Presbyterian Coalition, Inc., Form 990, Internal Revenue Service, 1997.

420 Robert P. Mills, "'For Such a Time as This': Gathering III Draws 600 Presbyterians to Dallas," *The Presbyterian Layman,* December 11, 1998, www.layman.org/the-layman/1998/nov-dec/such-a-time-as-this.htm.

421 Presbyterian Coalition, Inc., Form 990, Internal Revenue Service, 1994.

422 *Ibid.*

423 On the Genevans' "Reform and Representation Plan" to decentralize the General Assembly Council by expanding it from 67 members to over 1,000, see *The Genevan,* January 1995.

424 Daryl Fisher-Ogden, letter to "All Genevans' Members and Friends," January 3, 1995.

425 David Snellgrove, memo to "Fellow Presbyterians," March 26, 1993.

426 Tom Bailey Jr., "Presbyterians Critical of Report on Sexuality," *The Commercial Appeal,* February 13, 1991, p. A1.

427 "Ordination Ban Reaffirmed," *The Presbyterian Layman,* July/August 1993, p. 1.

428 The Presbyterian Coalition, letter to "Fellow Presbyterians," 1994.

429 Presbyterian Coalition, letter to "Fellow Presbyterians," Autumn, 1998.

430 Presbyterian Coalition, letter to "Fellow Presbyterian Leaders," undated (fall 1996).

431 "Coalition to Host Chicago Gathering," *The Presbyterian Layman,* July/August 1996, p. 11.

432 Presbyterian Coalition, Inc., Form 990, Internal Revenue Service, 1996.

433 Presbyterian Coalition, letter to "Presbyterian Friends," Autumn 1998.

434 Presbyterian Coalition, Inc., Form 990, Internal Revenue Service, 1996, 1997.

435 Parker T. Williamson, "1,100 Presbyterians Come to Dallas for Gathering II," *The Presbyterian Layman,* November/December 1997, p. 1.

436 The Presbyterian Coalition, "Releases Declaration and Strategy Paper," October 20, 1998, www.presbycoalition.org.

437 "Presbyterian Coalition Moderator Jack Haberer Answers Questions About 'The Gathering III,'" *The Presbyterian Review, op. cit.*

438 The Presbyterian Coalition, "Releases Declaration and Strategy Paper," *op. cit.* See also "The Presbyterian Coalition," *The Presbyterian Layman,* letter dated April 30, 1998, www.layman.org/layman/news/declaration/ letter-16member. html.

439 "The Radical Center," *The Presbyterian Layman,* May/June 1998, www.lay man.org/ layman/the-layman/1998/may-june/editor-radical-center.htm.

440 See "Presbyterian Coalition Moderator Jack Haberer Answers Questions About 'The Gathering III,'" *The Presbyterian Review, op. cit.*

441 "Unlocking the Conversation," *reNews,* December 1997, pp. 3–4.

442 "PC(USA) Joins AD 2000 and Beyond Movement," *reNews* insert, September 1995.

443 According to Purves and his seminary colleague Charles Partee in their presentation at Gathering II in Dallas, "Christian Sexual Morality is under attack by those who would replace Scripture and the witnesses of our confessions with the present and evolving values of left-wing American culture." See "Rooted and Grounded," *reNews,* December 1997, pp. 7–15.

444 A case in point is Gary North's history of Presbyterian conflict in the early 20th Century, *Crossed Fingers, op. cit.* North, a major intellectual force in the Christian Reconstructionist movement, is deeply concerned with mainline Presbyterian Church history and the legacy of struggles within the church. In fact, his book can be viewed as a call for the kind of agenda to reclaim the church that is set out in the Coalition's *Declaration and Strategy Paper.* Frederick Clarkson's emphasis on Reconstructionism's influence beyond the small network of hardcore theorists is crucial to understanding mainline theological conflicts, notably the growing Calvinist movement within the Southern Baptist Convention (see *Eternal Hostility, op. cit.,* chs. 4–5).

445 Deborah Kovach Caldwell, "Gay Ordination Goes to Vote," *The Dallas Morning News,* June 29, 1999.

446 Andrew Purves and Charles Partee, "Rooted and Grounded: The Love of Christ," *reNews,* December 1997, p. 8

447 *Ibid.,* p. 7.

448 *Declaration & Strategy Paper of the Presbyterian Coalition,* October 1998, p. 1.

449 Presbyterian Coalition Visioning Team, "Proposed Declaration & Strategy Paper," April 30–May 1, 1998, p. 13.

450 *Declaration & Strategy Paper of the Presbyterian Coalition, op. cit.,* p. 8.

451 Jay and Olga Gary, *The Countdown Has Begun: The Story of the Global Consultation on AD 2000,* Rockville, Va: AD 2000 Global Service Office, 1989, p. 32.

452 "Strategic Mobilization Task Force," January 27, 2000, www.ad2000.org/tracks /smtf.htm.

453 A memo dated May 17, 1999, by Peter Wagner, the leader of the spiritual warfare component of AD 2000 and Beyond, can be found on AD 2000 and

Beyond's web site, December 22, 1999, www.ad2000.org/re90714.htm.

454 *Declaration and Strategy Paper of the Presbyterian Coalition, op. cit.*, p. 10.

455 *Ibid.*, p. 11.

456 Robert T. Henderson, "Semper Reformanda: Liberating the 'Evangelical,'" *Catalyst*, vol. 26, no. 1, November 1999, p. 7.

457 *Ibid.* For a broad discussion of the Coalition's *Declaration and Strategy Paper*, see *Taking Aim: Conservatives' Bid for Power in the Presbyterian Church Entering Advanced Stage*, New York: Institute for Democracy Studies, October 1999.

458 *Declaration & Strategy Paper of the Presbyterian Coalition, op. cit.*, p. 11.

459 *Ibid.*, p. 13.

460 For a detailed discussion, see Russ Bellant, "Promise Keepers and the Christian Shepherding Movement," *PK Watch*, vol. 1, no. 1, March 1997, p. 9 (available from the Institute for Democracy Studies).

461 *Declaration & Strategy Paper of the Presbyterian Coalition, op. cit.*, p. 13.

462 William Lewis, "A Theological Guide for Pastoral Nominating Committees," *Theology Matters*, January–February 1999, pp. 1–13. *Theology Matters* is essentially a forum for conservative renewal theologians and teachers attempting to delineate the boundaries of Christian orthodoxy in relation to contemporary life.

463 Rev. George T. Hobson, "How to Examine a Candidate's Theology," July 7, 1999, www.presbycoalition.org/Forum070799.htm. Hobson is pastor of the First Presbyterian Church in George, Iowa, and has served as a member of the church discipline task force of the Presbyterian Coalition.

464 Presbyterian Coalition, "The Gathering III," Presbyterian Coalition web site, November 2, 1998, www.presbycoalition.org/G3addresses/G3report.htm.

465 *Ibid.*

466 "Highland Park pastor moderator of the Coalition," *The Presbyterian Layman*, January/February 1999, p. 7.

467 The Presbyterian Forum, "The Gathering IV—Day 1," *The Presbyterian Review*, September 20, 1999, www.pforum.org/wupdates/gather1.htm.

468 Lewis C. Daly, "Spiritual Warfare in the Presbyterian Church," *IDS Insights*, vol. 1, no. 1, 2000, p. 6.

469 Presbyterian Coalition Gathering IV, conference tape, "The Future of the Church," September 21, 1999.

470 Presbyterian Coalition, leaflet, received September 22, 1999.

471 Presbyterian Coalition, letterhead, January 1, 1999.

472 Presbyterian Coalition, December 3, 1999, www.presbycoalition.org.

473 Anita Bell, letter, January 31, 2000, www.presbycoalition.org/GatheringV-announcement.htm.

474 Chris Petrikin, "'Grill' Inspires 'No Man' pic," *Daily Variety*, May 16, 1997, p. 5.

475 First Presbyterian Church of Orlando, "Meet our Ministry Staff," First Presbyterian Church of Orlando web site, July 19, 1999, www.ourfrontporch.com.

476 "PPL elects two new board members," *Presbyterians Pro-Life News*, Winter 1999, p. 7.

477 Jon Sawyer, "Presbyterians Elect Leader on Second Ballot," *St. Louis Post-Dispatch*, June 6, 1991, p. 1C. Edington was a last minute replacement for John Huffman, who withdrew for family reasons (Jon Sawyer, "Sexuality Debate Threatens Church," *St. Louis Post-Dispatch*, June 5, 1991, p. 1B). This was the year of the controversial report on human sexuality, which Edington believed should be rejected without compromise.

478 Mark I. Pinksy, "Christians See Orlando as New Promised Land," *The Orlando Sentinel*, November 8, 1998, p. A1.

479 Mark I. Pinsky, "He Invests in Souls," *The Orlando Sentinel*, March 20, 1996, p. E1.

480 Harry Wessel, "He Gives Life a Game Effort," *The Orlando Sentinel*, October 31, 1997, p. E1.

481 Mark I. Pinksy, "Prayer Day to Bring Many 'Amens,'" *The Orlando Sentinel*, May 1, 1997, p. D3.

482 Fasting & Prayer '99 web site, November 17, 1999, www.fastingprayer.com/executive-committee/index.html.

483 *Ibid.*

484 *Ibid.*

485 John Dart, "Coalition Offers Ministers a Network of Support, Prayer," *Los Angeles Times*, May 3, 1997, p. B4.

486 Other right-wing leaders on the board of reference (1992) include Reconstructionist pastor Joseph Morecraft as well as Howard Phillips, organizer of the far-right U.S. Taxpayers Party (which changed its name in 1999 to the Constitution Party). See Ted Baehr, "Reclaiming Lost Territory," *Crosswinds*, vol. 1, no. 1, Winter 1992, p. 87.

487 Michael Johnston, "GA Sends Modified COCU Proposals to Presbyteries," *The Presbyterian Layman*, July/August 1996, p. 10.

488 Poppinga's pastor, the Rev. Paul Leggett, is the author of a December 1999 attack on the COCU published in *Theology Matters*, which is sent to every pastor in the PC(USA).

489 "Julius B. Poppinga," *Martindale Hubbell Law Directory*, 1999.

490 Hilary Appelman, "Dissenting Churches Oppose Appointment of Lesbian Minister," *Associated Press*, May 19, 1992.

491 Parker T. Williamson, "General Assembly calls for representation reform," *The Presbyterian Layman*, July/August 1995, p. 1.

492 Al Ruth, "Representation plan 'opens channels' for partnership," *The Presbyterian Layman*, September/October 1995, pp. 6-7.

493 Robert P. Mills, "GA has mixed reaction to Review Committee report," *The Presbyterian Layman*, July/August 1996, p. 18.

494 "Intercessor," CLS *Quarterly*, Spring 1996, p. B4.

495 "Issues and Matters Coming Before the 211th General Assembly in the Form of Overtures—A Digest and Commentary," undated.

496 "Past Presidents of the Christian Legal Society," CLS *Quarterly*, vol. 7, no. 3, Fall 1986, inside cover.

497 The late Herbert Ellingwood served as legal affairs secretary to Governor Reagan in California and would later direct the Office of Liaison Services in the Meese Justice Department [*The Complete Marquis Who's Who Biographies* (1999)]. Before working in the Justice Department, Ellingwood was the subject of a congressional inquiry focusing on his efforts to recruit and promote fundamentalist Christians for government posts as chairman of the Reagan administration's Merit System Protection Board (Lea Donosky and Glen Elsasser, "New Leader Unleashed on Hill," *Chicago Tribune*, February 15, 1985, p. C12). Ellingwood worked closely in his recruiting efforts with Rev. Tim LaHaye's ultrafundamentalist American Coalition for Traditional Values (David L. Kirp, "Serving the Lord," *The Nation*, June 29, 1985, vol. 240, p. 786). In 1986, Ellingwood worked for Pat Robertson, and served as a member of Robertson's presidential exploratory committee ("Robertson Hires Protégé of Meese," *Chicago Tribune*, October 17, 1986, p. C6). He was also a member of the board of Robertson's CBN University, later renamed Regent University.

498 Julius B. Poppinga, "In Remembrance of William H. Ellis Jr., 1932–1994," *Quarterly*, Winter 1994, p. 14.

499 Samuel B. Casey, "37 Years and Growing: Reflections on History at CLS," Christian Legal Society web site, August 2, 1999, www.christianlegalsociety.org. The CLS's budget grew threefold between 1980 and 1982.

500 Coalition on Revival, brochure, 1986.

501 Ericsson left CLS in 1991 after ten years to do liaison work with legal activists in Bulgaria and Albania with Advocates International. The Advocates International program for 1999 included a trip by Ericsson to "lead a delegation from several major evangelical relief organizations that want to help postwar Albania," as well as a law conference in that country. See Advocates International web site, August 2, 1999, www.advocatesinternational.org/1999_projectsfrm.htm; and www.advocatesinternational.org/Newsletters/newsjun99.htm.

502 Samuel B. Casey, "37 Years and Growing," www.christianlegalsociety.org. Prior to taking up his position under Poppinga at CLS, Ericsson served from 1977 to 1980 as counsel and chief of staff for Grace Community Church, the largest fundamentalist church in Los Angeles, which was used as a model for how to run men's shepherding networks in the early literature of the right-wing men's organization Promise Keepers (see Pete Richardson, *Focusing Your Men's Ministry: A Strategy for Lay Leaders and Pastors*, Boulder, Co.: Promise Keepers, 1993, pp. 46–48). In 1985, Ericsson served as a CLS defense lawyer for Grace Community Church in a clergy malpractice suit brought by the family of Kenneth Nally, who committed suicide while under the pastoral care of the church (see Bill Girdner, "Did Pastors Spur Suicide?," *The National Law Journal,* May 13, 1985, p. 6). Ericsson also launched a crisis pregnancy center in 1990 and remains active in its leadership. Before Poppinga brought him into CLS, Ericsson also served with the California Religious Organization Law Reform Commission. In 1983 Ericsson filed separate *amicus* briefs to the Supreme Court on behalf of CLS. One sought to defend Rev. Sun Myung Moon against criminal charges of tax fraud (the Supreme Court declined to review the case and Moon went to prison). In the other case, CLS sided with Bob Jones University in *Bob Jones University vs. U.S.* (USSC 1983) when the IRS revoked the school's tax exemption on the grounds that it engaged in racial discrimination (see Ericsson's *curriculum vitae* on Advocates International web site, August 2, 1999, www.advocatesinternational.org/ericssoncv.htm). For a discussion of the Moon tax case and the wider politics of Moon's Unification Church, see Frederick Clarkson, *Eternal Hostility, op. cit.*, chapter 3, *passim.*

503 Whitewater special prosecutor Kenneth Starr currently serves on the 13-member board of Advocates International, as does Ron Nikkel, the president of Charles Colson's Prison Fellowship International. Its chairman is John E. Langlois, a deputy of parliament on the Isle of Guernsey (see www.advocatesinternational. org/boardfrm.htm, August 2, 1999). Among the items listed on the 1997 financial disclosure form released in October 1998 by Starr was a $20,000 personal loan to Advocates International Inc. (see "Inadmissible," *Legal Times,* October 26, 1998). In 1994, Kenneth Starr introduced Samuel Casey at a reception in honor of his appointment as executive director of CLS. This event was co-sponsored by Sen. Dan Coats (R-IN) and Rep. Frank Wolf (R-VA) (see "Metro DC Chapter Welcomes CLS Executive Director," CLS *Quarterly,* Fall 1994, p. 16).

504 For instance, in 1997 Ericsson "[f]acilitated briefs and pro-life strategy" in South Africa (www.advocatesinternational.org/ericssoncv.htm).

505 Advocates International board list, *op. cit.*

506 Kathryn J. Sides, "CLS at 25: Reflections on Our First Quarter Century," *Quarterly,* Fall 1986, p. 12.

507 Tiffany is currently a member of COR's Church Council Steering Committee (letterhead, November 1999). For more on COR, see Glossary.

508 John Whitehead was a protégé of Rousas John Rushdoony, the founder of the Christian Reconstructionist movement (See Frederick Clarkson, *Eternal Hostility, op. cit.*, p. 93).

509 Christian Legal Society, "Fact Sheet: Center for Law and Religious Freedom," undated.

510 In late April 2000 Senate Majority Leader Trent Lott (R-MS) kept the RLPA from coming to a vote in the Senate. Focus on the Family's *The Pastor's Weekly Briefing* (March 3, 2000) noted at the time that "What began as a scare for some in the religious community last week turned out to be more of a procedural hiccup that delayed the U.S. Senate's consideration of a major religious-freedom bill."

511 Kristian D. Whitten, "Chipping Away at the Wall of Separation," *The Connecticut Law Tribune*, August 2, 1999.

512 *Ibid.*

513 Thomas B. Edsall, "Christian Right Lifts Ashcroft," *The Washington Post*, April 14, 1998, p. A1.

514 Americans United for Separation of Church and State has published detailed criticism of "charitable choice" on its web site, www.au.org/cc-leg.htm. Among other things, AU argues that, "[t]he religious freedom of beneficiaries would be violated by subjecting them to religious indoctrination while they are attending a religious organization to obtain their government benefits"; that "[c]haritable choice permits religious institutions that receive government funds to discriminate in their employment on the basis of religion"; and that "[c]haritable choice adversely affects the religious mission of houses of worship, by subjecting them to government rules that inevitably follow the granting of federal funds."

515 "CLS Member Helps Craft National Legislation," *The Defender*, December 1995.

516 "Plan to Boost Churches' Role Passes House," *Associated Press*, November 5, 1999.

517 Mike Crissey, "Texas Religious Leaders Criticize 'Charitable Choice' Campaign Proposals," *Associated Press*, November 3, 1999.

518 For an overview of the Christian Right legal movement, see Sara Diamond, "The Religious Right Goes to Court," *The Humanist*, vol. 54, no. 3, May 1994, p. 35.

519 National Legal Resource Center web site, www.nlrc.org.

520 Doug Vande Griend, "CLS' National Legal Resource Center," CLS *Quarterly*, Summer 1995, p. 8–9.

521 Derk Arend Wilcox, ed., *The Right Guide, op. cit.*, pp. 95, 316.

522 "Religious Freedom Defenders Join Forces," CLS *Quarterly*, Summer 1995, p. B1. This affiliation marks CLS's move into direct litigation at the trial and administrative level. Steven McFarland, then director of CLS's Center for Law and Religious Freedom, has asserted that "[with] this link-up, we can be involved in even more religious liberty efforts by shaping important test cases when they begin—rather than waiting until they reach the U.S. Supreme Court." In 1999 McFarland was appointed executive director of the United States Commission on International Religious Freedom, created as a provision of the International Religious Freedom Act of 1998. This legislation, designed to afford greater government involvement in protecting religious activity abroad, was supported by such Christian Right organizations as the Christian Coalition, the Family Research Council, the Rutherford Institute, and Advocates International. See congressional co-sponsor Frank Wolf's web site for the full roster, www.house.gov/wolf/ free/groups.htm.

523 Tracey Jefferys-Renault and Jerry Sloan, *Without Justice For All, op. cit.*, p. 51.

524 Ball was also a member of the Order of St. Gregory the Great, a papal knighthood (see Wolfgang Saxon, "William Bentley Ball," *The New York Times*, January 18, 1999, p. B7). He served on the advisory board of the Catholic League for Religion and Civil Rights as well. Prior to his rise in prominence as a Christian Right legal activist, Ball worked as an attorney for W. R. Grace & Company. On the right-wing activities of W. R. Grace chairman J. Peter Grace, see Françoise Herve, "Knights of Darkness: The Sovereign Military Order of Malta," *Covert Action Information Bulletin*, Number 25, Winter 1986, pp. 28, 35–37.

525 Presbyterian Coalition, Inc., Form 990s, Internal Revenue Service, 1994–1997.

526 Presbyterian Coalition, letter to "Presbyterian Friends," Autumn 1998.

527 Robert P. Mills, "'For Such a Time as This': Gathering III draws 600 Presbyterians to Dallas," *The Presbyterian Layman* web site, www.layman.org/layman/the-layman/1998/ nov-dec/such-a-time-as-this.htm.

528 For a general summary of the renewal effort at Fort Worth, see Jennifer Files, "Conservative groups organize to influence Assembly debates," *The Presbyterian Outlook* web site, July 28, 1999, www.pres-outlook.com/211_organize.html.

529 Kennedy McGowan, E-mail correspondence, August 30, 1999. McGowan is pastor of Brentwood Presbyterian Church of Long Island, N.Y.

530 See Rev. Al Sandalow's overview of the politics of the Coalition in "Learning to be a Coalition," *The Presbyterian Review*, July 28, 1999, www.pforum.org/sandalow.htm.

531 The Presbyterian Forum, "The Certain Trumpet," *The Presbyterian Review*, June 11, 1999, www.pforum.org/trumpet.htm.

532 *Ibid.*

533 *Ibid.*

534 Kennedy McGowan has affirmed this as follows: ". . . the Forum was formed out of a desire to see a more politically active role for evangelical-conservatives at General Assembly and frustration that other more established groups on the right side of the aisle were not moving fast enough in that direction. . . . There was a general sense that the conservative[s], particularly the Coalition leadership, were not seizing the moment with a reluctance in becoming too 'political'" (e-mail correspondence, August 30, 1999).

535 The 1997 General Assembly was characterized as an "unabashed arena for special interest politics" by *The Presbyterian Layman* (July/August 1997, p. 1). Perhaps more important for the renewal movement generally was the rejection of former PC(USA) moderator David Dobler, who later served as vice moderator of the Presbyterian Coalition, in his bid for election to the Permanent Judicial Commission. In a departure from protocol, his nomination was attacked from the floor, and this probably swung the vote against him, 280-252. A second conservative candidate, Philip Hull, was also defeated (Parker T. Williamson, "General Assembly Rejects Dobler," *The Presbyterian Layman*, July/August 1997, p. 1).

536 The Presbyterian Forum Foundation, Form 1023, Internal Revenue Service, May 5, 1998.

537 Tax-exempt directory, Internal Revenue Service web site, July 26, 1999, www.irs.ustreas.gov/cgi/eosearch.

538 The Presbyterian Forum Foundation, "Trust Agreement," Internal Revenue Service, May 21, 1997.

539 Doug Pride, "The Shepherds," *The Presbyterian Review*, July 2, 1999, www.pforum/org/shepherds.htm.

540 Robert P. Mills, "Resourcing Renewal," *The Presbyterian Layman*, January/February 1999, p. 21; John H. Adams, "Presbyterian Forum: PC(USA) Evangelicals on the Internet," *The Presbyterian Layman*, January/February 1998, p. 18.

541 Jennifer Files, "Conservative groups organize," *op. cit.*

542 Doug Pride, "The Shepherds," July 2, 1999, www.pforum.org/shepherds.htm.

543 Robert P. Mills, "Resourcing Renewal in the PC(USA)," *op. cit.*, p. 21.

544 The Presbyterian Forum, "The Certain Trumpet," www.pforum.org/trumpet.htm.

545 Jennifer Files, "Conservative groups organize," *op. cit.* Bob Davis was the main spokesman for this story and is characterized by Files as a "chief conservative strategist."

546 The Presbyterian Forum, "The Certain Trumpet," www.pfo rum.org/trumpet.htm.

547 Bob Davis characterizes the Forum as a political operation: "Most people are going to tell you that a church shouldn't be political. But as soon as you start having votes to determine the direction of the church, the process is political." See Jennifer Files, "Conservative groups organize," *op. cit.*

548 Robert P. Mills, "Resourcing Renewal," *op. cit.*, p. 21.

549 "General Assembly News Briefs," *The Presbyterian Layman,* July/August 1997, p. 7.

550 Robert P. Mills, "Resourcing Renewal," *op. cit.*, p. 21.

551 Presbyterian Coalition, letter to "Presbyterian Friends," Autumn 1998.

552 Jennifer Files, "Conservative groups organize," *op. cit.*

553 The Presbyterian Renewal Network, "A Pre-Assembly Meeting to Prepare for the 1999 General Assembly (1999)," The Presbyterian Renewal Network web site, April 27, 1999, www.presbyrenewal.org/Events.

554 The Presbyterian Renewal Network, "A Manual to Help Prepare for the 1999 General Assembly (1999)," The Presbyterian Renewal Network web site, July 15, 1999, www. presbyrenewal.org/ Manual/Table.html.

555 It is debatable whether the decision taken on the NNPCW—continued funding but more rigorous oversight—was a defeat for the renewal movement. The Presbyterian Lay Committee certainly wanted much more, but the fact remains that NNPCW will be greatly inhibited in its more exploratory currents due to the renewal campaign. Neutralization is no less effective than elimination, and far less controversial—a point of strategy which arguably distinguishes the moderate sectors of the renewal movement from the more extreme.

556 Pride is pastor of Clearfield Presbyterian Church, Clearfield, Pennsylvania.

557 Doug Pride, "The Shepherds," July 2, 1999, www.pforum.org/shepherds.htm.

558 Mountain View Presbyterian Church, "Reverend Robert Dooling," Mountain View Presbyterian Church web site, July 2, 1999, www.frii.com/~mvpc/ bobd_bio.html.

559 "Shepherds' sought for General Assembly," *The Layman Online,* January 7, 2000, www.layman.org/layman/news-from-PC(USA)/presbyterian-shepherds. htm.

560 Stanley M. Burgess and Gary B. McGee, eds., *Dictionary of Pentecostal and Charismatic Movements,* Grand Rapids, Mich.: Zondervan, 1988, pp. 783–785; and Sara Diamond, *Spiritual Warfare, op. cit.*, pp. 111–120. For more on shepherding and the Catholic Word of God community, see Russ Bellant, "Word of God network wants to 'save the world,'" *National Catholic Reporter,* November 8, 1988. This article is reprinted as an appendix in Russ Bellant, *The Religious Right in Michigan Politics,* Silver Spring, Md.: Americans for Religious Liberty, 1996, pp. 107–133. (This book also features a further appendix, "Mania in the Stadia: The Origins and Goals of Promise Keepers.")

561 *Ibid.*

562 Douglas DeCelle, "Promise Keepers: What's It All About," *reNews,* June 1996, p. 13. This issue of *reNews* is dedicated to the question of "covenants," a key term in the shepherding movement. Two articles on "covenant groups" by Gareth Icenogle, former director of the doctoral ministry program at Fuller Theological Seminary, lay out a rationale and strategy for covenant group development. Emphasizing carefully developed leadership, emotional prostration, and religious as distinct from secular structures of commitment, this material overlaps with the ideas and methods of shepherding in its right-wing parachurch forms: "We must get back in touch with our apostolic small group roots during this age of secular pagan ambivalence and hostility to the Church..." writes Icenogle. "And the hunger for human healing cries out for the Church to create small communities of love where it is safe to be vulnerable and con-

fessional. Many people have not learned to be self-disciplined, balanced, and healthy because their families of origin are distressed, distorted, and diseased. In these myriad cases, the Church must provide for them 'a new family,' a well-mentored covenant group that re-parents them and reasserts good human values." See Gareth Icenogle, "Why Covenant Groups Are Imperative for the Church of the 21st Century," and "How to Start a Covenant Group Ministry in Your Congregation," *reNews*, June 1996, pp. 10–12.

563 Russ Bellant, "Promise Keepers and the Christian Shepherding Movement," *PK Watch, op. cit.* On the Word of God community, see also Stanley M. Burgess, et al., ed., *Dictionary of Pentecostal and Charismatic Movements,* Grand Rapids, Mich.: Regency, 1988, pp. 110–125, 219, 583.

564 John H. Adams, "GA won't commend Promise Keepers," *The Presbyterian Layman,* August 2, 1999, www.layman.org/layman/news/news-from-PC(USA) /ga99-promise-keepers.htm.

565 Ted Nissen came out of Hollywood First Presbyterian Church, where fundamentalist Henrietta Mears had developed a renowned Christian Education program that influenced many college students. Other evangelical Presbyterians mentored by Mears include Christian right leader Bill Bright as well as Don Moomaw, longtime pastor to the Reagans at Bel-Air Presbyterian (1964–1993). Presbyterians for Renewal devoted substantial space in the December 1998 issue of *reNews* to Mears' legacy for the renewal movement. Left unmentioned in this celebration of Mears' influence is her background at First Baptist Church in Minneapolis, where she directed the Sunday school program in the late 1920s. This was the church of notorious right-wing fundamentalist preacher Rev. W. B. Riley, who in the 1930s distributed the *Protocols of the Learned Elders of Zion,* the notorious anti-Semitic forgery. Riley was also closely associated with the overtly pro-Nazi fundamentalist Gerald Winrod. On Riley, see Ralph Lord Roy, *Apostles of Discord,* op. cit., pp. 46–47.

566 The campaign for the legislation was spearheaded by GOP state Rep. Tony Perkins. Perkins was the campaign director of far-right state Rep. Louis "Woody" Jenkins' senatorial bid in 1996. Both are members of the Council for National Policy of which Jenkins has served as executive director. Jenkins is also a Christian television entrepreneur and a top figure in Richard De Vos's Amway Corporation. Jenkins' organization, Friends of the Americas, funneled private aid to the Contras in Nicaragua in 1987. See Bill McMahon, "Candidate Affiliations Differ Greatly," *Capital City Press,* October 20, 1996, p. 8A.

567 Jeff Hooten, "Tying the Knot a Whole Lot Tighter," *Citizen,* August 3, 1999, www.family.org/cforum/ citizenmag/coverstory. *Citizen* is the monthly political magazine of James Dobson's Christian Right media empire Focus on the Family. See also Frederick Clarkson, "Takin' It to the States: The Rise of Conservative State Level Think Tanks," *The Public Eye,* Fall 1999.

568 Jeff Hooten, "Tying the Knot a Whole Lot Tighter," *op. cit.*

569 *Ibid.*

570 *Ibid.*

571 Gary Miller, "Commissioner's Report to the Presbytery," Voices of Orthodox Women web site, July 8, 1999, www.vow.org/gary-miller.html.

572 "Dooling Manufacturing, Inc.," *US Business Directory,* 1999.

573 Mountain View Presbyterian Church, "Reverend Robert Dooling," Mountain View Presbyterian Church web site, July 15, 1999, www.frii.com/-mvpc /bobd_bio.html.

574 *Ibid.*

575 Presbyterian Coalition, Inc., Form 990, Internal Revenue Service, 1994.

576 Mountain View Presbyterian Church, "Reverend Robert Dooling," www.frii. com/ -mvpc/bobd_bio.htm.

577 "Locally Produced 'World Wide Pictures' Segment Will Air on IFC's 'Split Screen,'" *PR Newswire,* May 13, 1999.

578 John H. Adams, "Presbyterian Forum," *The Presbyterian Layman, op. cit.*

579 In a 1999 interview, Kennedy McGowan states, "In a casual conversation that I had with Mr. Reed in Charlotte in 1998, it was clear to me that he has been very helpful financially to the Forum in getting it started. I remember him saying on that occasion in Charlotte that during the battle over Amendment B, the Forum would call him for financial help, and he would send them a check. From this conversation, I gained the distinct impression that the principal funder of the Forum is Mr. Reed" (e-mail correspondence, August 29, 1999).

580 *The Genevans Newsletter,* Winter 1996–1997.

581 Presbyterians for Democracy and Religious Freedom, letterhead, 1988, 1989; annual report, 1991.

582 Presbyterians for Democracy and Religious Freedom, annual reports, Tennessee secretary of state, 1990, 1991.

583 Lee Walczak and Richard S. Dunham, "The Governors Try to Take Charge," *Business Week,* December 7, 1998, p. 88.

584 Tom Baxter, "On Politics: Barry Goldwater, 1909–1998," *The Atlanta Journal and Constitution,* May 30, 1998, p. 8A.

585 David M. Shribman, "The Life of the Party," *The Boston Globe Magazine,* August 11, 1996, p. 12.

586 Q. Whitfield Ayres, "Georgia GOP Has Best Year in Election History," *The Atlanta Journal and Constitution,* November 29, 1992, p. H1. Q. Whitfield Ayres, an influential Republican pollster and Presbyterian Lay Committee leader, has emphasized the broadly racial character of ascendant Republicanism in the South. Ayres reports that South Carolina GOP Gov. Carroll Campbell's gubernatorial victory in 1986 marked a decline in white Democratic Party support to 15 percent of the white electorate.

587 On Reed's party politics, see Tanya Melich, *The Republican War Against Women,* New York: Bantam Books, 1996, pp. 26, 36, 42, 55, 61, 151.

588 David M. Shribman, "The Life of the Party," *The Boston Globe Magazine,* August 11, 1996, p. 12.

589 Jack Elliot Jr., "Miss. GOP Eyes Ex-Chief," *The Commercial Appeal,* February 14, 1995, p. 4B; Jim Yardley, "Mississippi Governor Still Recovering From Crash," *The Atlanta Journal and Constitution,* December 19, 1996, p. 01D.

590 Curtis Wilkie, "Miss. Flogging Debate Opens Old Wounds," *The Boston Globe,* February 21, 1995, p. 1.

591 Clyde Woods, *Development Arrested: Race, Power, and the Blues in the Mississippi Delta,* New York: Verso, 1998, pp. 272–273.

592 *Ibid.,* p. 273.

593 *Ibid.,* p. 277.

594 Council of Conservative Citizens, leaflet, undated (ca. February 26, 1996).

595 Adam Clymer, "Race Raised as an Issue in Mississippi House Contest," *The New York Times,* October 14, 1982, p. B12. On Reed's campaign contributions, see the FECInfo web site, www.tray.com/cgi-win/_allindiv.exe.

596 Council of Conservative Citizens, leaflet, undated (ca. February 26, 1996).

597 FECInfo, PAC And Party Committee Contributors, www.tray.com/cgiwin /_paccontr.exe. In 1998 Reed gave $1,000 to Delbert Hosemann, a wealthy Jackson attorney, for his unsuccessful congressional campaign. FECInfo, Individual Contributors, www.tray.com/cgi-win/_allindiv.exe. Like Kirk Fordice, Hosemann received substantial support from white evangelical and Pentecostal churches as well as the Christian Coalition. Mary Ann Akers, "Candidates Vie for White Evangelical Vote," *The Washington Times,* October 31, 1998, p. A2.

598 Reed Branson, "New Wildlife Group Shuns Liberalism," *The Commercial Appeal,* December 11, 1997, p. B2.

599 Clyde Woods' book, cited above, details the continuing history of "plantation" politics in the deep South.

600 See Lewis C. Daly, "Renewal Unto Death: The Presbyterian Lay Committee in Context," Master of Divinity Thesis, Union Theological Seminary, 1999.

601 The Presbyterian Forum Foundation, Form 1023, Internal Revenue Service, May 5, 1998.

602 A more detailed chronology of these cases is presented in *The Trials of 1999: The Cutting Edge of Right-wing Power in the Presbyterian Church (USA),* New York: Institute for Democracy Studies, November 1999. All four cases were related to the enforcement and/or interpretation of Amendment B, the denomination's constitutional ban on gay ordination. As of January 2000, the Stamford case, where the complaint was upheld with qualification at the synod level, has not been appealed. The Northern New England case, where the complaint was upheld at the synod level, has been appealed to the General Assembly Permanent Judicial Commission (PJC). The complaints in both the Hudson River and West Jersey cases were denied by the synod-level PJC and have been appealed to the General Assembly PJC

603 John H. Adams, "A PC(USA) Court Primer," *The Presbyterian Layman,* May 13, 1999, www.layman.org/layman/news/news-from-PC(USA)/PC(USA)-court-primer.htm.

604 The Presbyterian Coalition, "The Renewal of Church Discipline," *Turning Toward the Mission of God: A Strategy for the Transformation of the P.C. (U.S.A.),* 1999.

605 *Ibid.,* "The Renewal of Polity."

606 One By One, based in Rochester, N.Y., is a newer Presbyterian renewal group that promotes so-called gay conversion therapy. The Coalition's disproportionate emphasis on sexuality is reflected in its inclusion of direct statements about sexuality in its theological charter, *Union in Christ* (see Andrew Purves and Mark Achtemeier, *Union in Christ: A Declaration for the Church,* Louisville, Ky.: Witherspoon Press, 1999, p. xvi).

607 The Presbyterian Coalition, "The Renewal of Church Discipline," *Turning Toward the Mission of God, op. cit.*

608 Presbyterian Coalition Gathering IV, conference tape, task force "Reports," September 22, 1999.

609 *Ibid.*

610 "Robert L. Howard," *The Presbyterian Layman,* January/February 1998, www.layman.org/layman/the-layman/1998/january-feb/bob-howard.htm. Hoffman is a spiritual mentor to Lay Committee chairman Robert Howard.

611 Rocky Lantz, "Kime Thinks Tenure Limited," *Parkersburg News,* January 15, 1995, p. A1. In 1996, the state Republican convention in West Virginia, which was chaired by Robert Fish, featured a prayer breakfast keynoted by Dale Berryhill of the right-wing Accuracy in Media organization, who presented an address on "The Biblical Case for Christian Involvement." See Jack McCarthy, "Pitt and Underwood in Weekend Spotlight," *The Charleston Gazette,* July 18, 1996, p. 5B.

612 Information and quotes from Presbyterian Coalition Gathering IV, conference tape, task force "Reports," *op. cit.*

613 Paula R. Kincaid, "PJC Decides Stamford Church May Install Gay Elder," *The Presbyterian Layman,* March 8, 1999, www.layman.org/layman/news/news-from-PC(USA)/stamford-decision.htm.

614 The Presbyterian Renewal Network, "Response to NNPCW Task Force Report," Presbyterian Renewal Network web site, October 21, 1999,

www.presbyrenewal.org/ NNPCW.htm.

615 Other signatories to the Presbyterian Renewal Network's position on NNPCW included Parker Williamson (Presbyterian Lay Committee), Terry Schlossberg (Presbyterians Pro-Life), Robert Dooling (Presbyterian Forum), and Z. Bradford Long (Presbyterian and Reformed Renewal Ministries International). The Presbyterian Renewal Network, increasingly politicized under the influence of the Presbyterian Forum, plans to hold its second annual pre-Assembly training retreat in May 2000, in Long Beach, California.

616 "PPL President Ben Sheldon Retires," *Presbyterians Pro-Life News,* Winter 1996, p. 12.

617 Phone interview with Walter Baker, October 29, 1999. Baker's involvement in the Stamford case predates his membership on the Coalition's task force on church discipline. In an earlier phone interview, he stated that the Presbyterian Coalition had "nothing whatsoever" to do with bringing the case.

618 Salomon Inc., *SEC Online,* December 31, 1989.

619 Alan Cowell, "South Africa's Gold Colossus," *The New York Times,* November 18, 1985, p. D1. Baker was appointed controller of Engelhard Minerals & Chemicals Corporation back in 1978, which had earlier merged with Philipp Brothers (see Oil & Gas Journal, September 18, 1978, p. 220). Charles Engelhard, who founded the Newark-based firm in 1907, was a close ally of Harry Oppenheimer in his building of the DeBeers and Anglo-American empire in South Africa (see Barbara Phillips, "Is the Diamond Mystique About to Crumble?," review of *The Rise and Fall of Diamonds,* by Edward Jay Epstein, in *The Christian Science Monitor,* July 7, 1982, p. 17).

620 Philipp Brothers, Inc., corporate record, California secretary of state, March 5, 1998; interview with Walter Baker, October 29, 1999.

621 Rev. Samuel A. Schreiner III, "God's Good Plans for LPC," Londonderry Presbyterian Church web site, October 27, 1999, www.lpcnh.org/ sermons/Sermon19990808.htm.

622 *Ibid.*

623 Brad Long, "PRRMI's Call to Continue the Work of Prayer," *Moving with the Spirit,* Issue 56, August 1999.

624 Presbyterian & Reformed Renewal Ministries International, letter to "Intercessors," July 27, 1999.

625 Presbyterians Pro-Life, "What Do Presbyterians Believe About Discipline?" Presbyterians Pro-Life web site, October 26, 1999, www.ppl.org/ Discipline_Spring1999. html.

626 Presbyterians Pro-Life Research, Education and Care, Inc., Form 990s, Internal Revenue Service, 1991, 1992, and 1993. Presbyterians Pro-Life Research, Education and Care, Inc., corporate record, Virginia secretary of state, June 10, 1993.

627 Presbyterians Pro-Life Research, Education and Care, Inc., Form 990s, Internal Revenue Service, 1991, 1992, 1993.

628 Christian Legal Society, 1996 Directory.

629 Hilary Appelman, "Dissenting Churches Oppose Appointment of Lesbian Minister," *Associated Press,* May 19, 1992.

630 "Past Presidents of the Christian Legal Society," CLS *Quarterly,* vol. 7, no. 3, Fall 1986, inside cover.

631 Presbyterian Coalition Gathering IV, conference tape, task force "Reports," *op. cit.*

632 For a detailed news account of the Synod-level verdicts in this case, see Ronald Smothers, "Presbyterian Court Denies Two Efforts Against Gays," *The New York Times,* metro edition, November 23, 1999, p B5.

633 Gary North, *Crossed Fingers, op. cit.,* 1996.

634 *Ibid.*, pp. 1–31.

635 *Ibid.*, p. xvi.

636 "Gary North Interviews Paul Pressler," *Firestorm Chats,* Colleyville, Tex.: Dominion Tapes, Inc., 1988.

637 Deborah Kovach Caldwell, "Gay Ordination Goes to Vote; Presbyterian Committee Recommends Abolishing Ban," *The Dallas Morning News,* June 24, 1999, p. 24A.

638 James R. Edwards, "What Ever Happened to the Great Ends of the Church?" *Theology Matters,* vol. 4, no. 3, May/June 1998, p. 10.

639 Some American Christian Rightists already envision themselves as engaged in an actual or potential religious war against constitutional democracy on behalf of the faith. See Frederick Clarkson, *Eternal Hostility, op. cit., passim.*

640 *Ibid.,* pp.85–86.

641 Presbyterian Coalition Gathering IV, conference tape, task force "Reports," *op. cit.*

Oxnam, Bishop G. Bromley, 16, 19
    attempts to thwart conservative control of NCC, 19

Paleo-conservatism, 29, 113, 124
Partee, Charles, 78, 139
Peacock, Rev. Dennis, 50
Pelley, William Dudley, 14
Perkins, Rev. John, 60–61
Permanent Judicial Commission, 113–114
Pew, J. Howard, 119, 120
    American Liberty League, role in, 14–15
    anti-mainline church activities in 1940s, 15–16
    Christian Freedom Foundation, funding of, 30
    Christianity Today funding, 137
    ecumenical movement, opposition to, 16–20
    federal aid to education, opposition to, 118
    Grove City College, affiliation with, 31
    John Birch Society, role in, 121
    National Council of Churches and, 17–19
    National Lay Committee, role in, 17–20
    Presbyterian Lay Committee, role in, 12–15, 20–21
Pew, J. Howard, Freedom Trust
    PLC funding, 39
    Presbyterian Layman funding, 30
Philbrick, Herbert, 119
Philipp Brothers, 102, 149
Phillips, Howard, 32, 124, 141
    quoted, 30
Plymouth Rock Foundation, 66
    background, 29
Poppinga, Julius (Jay), 8
    Christian Legal Society (CLS) and, 83–86
    Christian Right legal movement, leader of, 83–86
    church discipline, enforcement of, cases, 100–104
    profile, 82–83
Prentis, Henning, 18
Presbyterian Action for Faith and Freedom, 5, 49, 51, 69, 94, 114
Presbyterian Center for Mission Studies, 6, 27
Presbyterian Charismatic Communion, 59
Presbyterian Church in America (PCA), 20, 25, 43, 53, 58, 66, 114
Presbyterian Church in the United States (PC(US)), 5, 20, 114
    1983 union with UPC(USA), 23
    political conflict within, 58
Presbyterian Church (USA) or PC(USA)
    (*See* specific listings throughout this index)
Presbyterian Churchmen United, 57
Presbyterian Coalition, 2, 3, 5, 6, 7, 8, 69–86
    authoritarian agenda, 76–77
    background, 70–72
    board of directors (1999), 80
    church discipline and, 77, 99–104
    Declaration and Strategy Paper, 6–7, 12, 69, 73, 75–77, 78, 80
    dominionist influences, 74
    funding, 86
    Gatherings, 73–74
    Gathering III, 78
    Gathering IV, 79

IDS Insights. (12-16 pgs.) Investigative newsletter highlighting anti-democratic groups and trends. $25 for 4 issues individuals and nonprofits. $50 other organizations. $20 students/low income.

A Moment to Decide: The Crisis in Mainstream Presbyterianism. May 2000 (170 pgs.) Details the right-wing renewal movement in the Presbyterian Church (USA). $25.

Antifeminist Organizations: Institutionalizing the Backlash. March 2000 (35 pgs.) Profiles five leading antifeminist groups. $15.

The Assault on Diversity: Behind the Challenges to Racial and Gender Remedies. Dec. 1999 (22 pgs.) Profiles five organizations using affirmative action as a wedge issue to promote a broader, anti-diversity agenda. $10.

The Trials of 1999: The Cutting Edge of Right-wing Power in the Presbyterian Church (USA). Nov. 1999 (11 pgs.) Provides background on the anti-gay trials of Nov. 1999 in the Presbyterian Church (USA). $5.

Taking Aim: The Conservatives' Bid for Power in the Presbyterian Church Entering Advanced Stage. Oct. 1999 (7 pgs.) Exposes efforts by the right-wing Presbyterian Coalition and others to take over the Presbyterian Church (USA) and purge its liberal elements. $5.

Priests for Life: A New Era of Anti-Abortion Activism. Oct. 1999 (17 pgs.) Profiles a growing international Vatican-sponsored anti-abortion rights organization. $10.

The American Life League Enters Mexico: Recruiting Anti-Choice Activists for U.S. Right-wing Goals. July 1999 (23 pgs.) Investigates a major U.S.-based anti-abortion rights organization. $5.

(Video) Promise Keepers: The Third Wave of the American Religious Right. 1997 (20 min.) Powerfully documents the men-only religious revival network, Promise Keepers, in action. $15.

(Video) Submission: Women's Groups of the Religious Right. 1997 (20 min.) Features interviews with members of women's groups promoting submission of women to men. $15.

Promise Keepers: The Third Wave of the American Religious Right. Nov. 1996 (23 pgs.) Explores the background and political agenda of Promise Keepers in depth. $15.

PUBLICATIONS AND RESOURCES AVAILABLE FROM THE INSTITUTE FOR DEMOCRACY STUDIES

ORDERING INFORMATION

Please send a check or money order payable to the **Institute for Democracy Studies** to 177 East 87th Street, Suite 501, New York, NY 10128. Be sure to include the title of the item(s) and indicate how many. All prices include shipping. Please allow three to four weeks for delivery. Thank you.

ABOUT THE INSTITUTE FOR DEMOCRACY STUDIES

The Institute for Democracy Studies is a non-profit, tax-exempt research and educational center that studies anti-democratic religious and political movements and organizations in the U.S and internationally. IDS is dedicated to publishing carefully documented studies of these entities in the interest of furthering informed public discussion and fuller reporting in the media on these major challenges to constitutional democracy and human and civil rights.

Founded in 1999 in New York City, the Institute currently maintains interdisciplinary research programs focusing on religion, reproductive rights, and law:

The *Religion and Democracy Program* investigates the resurgence of extremism that is transforming mainstream theology and religious institutions in the U.S. These anti-democratic trends are often rooted in intolerant fundamentalist ideologies, and increasingly influence the debate on public policy issues.

The *Reproductive Rights and Democracy Program* engages in domestic and international research on the major structures opposed to reproductive rights, from abortion to contraception and sexuality education. As part of the Institute's global commitment to reproductive freedom, the Mexico Reproductive Rights Initiative provides essential information to the media and leading organizations in Mexico.

The *Law and Democracy Program* conducts research on litigation and legal organizations that challenge mainstream American democratic jurisprudence and constitutional rights in such areas as the separation of church and state, reproductive rights, and racial and gender justice.

IDS has issued briefing papers in each program area as forerunners to more in-depth studies to be published in 2000. The Institute will also launch an investigative newsletter called IDS *Insights* in April 2000.

ABOUT THE DENOMINATIONAL STUDIES SERIES

This study of the conservative renewal movement in the Presbyterian Church (USA) is the first in the Denominational Studies Series, which is a project of the IDS Religion and Democracy Program. Strong conservative "renewal" movements aiming for an historic realignment of moderate and liberal mainline Protestantism with conservative evangelicalism are also active in a number of other denominations, including the Episcopal Church and the United Methodist Church, the subjects of forthcoming studies in the series. The Denominational Studies Series was conceived of and the research is directed by Lee Cokorinos. The general editor of the series is Frederick Clarkson.